GUITAR FINISHING
STEP-BY-STEP 2nd Edition

Acknowledgments

To all our friends in luthiery, and countless Stewart-MacDonald customers (many of whom we've met only on the phone) for interacting with us and over the years sharing their finishing experiences—both good and bad—we thank you! This book benefits from the experiences of the entire luthier community.

Many people acted as special consultants for this book. We can't thank the following people enough for giving us many hours of their valuable time: Peter Beck, Bill Gutteridge, Albert Garcia, Bill Antel, Joe Glaser, Michael Dresdner, Mark Huizinga, John Allison, Bill Collings, Bob Flexner, Pete Moreno, Frank Ford, Ren Ferguson, Richard Johnston, Bryan Galloup, Tim Klimefelter, George Fullerton. Steve Gilchrist, Thomas Humphrey, Yasuhiko Iwanade, Jeff Jewitt, Mike Spicer, Dave Fox, Fred Stuart, Alan Hamel, Jonathan Kemp, Richard Smith, Ron Lira, John Arnold, Steve Ryder, Julius Borges, Marv Lamb, Clay Harrell, Mike Lennon, Mark Piper, Dana Bourgeois, Tom Marcell, Chris Minick, Tom Murphy, Scott Lentz, Hank Risan, Paul Rossi, Dan Shin, Michael Stevens, T.J. Thompson, Michael Hornick, Jeff Traugott, and Dave Hussong.

Over the years we've learned from more than just the folks listed above—if you're one of them, and we haven't officially thanked you here, in print, that does not diminish our appreciation for all the large and small things we've learned from you. Thanks!

The most special thanks of all goes out to Joan Erlewine and Nicki MacRostie for their support during the years of development it took to bring this book into existence!

Dan Erlewine
Don MacRostie

©2006, 2005, 1998 by Stewart-MacDonald
21 N. Shafer Street, Athens, OH 45701
Printed in USA

All rights reserved. No part of this book may be reproduced in any form without written permission from the publisher, except by a reviewer who may quote brief passages in a review.

The following manufacturers and product names appearing in this book are trademarks: 3M®, Armor All®, Bondo®, Dry-lube®, Durham's Rock Hard Water Putty®, Elmer's®, Fre-Cut®, Imperial®, Les Paul®, Plastic Wood®, Scotch-Brite®, Stratocaster®, Telecaster®, Tints-All®, Titebond®, TransferRite®, Tru-Oil®, Unigrit®, Velcro®, Wet-or-Dry®, Windex®, X-Acto®.

GUITAR FINISHING STEP-BY-STEP 2nd Edition

Table of Contents

About the Authors vi
Introduction vii
Safety Precautions viii

Chapter 1 — Topcoats and Solvents
Evaporative Finishes 1
Reactive Finishes 6
Coalescing Finishes 9
Solvents and Thinners 12

Chapter 2 — Grain Filler, Wood Putty, and Wood Dough
Grain Filler 16
Wood Doughs and Putties 18
Grain Filler Colors 19

Chapter 3 — Finish Colorants
A Short History of Guitar Coloring 21
A Little Bit of Color Theory 24
The Most Common Methods of Coloring Guitars 26
Colorant Types Used in Guitar Finishing 28

Chapter 4 — Tools and Materials for Applying Finishes
Aerosol Spraying 32
Compressed-air Spraying 32
Spray Booths 36
Devices for Holding the Work 38
Masking Supplies 40
Miscellaneous Tools and Supplies 41

Chapter 5 — Abrasives and Smoothing Tools
Sandpapers 43
Power Sanders 49
Scrapers 50
Other Tools 51

Chapter 6 — Materials and Tools for Buffing
Compound and Polish Types 53
Tools Used for Buffing 55

Color Pages
Finish Recipes: Example Guitars
Stain Mixing Charts: Two-color Blends
Color Density
8-Day Schedule: Martin-style Finish

Chapter 7	**Spraying Basics**	
	Thinning Lacquer	57
	Air Pressure	59
	Spray Gun Maintenance	60
	Spraying Techniques	64
Chapter 8	**Sanding and Buffing Techniques**	
	Techniques for Sanding Wood	68
	Techniques for Sanding the Finish	70
	Techniques for Buffing the Finish	73
	Sanding Schedule Example	75
Chapter 9	**Ten Basic Finishing Steps**	
	Step 1: Wood Preparation	77
	Step 2: Transparent Stains on Bare Wood	83
	Step 3: Wash Coating (optional)	85
	Step 4: Filling the Grain	87
	Step 5: The Sealer Coat	89
	Step 6: Vintage "Primer" Under Solid Colors	91
	Step 7: Solid Color Coats	92
	Step 8: Shading, Sunbursting, Toning, & Touch Up	92
	Step 9: Clear Topcoats	98
	Step 10: Final Sanding and Rubbing Out	99
Chapter 10	**Finishing Recipes**	
	Get A Vintage Finish To Reveal Its Recipe?	101
	Weights and Measures	103
	Recipe 1: Fresh Mixed Shellac	104
	Recipe 2: Antique Binding Toner	104
	Recipe 3: Blackening The Peghead Face	105
	Recipe 4: Shop-made White Lacquer	108
	Recipe 5: Sonic Blue Pastel	109
	Recipe 6: Fiesta Red	109
	Recipe 7: Solid Color Spraying With Aerosols	110
	Recipe 8: Basic Gold Bronzing Lacquer	113
	Recipe 9: Metallic Blue—As Blue As Lake Placid	113
	Recipe 10: Gold Top Finish	115
	Recipe 11: Candy Apple Red	117
	Recipe 12: Basic Martin-style Finish—Nitrocellulose	118
	Recipe 13: Basic Martin-style Finish—Waterbase	119
	A Brief History of Gibson Guitar Finishing	121
	Recipe 14: ES-125 Tobacco Sunburst	128
	Recipe 15: Modern Factory Color Job	129
	Recipe 16: Top O' The Line Shaded Finish	130
	Recipe 17: Vintage Sunburst	132
	Very Cherry Reds	134
	Recipe 18: Cherry Red Grain Filler	135
	Recipe 19: '58 Vintage Cherry Sunburst	136
	Recipe 20: Cherry Red 335	137

SG Reds 139
Recipe 21: Close-to-the-wood Cherry Red 139
Recipe 22: Modern Factory Cherry Red 140
Recipe 23: Easier Cherry Red 140
Recipe 24: Mostly Waterbase Cherry Red.................141
Recipe 25: Faded Cherry Red On Mahogany............141
Recipe 26: Tv Yellow 143
Fender: Chasing After Blonds 146
Recipe 27: E-Z-Make Blond 151
Recipe 28: Good Looking Old Blond 152
Fender Sunbursts, According To "Yas"................154
Recipe 29: Pre-'64: Yellow Stain 160
Recipe 30: Post-'64: Yellow Toner.............................161
Recipe 31: Dark Salem Maple Shader 161
Recipe 32: Pre-'56 Two-tone Sunburst 162
Recipe 33: Post-'56 Two-tone Or Pre-'64 Three-tone ...163
Recipe 34: Post-'64 Three-tone Sunburst 164
Recipe 35: Finishing A Bolt-on Maple Neck 165
Recipe 36: Gretsch's Flagship Finishes.....................166
Recipe 37: PRS Vintage Sunburst..............................168

Index 170

About the Authors

Dan Erlewine: repairman, author, video producer, tool inventor.
Who could estimate the number of luthiers whose careers were started through lessons with Dan? With his books, his articles in Guitar Player and other luthiery magazines, and his library of guitar repair DVDs, Dan shares the trade secrets of guitar repair with everyone who wants to learn. His teaching style is "come on in and let's talk," and his lessons come right from the workbench: real customer jobs with solutions to problems that show up in repair shops every day. Dan has authored several books: *The Guitar Player Repair Guide*; *How To Make Your Electric Guitar Play Great!*; *Fretwork Step-By-Step*, and *Trade Secrets*. His DVD series on guitar repair includes nine volumes as of this writing.

Don MacRostie (left) and Dan Erlewine

Don MacRostie: ingenious creator of a whole shopful of luthiery tools. As Director of Product Development at Stewart-MacDonald, Don is always developing new tools, new kits, and new products for the world of luthiery. MacRostie-designed tools are used throughout the instrument building and repair industry. Don also makes renowned Red Diamond mandolins, and has created some of the world's finest sounding and most beautifully finished mandolins. His sunbursts have set a new standard of quality.

If you build or repair stringed instruments, you're probably already using tools developed by Don MacRostie and Dan Erlewine every day. For the latest tools, products, and information from Stewart-MacDonald, visit stewmac.com online.

Introduction by Dan Erlewine

New in this second edition: *We've updated our information on getting great results with waterbase finishes, which are becoming the norm in so many shops. (For a Martin-style finish using waterbase lacquer, see Recipe 13 and the photo story in our new color section.) Stain mixing charts for custom colors are here now, too! – Dan Erlewine, 2005*

This book is for anyone who wants to finish or repair the finish on a guitar, though much of it can be applied to finishes on banjos, mandolins, dulcimers, and related stringed instruments. It answers the questions that books on furniture finishing really can't, considering that so many techniques and many materials used for musical instrument finishing are unique to our trade. Furniture finishers seldom worry about how good a chair sounds!

Once you have a basic understanding of how musical instrument finishes are applied, you'll be able to finish new work from scratch, refinish old work, and approach touchups and repair work with confidence.

Almost everybody at Stewart-MacDonald has tried a hand at finishing; Don MacRostie and I have tried both hands and both feet, jumping off the deep end together. When I joined Stewart-MacDonald in 1986, we each had a couple of decade's experience with instrument building and repairing. We've spent the years since sharing our experiences as StewMac's R&D team. It's amazing how our discussions always end up on the topic of finishing. This book was inevitable!

Most of the finishing tools, products, and techniques we discuss revolve around nitrocellulose lacquer, the most common guitar finish in use since the 1930s. We also give you plenty of information on alternative products, such as automotive or waterbase lacquers, which don't require too many changes in technique. Because they are viable options in many situations—especially for those of you who will be finishing instruments other than guitars—we couldn't help but touch on several hand-applied instrument finishes such as oil, French polish, and varnish.

Finishing materials are rapidly evolving due to technological advances and environmental requirements. Most of these changes spell good news. With today's products and tools, you'll achieve a dizzying array of effects, but won't get so dizzy doing it! These changes by no means eclipse the past; you can still duplicate the best classic finishes and sometimes go them one better.

This book takes you from understanding tools and terminology to finishing an instrument like a pro. Finishing materials and equipment are explained in terms that you needn't be a chemist to understand. By studying the advantages and disadvantages of each, you'll learn when to use a particular finish and why. To get you started we've added a recipe section showing how we would approach the reproduction of some popular guitar finishes, such as those used by Martin, Gibson, Fender, and others. Use these as a launching pad for your own creativity.

Even if you're no nut for details and put "breathing dust and fumes" last on your list of fun ways to spend a weekend, finishing can be fun. And it certainly can't be avoided if you're going to be in, or even dabble in, this business.

No job's done until it's finished, right?

Dan Erlewine
Athens, Ohio
1998

Safety Precautions

Before going any further in the book, read this important notice about safety. You can't be too careful in a wood shop—especially if you keep flammables around and you're doing finishing work. Varnish, oils, shellac, lacquer, lacquer thinner, mineral spirits, denatured alcohol, and other solvents are toxic and flammable. They must be handled with knowledge and care in an extremely well-ventilated, explosion-proof area. Pay special attention to *all* the safety precautions throughout this book, including the following:

- Establish better-than-adequate ventilation in your work and drying areas. Fresh air intake and a nonsparking, explosion-proof fan are a must for any shop. You can get UAL-approved fans and other spray equipment from the Grainger Company in the United States.
- Keep fire extinguishers in every room and check them routinely.
- Keep charcoal-filtered respirators, rated for the solvents and finishes you spray, at hand and wear them while mixing and spraying solvent-based finishes and while the solvents are evaporating in the spray area.
- Wear a dust mask during the wood preparation (sanding) stage and also during dry sanding of solvent-based finishes.
- Wear rubber safety gloves when handling solvents, epoxies, superglues, and all solvent-based materials.
- Store finishing materials in a cool, dry place away from heat sources, sparks, flames, or children. We prefer steel cabinets with locking doors.
- Wear eye protection when working, especially when using tools or handling chemicals.

CHAPTER 1

Topcoats and Solvents

We start by describing the most common of these finishes you're likely to use, and what they're made of. We touch on some of the other finish types, and there's also an entire family of solvents, thinners, and other chemicals for guitar finishing that we will explain and demystify. Of the three basic finish types, each has solvents that work particularly well with them. If you understand just how these finishes and solvents work, you'll do a better job of finishing your guitar.

There are three basic kinds of finishes, differentiated by the way they dry: **evaporative, reactive, and coalescing**. Though the reactive finish certainly has a place in traditional instrument finishing (varnish and oil finishes), the coalescing (waterbase or "water-borne" lacquer), and especially the evaporative (nitrocellulose lacquer), are the finish types this book covers most thoroughly. Nitrocellulose lacquer has been the mainstay of the guitar finishing business since the late 1920s, so we begin there.

Evaporative Finishes

Evaporative finishes are solids (nitrocellulose, vinyl and acrylic pellets, shellac flakes, or other natural or synthetic resins) dissolved in their appropriate solvent. On contact with air, the usually fast-drying solvent evaporates and the resin returns to its original solid state. Having been dissolved by the solvent, the solids stick together in a unified film on the wood's surface. Evaporative finishes have the least scratch and dent resistance, and are sensitive to moisture and solvent penetration because the molecules are only bonded, not cross linked. With the handling and care most musical instruments receive, these shortcomings are usually not a problem.

Evaporative finishes are the easiest to apply, however, because they dry fast, sand easily, and buff nicely to a high gloss. Repairing evaporative finishes is a breeze, too, because they redissolve themselves leaving no "witness" line when new finish is applied over the old.

Perhaps the first evaporative finish was shellac. For centuries shellac makers in Indochina have collected residue that the lac insect has deposited on tree limbs, and cleaned and dissolved it in alcohol to make shellac. Solvent lacquer and shellac are the most common evaporative finishes available today.

Nitrocellulose lacquer

Nitrocellulose lacquer is the standard wood lacquer traditionally used by furniture and instrument makers. If you learn to use lacquer now, you'll have no trouble changing with it as it evolves, and many of the same techniques will apply to other finishes.

Clear nitrocellulose lacquer is often referred to as water-white lacquer (not to be confused with waterbase lacquer!). Water-white is the term used to distinguish the nonyellowing version of nitrocellulose from the older lacquers which yellowed with age. In general, you want a lacquer that is clear, hard yet flexible, will buff to a high gloss, and is resistant to cold checking. (Cold checking is what can happen to a brittle lacquer finish if a guitar sits in an unheated UPS truck over the weekend in Montana during the wintertime—the finish may become riddled with cracks). The lacquer you choose for guitar finishing should be made for finishing wood, not metal (lacquers are formulated for spraying over many different surfaces). A high-solids lacquer is best because it will build faster. Most furniture lacquers have a solids content of 18% to 28%, with 21% to 23% being most common. Today's ready-to-spray guitar lacquers are high-solids lacquers formulated for spraying with little or no thinning.

ADVANTAGES OF NITROCELLULOSE LACQUER
- Easy to use
- Used on many factory instruments and is easily repaired
- Dries fast and hard
- Buffs easily to a high gloss
- Superior acoustical properties

DISADVANTAGES
- Lacquer thinners are volatile organic compounds (VOCs), which are harmful to the environment and to the finisher confined in a room with these chemicals
- You must spray on most lacquers requiring a sizeable investment in equipment
- Not hardy enough to withstand neglect or certain elements

Lacquer sanding sealer

Lacquer sanding sealer is clear lacquer with powder-like soap or stearate lubricant added to make it sand easily, and a clear pigment or bulking agent to make it build fast and bridge, or fill the rough surface of raw wood. Lacquer sanding sealer usually requires thinning and *must be stirred well to get the suspended stearates into the finish!* The big advantage of sanding sealer is that it's easier to sand than clear lacquer. Many finishers use sanding sealer for the initial layer of finish to produce a "build" and thus a flat level surface quickly. They follow with clear lacquer as a topcoat.

We regard sanding sealer as a material designed to speed up the finishing process in factories, and we recommend using it in moderation or not at all. Lacquer alone will thoroughly seal the wood and so will shellac, vinyl wash coat, and vinyl sealer. The sealing process is detailed in Chapter 9.

Too much sanding sealer can impair adhesion. A thick layer of sanding sealer produces an undercoat that is too soft for the harder lacquer to follow. This can allow the hard topcoat to crack or craze. It can also cause lifting around tuning-key holes or other routed or drilled openings. Even though apparently clear, sanding sealer is less transparent than lacquer, thus it reduces the clarity of the final finish depending on how much is used.

If you have no deadline to meet on your project, take the time to create your build with clear lacquer. You'll be rewarded with a wonderfully clear finish. If you're getting into finishing on a full-scale basis however, where time is a factor, become familiar with sanding sealer so you can make up your own mind. Note, however, that today's lacquers sand more easily than they once did, sand papers have improved markedly, and finishing tastes have become more refined. Today's "old-time" finishers, who used lots of sanding sealer in the '60s and '70s, are now more willing to sand the clear lacquer.

ADVANTAGES OF SANDING SEALER
- Builds quickly and sands easily
- Dries fast because it's usually sprayed quite thick, with little thinner added

DISADVANTAGES
- The stearate in it does not promote good adhesion
- Softer and less transparent than lacquer (it has a milky character), thus more likely to dull a great acoustic instrument's tone

Vinyl sealer—a barrier coat

Vinyl sealer is a general term for vinyl-modified lacquer, or lacquer into which clear vinyl pellets are dissolved for the purpose of increasing its moisture resistance and to make it impermeable. A barrier coat is a finish material that won't be dissolved (or at least not completely) by the topcoat finish sprayed over it. It is compatible with that finish and any stain, grain filler, or natural wood dye used under or over it.

The most popular vinyl sealer is a thin, low-solids, nonstearated, crystal clear, ready-to-spray vinyl wash coat. It's used as a barrier wash coat for several reasons: As a moisture barrier, a vinyl wash coat locks in bare wood (rosewood in particular), which tends to bleed color naturally. It locks in applied colorants that may bleed up into the topcoats. It blocks contaminants such as oil and silicone in the wood from migrating up into the finish (a cause of fisheyes, craters, and other problems). It also keeps the topcoats from soaking down into the bare wood, the colorants, or the grain filler, preventing the topcoats from muddying the clarity of the finish.

There also are good vinyl sanding sealers available. These have some stearate added, and they're clearer and harder than traditional lacquer sanding sealers. These vinyl sealers are worth consideration if you're looking for build coats (as opposed to a wash coat). They have all the barrier-coat properties not found in traditional lacquer sanding sealers.

ADVANTAGES OF VINYL SEALER
- Promotes good adhesion for successive coats
- Has great moisture resistance
- Tends to be clearer than traditional sanding sealer
- Good for sealing in color
- Builds fast and sands a little easier than clear lacquer

DISADVANTAGES
- It has a tendency to lift from oily woods such as rosewood if the sealer is not properly thinned, is sprayed too thick, or if too many coats are sprayed too fast
- Vinyl sealer will not adhere well if uncured wood filler lies beneath

TECH TIP

Martin uses a vinyl wash coat over raw, unstained rosewood before filling the grain with a dark wood filler. Vinyl sealer keeps the dark filler from coloring the natural rosewood, and it controls rosewood's tendency to bleed color into clear lacquer coats or over white binding.

Satin lacquer

Satin lacquer, or dull-rub lacquer, is just what the name implies—it produces a matte finish with a soft look. You can turn gloss lacquer into satin by adding flattening agent (available from industrial finish suppliers, mail-order tool companies, or well-stocked finishing stores). You can obtain a similar look by steel-wooling gloss lacquer, but most finishers prefer satin lacquer because they don't like the somewhat scratchy look of a steel-wooled finish, and the fact that the gloss will return in areas that get a lot of wear. A dull-rub lacquer has the satin look, but retains the professional quality of a well-sprayed, smooth, level finish. Dull-rub lacquer is often preferred as a neck finish, because it has less drag to the playing hand than a high gloss finish. Satin lacquer has the welcome advantage of not requiring buffing.

Acrylic lacquer

Acrylic lacquer appeared in the late 1950s, replacing nitrocellulose lacquer as the standard automotive finish. For years we used acrylic lacquer to match certain vintage custom colors when a nitrocellulose color was unavailable. Today, however, acrylic lacquer is quickly being replaced by high-tech products using catalysts and fewer VOC-emitting solvents. We are not discussing or recommending acrylic lacquer products in this book because in many areas they are unavailable.

Shellac

Mixed fresh from flakes, shellac is an excellent sealer under lacquer. It's a favorite in the repair shop as a sealer over repair work, or whenever oils, silicone, and other fisheye-causing contaminants may be present. Shellac makes a fine finish by itself when applied by French polishing, the preferred technique of many classical guitar makers. It can be brushed or sprayed, though it can't be applied very thick (compared to lacquer). Every serious builder and repairman should buy some shellac and denatured alcohol (Behkol, for example) and experiment.

The term "cut" is used when referring to the amount of alcohol added to dry shellac flakes to dissolve them (one pound of shellac flakes dissolved in one gallon of alcohol gives a well-thinned one-pound cut). Store-bought shellac is usually sold in a heavier three- to four-pound cut, and then thinned accordingly. (Four pounds of shellac flakes thinned with one gallon of alcohol produce a four-pound-cut shellac.) Common shellac thinning ratios range from a two- to a five-pound cut.

Once shellac flakes are mixed with alcohol, the mixture has a shelf life of no more than a year and a half. Most of us discard shellac if it's more than six months old, however. Keeping it cool will increase mixed shellac's shelf life. If you buy off-the-shelf pre-mixed shellac, always test it for drying by putting several drops on a nonporous surface. Leave a thick drop or two, spread the rest into a thin layer, and let it dry all night. By the next day, the thin layer should be dry and sandable. The thicker drop shouldn't easily take an imprint from your thumbnail. If it does, it may be usable but questionable—give it another day or two of test-drying before using it.

ADVANTAGES OF SHELLAC

- Excellent sealer because it sticks to almost anything
- Golden color and a quality that makes wood look beautiful
- Can be brushed, sprayed, or French polished
- Blocks out, or seals in, trace amounts of oil, wax, and silicone
- Easily repaired

DISADVANTAGES

- Shellac finishes are sensitive to hot objects, and are easily marked by water and alcohol (this isn't necessarily a problem with musical instruments)
- Short shelf life (always test-dry pre-mixed shellac)

Spirit varnish

Spirit varnish is made by dissolving resin, usually shellac, in solvent, usually alcohol or turpentine (hence the "spirits"), without oil. It is evaporative and is one of the earliest instrument finishes. (Technically, one could say that lacquer is a spirit varnish, since it too is made by dissolving resin in solvent). A spirit varnish called piano varnish was used in the early 1900s for finishing pianos and furniture as well as guitars. It contained shellac, natural resins, and other additives, a blend that improved its moisture and heat resistance. One violin expert believes this enhanced shellac became popular at the turn of the century to make the finish easier to remove at a future date—pointing out that shellac is impossible to remove or dissolve after it oxidizes over a long period of time, perhaps 50 years. Behlen's Violin Varnish is a modern version of such an enhanced shellac-based varnish.

Spirit varnish is the basis of a technique called French polishing. Until the late 1920s, guitars were generally finished with spirit varnish. Consisting of shellac dissolved in alcohol, usually with natural plant resins such as copal or sandarac added to make the film harder, the varnish was applied by a brush and polished to a final shine. The technique became know as French polishing. Guitar finishers using it apply multiple coats of spirit varnish by rubbing it onto the wood using a ball of cotton wrapped in linen with a dab of a nondrying oil, such as mineral oil, as a lubricant. Because the oil doesn't dry or polymerize, it rises to the surface of the coats of shellac and is removed with pure alcohol during a process known as spiriting-off. Commercially, French polishing gave way to spray finishing with nitrocellulose lacquer in the early 1930s because lacquer is faster and easier to apply, is more durable, and needs less upkeep.

Many hand builders today believe nothing is more beautiful than a nicely applied, French polished spirit varnish finish. Some say that French polished instruments have the best tone because, along with being flat and level, the finish is thin. Some makers French polish only the sound board, then spray the sides, neck, and back with lacquer. French polishing also offers a great way to repair and touch up shellac and lacquer finishes.

ADVANTAGES OF SPIRIT VARNISH

- With its pre-mixed resins, it is easy to use and ready to apply
- Makes an excellent finish for a spruce soundboard

TECH TIP

The violin world is very conservation-conscious, doing to an instrument only things that can easily be undone—a practice that most guitar restorationists are now discovering. Spirit varnish or plain shellac is used more for touchup and restoration work on violins because it is reversible—meaning it can be removed from oil varnish (using alcohol) without harming the original varnish. (Shellac will lay on top of oil varnish but won't dissolve into it.)

- Not quite as sensitive to moisture as a straight shellac finish

DISADVANTAGES
- Short shelf life (test that it dries)
- Sensitive to hot objects, and are easily marked by water and alcohol (this isn't necessarily a problem with musical instruments)

Padding lacquer

Padding lacquer is commercially made for French polishing. It's shellac with a lubricant added so that it's ready to use (Qualasole is one popular brand). Padding lacquers do an adequate job of imitating a French-polished shellac finish, with all the same pluses and minuses, and they don't need to be spirited off.

Reactive Finishes

Reactive finishes include the penetrating oils, oil varnishes (the most common reactive finishes), catalyzed urethanes and acrylics, polyesters, and polyurethanes. They dry, or cure, in one of two ways: either the resins **polymerize** from a reaction with oxygen as the thinner evaporates (oxidation), or they **catalyze** when a hardener (catalyst) is used. In both polymerization and catalyzation, chemicals cross link into a solid film. This means that there are no spaces between the molecules for water or solvents to penetrate to the wood surface. Because of cross linking, reactive finishes are more resistant than the other two types to scratches, heat, solvents, and moisture penetration.

Reactive finishes also are more difficult to apply, however, because they cure slowly, don't sand well, don't rub out easily, and do not bite, or melt, into previous coats. The first coat must be dry before you apply additional coats, and you need to sand between coats so that all coats adhere well together. Polymerizing finishes (such as oil varnish) must be applied thin, because they cure from the top down. If the top skins over on a coat that's too thick, the rest of the film will have trouble drying (as opposed to a catalyzed finish, which would cure anyway).

Reactive finishes are difficult to remove by sanding or stripping. When you try to strip a cross-linked finish you get a sticky, thick mess. Also, cross-linked finishes are the hardest to repair since they don't redissolve with their own solvent. Touchup work on these finishes leaves a telltale line where new finish meets the old.

Oils

Several oil types are used in guitar finishing, but not as finishes per se: Nondrying, semi-drying, and drying oil. **Nondrying oils** such as mineral oil and paraffin oil are used as a lubricant to apply shellac when French polishing. They don't remain as part of the finish but rather are spirited off with alcohol.

Semi-drying oils such as walnut, safflower, and soybean, are modified for use in the manufacture of synthetic oil varnish. Some finishers prefer walnut oil rather than nondrying mineral oil as a lubricant for French polishing. They feel walnut's semi-drying nature adds hardness and build to the shellac while simultaneously lubricating the French polishing process. Walnut oil is not removed completely during the spiriting-off stage of French polishing as are paraffin and mineral oil.

Drying oils such as linseed oil and tung oil, are the base for penetrating-oil finishes and for manufacturing traditional oil varnishes. Used by themselves as penetrating oil finishes, they go on by hand, are easy to use, and can be a valid choice for certain instruments that don't need the durability or glossy, wet look of modern factory film finishes. Most penetrating oil finishes are found either in a pure or a boiled polymerized form. In the boiled form they dry faster.

A hand-applied oil finish can be a good choice for first-time finishers, persons lacking spray equipment or those who prefer the look and feel of the simple, soft, satiny finishes found on some electric basses and certain folk instruments. In general, though, we don't recommended an oil finish for high performance acoustic instruments because, with their thin-walled tops, sides, and backs, they generally require a harder finish that dries fast and forms a film on top of the surface, instead of penetrating into the wood as oil finishes do. Like lacquer, such finishes enhance tone, protect against dents and scratches, and stop the absorption of body oils and moisture that might cause the thin wood to warp and crack.

Oil varnish

Along with shellac, oil varnish was among the earliest of musical instrument finishes. The consensus is that Stradivarius used oil varnish, although some well-respected makers insist that it was spirit varnish. Oil varnish was in wide use at the time, and formulas for its making abound in the old literature.

Oil varnish is a reactive finish made by melting resin and adding a drying oil (usually linseed or tung oil) to make it less brittle and a thinner to make it possible to brush. The reaction of oil and resin with oxygen (polymerization) causes the finish to dry and form a film as the thinner evaporates.

Oil varnish can be a beautiful-looking guitar finish with fine acoustical qualities, but it's fussy, hard to spray or brush, and very slow drying. Dust specks are inevitable, and even experienced finishers find it hard to use. It's difficult to buff to a gloss, and it doesn't repair as easily as lacquer. Still, some finishers who want to be historically correct use it.

The resins in oil varnish remain on the surface and are what gives it build after the solvents have evaporated, coalesced, or polymerized (reacted). They remain behind as a dry, hard, protective coat. Some oil varnishes, though certainly not as many as in the past, contain the traditional organic, insect or plant-derived resins—amber, rosin, damar, shellac, copal, sandarac, or mastic. Violins are generally finished with oil varnish made from these natural resins. Such oil varnishes can be purchased ready-to-use from violin supply houses, ready for you to mix. Another oil varnish type used on violins is turpine, a mixture of highly distilled turpentine and linseed oil heated without added resin.

The distilled turpentine forms its own resin, which combines with the polymerized linseed oil.

Tung oil/linseed oil

Pure (nonpolymerized) tung oil and linseed oil dries slower than the polymerized oils and with a nonglossy satin sheen. If you take the time to build up three to five coats of these oils and rub them out, however, you can get a gloss. Though guitar builders don't use an oil finish on the sound box, some favor a light tung oil finish on necks—especially necks made of maple—so that the true feel of the wood meets the player's hand.

Polymerized tung oil/linseed oil

Polymerized drying oil has been heated to 500°F to increase its gloss and speed the curing time upon contact with air. This is "gunstock" finish, of which Tru-Oil is the best-known brand. Polymerized oil gives great protection if you apply several coats. It dries fast and hard, has a good gloss, and doesn't penetrate too deeply. It could be a candidate for a simple neck finish that doesn't leave the feel of the natural wood but more the feel of a finish.

Danish oil

Danish oil is the name given to combination oil and varnish products made from natural tung oil or linseed oil that has various added dryers, thinners, and varnish resins. Since Danish oil actually has a finish in it, it builds faster than tung oil, and often one coat is sufficient. Because of the added varnish, the finish will be glossier than tung oil alone.

Gel finish

Modern gel finish, although not actually an oil but a high-tech polyurethane, falls into the penetrating-oil category because it's applied by hand and gives similar results (better, in our opinion). It duplicates the look and feel of penetrating oil finishes. Gel finish is the easiest and most versatile of all the above types to use, especially for novice finishers. You can buff it to achieve a semigloss or leave it unbuffed for a nice satin look like oil. Since gel finish dries quickly, dries hard, doesn't penetrate too deeply, and builds to a good film, it could be considered as a finish for an acoustic guitar.

"Hi-tech" finish (polyester and polyurethane)

"Polys" are the hi-tech finishes used by many motorcycle and automotive finishers. Many large guitar manufacturers—especially overseas companies—use polyester because it produces a tough film, builds quickly, sands easily, and buffs nicely. It produces low levels of volatile organic compounds since it is a catalyzed finish and requires little or no thinner (and is therefore less harmful to the environment). However, polyesters and polyurethanes require sophisticated equipment, prompt cleanup, extremely toxic hardeners and catalysts, and are beyond the scope of this book and the needs of most of its readers. You can learn about hi-tech finishing by consulting the best car or motorcycle painters in your area.

Coalescing Finishes

Waterbase lacquer

The third type of finish is the coalescing finish. Coalesce means to stick together or unify. The main coalescing finish for guitar finishing is waterbase, or "waterborne" lacquer. This finish has micro-pellets of an already cured resin suspended in water and glycol ether solvent. As the water evaporates, the slow-drying solvent softens the outer surface of the resin pellets, enabling them to stick together and connect into a film in much the same way as the evaporative finishes do. The water makes the finish applicable. It dilutes the slow-drying solvent to keep it from softening the resin and coalescing before the water has evaporated. Waterbase lacquer is nonflammable and doesn't produce unbearable fumes. For clear, hard finishes, waterbase lacquer does a great job, and it has proved itself to numerous guitar makers.

Waterbase lacquer generally consists of a resin (typically acrylic or urethane, or a blend of the two) that is not dissolved, but is in the form of microscopic particles suspended in the finish, and the following liquid components:

- Cosolvents required to dissolve or melt the resin
- Water to dilute the solvents and prevent them from coalescing prematurely, as well as to act as the "vehicle" for spraying
- De-foamers that keep the finish from trapping air bubbles as it is applied
- Emulsifiers to hold all of the disparate elements in a uniform suspension
- Small amounts of modifying elements that alter the resin to achieve good performance characteristics

Once the finish is applied (sprayed, brushed, wiped on with a rag), the water evaporates first. Next, the coalescing solvents concentrate and soften the resin particles, which enable them to merge together. Ideally there should be complete merging of all the resin particles. Without complete coalescing of the resin particles, there will be voids, which can diffract light and cause haze and cloudiness in the finish. These solvents also soften the surface of the coat they are applied to, allowing the newly applied topcoat to "burn in" or melt into its undercoat. Last, the cosolvents evaporate, and the resin cures.

Safety precautions

While waterbase lacquer greatly reduces the amount of volatile organic solvents per gallon over evaporative finishes, this does not mean that the chemicals in waterbase lacquer are any less toxic or harmful. In fact they are at least as much so as those in nitrocellulose lacquer, but they are present in much smaller amounts, and diluted with water rather than a solvent thinner.

Although waterbase finishes are non-flammable, thin and clean up with water, and are perhaps less toxic than the solvent lacquer we are used to, follow the same safety precautions used with solvent finishes: excellent ventilation, wearing an approved respirator, curing the finish in a separate room to avoid breathing evaporating fumes, and wearing protective gloves when contacting uncured finish while filling or cleaning your spray gun or when spraying a finish; also wear gloves when sanding—whether it be wet-sanding or dry-sanding. (Even though the cured finish is hardened acrylic, and is solvent-free, we prefer not to come in contact with sanding dust and residue). Spraying finish causes the atomized liquid to hang in the air, and a good vapor respirator is required to prevent inhaling this material. In addition, an exhaust fan should be used to evacuate the room of these harmful materials. Once a coating of finish is applied and drying, the cosolvents evaporate into the room. Avoid the vapors by working in a different room, or be sure that the room has adequate ventilation. Spray equipment should be cleaned after each spray session. That means emptying the contents of the spray cup into another container, and using warm water to clean all parts of the gun that came into contact with the liquid finish. Afterwards, dry all parts of the gun and cup. This doesn't take very long—far shorter than the amount of time needed to clean a gun that has had finish cure and harden in the fluid passageways.

Specifics about Stewart-MacDonald's ColorTone waterbase products

ColorTone waterbase finishes have been formulated to give a clear, hard, easy to apply, easy to repair alternative to the current solvent finish choices. The ColorTone Waterbase Guitar Lacquer line includes clear gloss acrylic topcoat, sanding sealer, retarder, and grain filler. These materials can be used together exclusively, or used under and on top of many other products, such as shellac or lacquer. Virtually any finish can be applied over wood filled with the ColorTone Waterbase Grain Filler. These products are highly compatible.

ColorTone waterbase products require a clean, dust-free, wax-free surface for optimum performance. New wood that has been vacuumed and blown dust free is an ideal surface to apply ColorTone finishes to. If in doubt, or if the surface has been contaminated with oils or waxes, wipe it down with denatured alcohol. When applying ColorTone over an old finish, we recommend wiping it with denatured alcohol too. Denatured alcohol can be mixed 50/50 with clean water to reduce the solvent bite, and it still has the de-greasing benefits.

Sanding sealer

Modern guitar finishes have a level, flat surface—even on the curves of a neck or heel. On porous woods (mahogany, rosewood, etc.), the open grain is filled with a grain filler to create a flat surface to begin with. Then multiple coats of finish are applied, leveled, and polished. Often, color is applied to the bare wood, or to early layers of the finish itself, during the finishing process. A level finish can only be achieved if the finish thickness, or "build," is thick enough to allow for level-sanding and buffing without sanding into bare wood or color layers.

Our **ColorTone Sanding Sealer** is a clear, tough, hard, shrink-resistant polyester/urethane lacquer sealer. Use it for the majority of your finish (65–75% of the final finish thickness should be sealer). The sealer has a 48-hour "burn-in" window, meaning that successive coats will bond best when applied within 48 hours of each other. When this time is exceeded, sanding with 320-grit paper is required to roughen the surface for good adhesion of the coats to follow, so try hard to stay on schedule!

Waterbase sealer coats do not melt into each other as the topcoat finish does, but they cling well to each other. If you sand through a layer of sealer you will expose a mark called a "witness line"—however, this will disappear with the following coat.

ColorTone Waterbase Guitar Lacquer is a crystal clear, acrylic waterbase lacquer that, unlike the sanding sealer, has 100% burn-in between coats without a time limit. That makes it repairable, much like nitrocellulose lacquer. It is a thermoplastic resin and will shrink and move around with the heat of buffing—that's why we don't recommend it for all of the build, but just the top 25–30% of the finish. It sands and buffs well to a high gloss, has good hardness and durability, and performs like the finishes you are used to on those fine old guitars. Use the same spraying environment as with the sealer, and same gun tips and air pressure also. Apply 3–4 topcoats in one to two days. Sand between coats (800-grit) only to remove defects such as runs, sags, or dust specks. The gloss topcoat dries (full chemical cure) in 150 hours. This can be accelerated slightly at an elevated temperature (100°F), but consideration should be given to what that temperature might do to the guitar. Remember, at a higher temperature the relative humidity can drop. A lower than ideal temperature can lengthen cure time.

Optimum spraying conditions

Both the sealer and the topcoat lacquer perform best at 70°F, and 45–50% relative humidity. Operating outside this environment can cause less than ideal results. For instance, spraying at an elevated temperature and/or reduced humidity will cause faster evaporation, and insufficient time for the cosolvents to coalesce the resins properly. On the other hand, reduced temperatures, and/or increased humidity, can slow drying to the detriment of the quality of the film. For a siphon feed gun, we recommend a tip size of 1.8; with a gravity feed gun, use a 1.3mm tip. This is important for proper atomization, and a proper wet film thickness. Dry, oil and dirt-free air is always a must for any spray finishing because the wet film will lay down nicely when the surface and the propellant air are free of contaminants. Contaminants break down or interrupt the surface tension of the material, and uniform surface tension is needed for excellent flow-out. Somewhere around 40–60 psi is recommended for gravity feed guns. Use the manufacturer's recommendation for gravity feed and HVLP guns.

ADVANTAGES OF WATERBASE LACQUER/SANDING SEALER
- Clarity: compares favorably to nitrocellulose lacquer
- Hardness: pencil "Scratch Hardness" of 6H, which is about the same as most nitrocellulose lacquers
- Less solvent, no VOCs
- Very mild fumes when drying

- Dries fast and sands easily
- Can be used to "drop-fill" nitrocellulose lacquer in repair work

  DISADVANTAGES
- Sanding through a sealer layer will expose a "witness line", though this disappears with the following coat

ColorTone Retarder

Retarder can be used when temperature and/or humidity conditions are causing the finish to dry too fast. Retarder is made up of a mixture of the cosolvent and water. It will slow the drying. If drying is not the problem, but thinning is desired to reduce the viscosity so the finish flows through the gun easier, we recommend just using clean water. For build coats, use up to 15% water, retarder, or a mixture of the two. For the very first wash coats, you can use as much as 50/50 water to finish without a problem, but this much thinning is not a good idea for build coats.

ColorTone Waterbase Brushing Varnish is an oil varnish in a water vehicle. It can be applied over shellac or ColorTone Sanding Sealer, and works just fine when used alone. The resin is a combination of a proprietary oil and urethane/acrylic blend, with many of the same characteristics as oil varnish. For instance, it has an amber tint, yellows with age, is flexible yet tough, has a chatoyance, or depth and iridescent luster, and has the odor of an oil varnish.

We recommend an inexpensive polyester bristle brush, available at most paint and hardware stores, for application. The biggest problem with brushing waterbase is brushing bubbles into the wet film, and this type of brush puts fewer and larger air bubbles into the film. The larger bubbles seem to rise out of the finish and pop easier than smaller ones. Buffing works well on this varnish, giving a lovely luster. The drying time and application schedule is similar to waterbase lacquer. Although this varnish has been formulated for brushing, spraying is an option. Keep in mind that it is a little thinner, and is retarded for brushing, so spraying would require thinner coats to be successful.

Solvents and Thinners

Solvents and thinners aren't necessarily the same thing, though the terms are used interchangeably by novices. Both solvents and thinners evaporate completely when the finish cures. A solvent is a liquid that dissolves a solid material and allows it to be used as a liquid. A thinner is a liquid that dilutes, reduces or thins an already-dissolved material. Sometimes the same liquid is used as a solvent and a thinner. Other times it is quite different. For example, shellac flakes are dissolved with alcohol, and they are also reduced to a different cut with the same alcohol. Lacquer thinner is a mixture of solvent and diluent, and is not the same as the primary solvent for nitrocellulose resin.

Thinner can also serve to clean spray guns and finishing equipment, as long as the finish hasn't cured. That's because it's miscible, meaning it mixes with or dilutes the liquid finish. A thinner reduces the viscosity and extends the amount of the finish. Add alcohol to

> **CAUTION!**
>
> Oil-soaked rags, wipes, and paper towels generate heat as they dry and can ignite by spontaneous combustion. Dispose of such rags by incinerating them or by hanging them, one layer thick, outdoors to dry. At the least, submerse them in water until you can dispose of them properly.

dissolved shellac, and you'll get a thinner "cut"—alcohol is the thinner in that case. Or, add mineral spirits to polyurethane varnish, and you get more varnish that sprays easier because it's thinner.

It's good to understand when a certain product will act as both thinner and solvent, and when it won't. Lacquer thinner, for example will dissolve shellac somewhat but it doesn't serve to thin it. Another example: Spill lacquer thinner or alcohol onto a hardened lacquer or shellac finish and you're in big trouble. On the other hand, neither lacquer thinner nor mineral spirits will soften a cured varnish finish.

Lacquer thinner

Lacquer thinner, a mixture of volatile organic compounds, is both a diluent and a mild solvent for lacquer. It's used to dilute the viscosity so that the lacquer will flow properly through the spray gun, and for cleanup afterwards. Lacquer thinner, which contains alcohol, is also a mild solvent for shellac and waterbase finishes, which makes it useful for cleanup of shellac and waterbase lacquer as well. It is not used to thin shellac or waterbase finishes, however. Another important use for lacquer thinner is to dissolve lacquer and oil-soluble aniline dyes and pigments.

Alcohol

The main uses of alcohol in finishing are to make alcohol-soluble stains, to dissolve shellac into liquid form, to thin shellac for spraying, and for use in French polishing. The commonly available alcohols are methanol (wood alcohol), isopropyl (rubbing alcohol), and ethanol (grain alcohol). Methanol is quite toxic and isopropyl is hygroscopic (absorbs water), so ethanol is preferred for finishing use.

Wood finishers commonly use ethanol, which contains poisons added by the manufacturer to make it undrinkable, untaxable, and therefore inexpensive. This **denatured alcohol** is what you buy at the hardware store as shellac thinner. Another good denatured alcohol is Behkol proprietary solvent.

Alcohol will soften lacquer and waterbase products, but not as well as lacquer thinner. Denatured alcohol is good for the initial cleanup of spray guns after using shellac and should be followed with lacquer thinner. Alcohol is also an excellent degreaser and wipe-down for bare wood.

Mineral spirits, naphtha, turpentine

These petroleum distillates are used mostly as thinners for varnishes, the oils (linseed, tung, Danish, and gel finish), and for thinning oil-base grain wood filler. Since naphtha, mineral spirits, xylene, or turpentine won't affect cured varnish, lacquer, or shellac finishes, we often degrease and clean lacquered instruments with them. Naphtha is the most accepted degreaser of all the petroleum products because it leaves the least oily film behind.

Petroleum distillates are also good for dissolving wax and removing silicone contamination. Do not use these products on waterbase finishes however!

Acetone

Acetone is sometimes an ingredient of lacquer thinner. Some experienced professional finishers will actually substitute pure acetone for lacquer thinner when they want the finish to dry faster, and lacquer formulators on the West Coast are using acetone-based lacquers to replace the more environmentally hazardous formulations. There are many uses for acetone in finishing, including cleaning and degreasing bare wood (watch out for plastics however, which will dissolve under the influence of acetone), removing white and yellow glue, and removing super glue.

Glycol ether

Glycol ether is a name you may hear, but the generic product is not generally available to the public. It's a resin solvent used in waterbase products and for nitrocellulose lacquer. Glycol ether is a bridging solvent, meaning it can make some otherwise incompatible substances compatible with each other. Glycol ether is commonly used to make waterbase finishes and to allow liquid dyes to dissolve in water, alcohol or lacquer based materials (for NGR stains).

There are two groups of glycol ethers—ethylene and propylene. Of the two groups, ethylene is the most toxic but also the most useful to guitar finishers. Use it when necessary but with great care.

Butyl Cellosolve

Butyl Cellosolve, one of the ethylene glycol ethers, is a primary solvent for lacquer and one of the key ingredients in lacquer retarders. One of the more toxic chemicals used in lacquer, Butyl Cellosolve should be handled with gloves and used in a well-ventilated area, as should all lacquer products. For repair on a lacquer finish, nothing beats Butyl Cellosolve for melting-in touchup finish. When spraying new finish over old, melting-in avoids a telltale lacquer line and prevents or eliminates blushes (more about this later under retarders).

Available only in gallons from larger suppliers such as Sherwin-Williams, Butyl Cellosolve can be added to normal lacquer thinner (or into already thinned lacquer) instead of normal retarder to make an even slower-drying mixture.

Retarder

Retarder is added to lacquer thinner in humid conditions to prevent blushing. Blushing is a white or bluish haze produced when moisture is trapped under the finish as the surface skins over. Some suppliers offer retarder-thinner (with the retarder already mixed in it). It has more primary solvent added to it than normal lacquer thinner. This retards the drying time so that trapped moisture can escape. Butyl Cellosolve is a key retarder ingredient. Retarders also remove blushes after the fact when carefully and lightly sprayed over a blushed finish.

Another plus of retarders is that they help control "orange-peel" (that grainy, pebbly look) caused by too-rapid drying before the finish has a chance to flow out. It doesn't hurt to add a capful or two to the lacquer on a regular basis to prevent blushing and orange peel.

TECH TIP

In repair work, the two-gun method uses Butyl Cellosolve in one gun to melt in the lacquer sprayed by a second gun—all done in very quick order. The first spraying of Butyl Cellosolve softens the lacquer finish so the repair lacquer can melt in more easily. This eliminates any possibility of a lacquer line or "witness mark" showing when the finish is dry. To melt in a finish, use Butyl Cellusolve almost straight, but with a dollop of clear lacquer added to keep it from running (1/8 ounce lacquer to two ounces Butyl Cellosolve).

> **TECH TIP**
>
> Retarder is added to the thinner before the thinner is added to the lacquer in the normal ratios. You should add 5%–10% retarder to the thinner—no more. For example, a quart (32 ounces) of ready-to-spray lacquer, thinned one-to-one with a thinner to which you add your own retarder, would be composed of 16 ounces of clear lacquer, mixed with 14.4 ounces of thinner, and 1.6 ounces of retarder. That amounts to 10% of retarder and a total of 16 ounces of retarder-thinner.

With proper experimentation, you can add retarder to regular spraying lacquer to make it brushable. Special brushing lacquers are available, however, that are better for this purpose. Because lacquer dries so fast, brushing lacquer is harder to use than mere paint. It dries fast, like shellac, and areas cannot be rebrushed without dragging the finish. With sanding, and successive coats, brushing lacquer can produce a good finish, albeit a softer one, but it's main usefulness to a guitar finisher would be for small repairs that don't warrant an elaborate spray setup.

Water

Water is the recommended thinner and initial cleanup solvent for waterbase finish. For best cleanup, follow with glycol ether and/or lacquer thinner. It is also used to dissolve water-soluble stains, soften and clean up glue residue, raise grain during the wood preparation stage.

CHAPTER 2

Grain Filler, Wood Putty, and Wood Dough

Most of us expect guitar and bass finishes to be level—free of ripples, imperfections, and especially the hundreds of little pits created when the finish sinks into the grain of the open-pore woods used in guitar making. The first thing we look for upon holding a guitar up to a backlight is a level, mirror-like finish. Perfectly level "piano-type" finishes, however, are the most difficult to produce and represent the height of musical instrument finishing to many connoisseurs, and they're what the typical player expects.

Hardwoods such as ash, rosewood, mahogany, and walnut, which are used for building guitars, have open pores, and a grain structure that must be filled flush with the wood's surface before you can apply a level finish. Unless the guitar is simply oiled, unfilled pores mar the finish with craters, pinholes, and air bubbles caused when air, solvents, and stains become trapped in the unfilled pores—flawing an otherwise excellent finish. Soft tone woods (such as spruce, alder, cypress, and cedar) and smooth hardwoods (such as cherry, maple, and most ebony) are closed-pore and don't require filling.

Guitar makers generally fill pores by working a grain filler into them or by applying a clear finish and sanding it back until the pores are filled level with the finish. Either method leaves a level surface for a top coat but grain filler is easier and faster to apply, has the right look for traditional finishes, and usually shrinks less than using finish. Clear finish used as filler is discussed briefly in this chapter.

A select few finishers, especially classic guitar makers, level the surface by French polishing with shellac, oil, and powdered pumice to sever the wood fibers and pack them into the pores. This book does not go into detail on French polishing techniques, however. The following section deals with grain fillers and clear finish filling.

Grain Filler

Grain filler, or grain wood filler, is a slurry of ground quartz (silex) suspended in either an oil or waterbase mixture and colored in wood tones to match or contrast with the surrounding wood. Grain filler is intended for filling pores only, and novice finishers would benefit from experimenting with each type. Grain filler is wiped and sanded off the surface before finish is applied over it.

Oil-base grain filler

Oil-base grain filler is an oil varnish-like base with added silex and thinned with either naphtha or mineral spirits. Naphtha-thinned filler dries faster than filler thinned with mineral spirits. The two solvents can also be combined to control the drying time. Oil-based filler is easier to apply than the waterbase version because it dries more slowly (it contains linseed oil to slow down the drying time of the naphtha or mineral spirits), allowing plenty of time to remove the excess filler from the wood surface. Once filled, the wood won't stain

TECH TIP

Many professionals only wait overnight before lacquering over an oil-base filler. This is risky unless you've finished many instruments and know your products. Some finishers will purposely add Japan drier to speed up drying (Japan drier is often used with artist's oil colors but is seldom used in guitar finishing). If you add Japan drier to the filler, start with only a few drops per quart and test it on scrap. It is very strong, and too much will ruin the filler and your project because, oddly enough, too much Japan drier can actually cause grain filler *not* to dry!

well, since the varnish base of the filler seals the wood. Therefore, sand-throughs into colored bare wood are difficult to repair, even with matching stain.

Oil-base filler dries in two stages. The hazing-over stage happens about five to fifteen minutes after application; the filler is partially dry and any traces left on the surface can be polished off without pulling the filler back out of the pores.

The second stage is the true drying time of the oily base; you must allow a *minimum* of three to five days pass before you apply any finish over it.

ADVANTAGES OF OIL-BASED FILLER

- Easier to apply than waterbase filler because it dries more slowly, giving you more time to apply it
- Time-tested and familiar
- Good colors are available

DISADVANTAGES

- Oil-base inhibits staining later
- Sand-throughs are tough to repair
- Takes several days or more to dry

Waterbase grain filler

ColorTone Waterbase Grain Filler is a urethane based heavy-bodied material that is excellent for grain filling using familiar techniques. The biggest difference is that the waterbase filler dries a lot faster, and dries more completely and much harder. It comes in clear, medium brown, and black. Pigmented colors such as ColorTone Liquid Pigments for waterbase lacquer can be used to color the filler or modify the brown to the particular tint desired. Using the pigments in amounts up to 15% with the filler will not alter the filler's performance, and should be enough to get any color needed. Filler can be used directly on the bare wood, or over a clear wash-coat of waterbase sealer, shellac or lacquer. Used directly on bare wood, the filler color penetrates the wood and changes the wood's color—practice on scrap to get a color that you like. Two applications are recommended for complete filling. Once filled and dried, the surface should be sanded lightly with 320-grit sandpaper.

ADVANTAGES OF WATERBASE FILLER

- Works well under waterbase finishes, which don't adhere well to oil-base filler
- It accepts stain
- Fast-drying
- It sands fairly easily if the majority of the excess left on the surface is removed before it hardens (which must happen within a matter of minutes)
- Cleans up with water

DISADVANTAGES

- Its fast-drying property can be a disadvantage on large surfaces

---

TECH TIP

Some finishers use the fact that waterbase grain filler accepts stain until it's fully cured to their advantage: They use a neutral grain filler, let it dry then sand it back to the surface, and then stain both wood and filler at once, by using a neutral filler and coloring it with one of the above-mentioned stains the same day that the filler is applied.

Clear finish as a filler

Clear lacquer (or other finish) can be used instead of grain filler to fill the grain. Wood filled with clear finish shows its natural color and has great depth and clarity. Filling open pores with finish is labor-intensive, however, and is not a conventional pore-filling technique for guitars. The wood prep for this type of finish must be impeccable because there's nowhere for mistakes to hide—not even a little scratch!

For filling pores, manufacturers that use a transparent finish (without stain or filler) generally prefer using a catalyzed finish—not a solvent-base (evaporative) finish. Because the finish cures and hardens, it fills the pores quickly and doesn't shrink. For example, some of Alembic's most beautiful basses are unstained and filled only with clear catalyzed polyester.

Producing the transparent look with lacquer as filler takes a lot of patience. The lacquer tends to disappear as it soaks into the open grain. Each new coat softens and swells the finish already in the pores before shrinking back. When it finally fills the pores, it tends to continue shrinking after it's cured, which means you may have to add more coats days later. For best results, use clear lacquer or fresh-mixed shellac. Spray several coats and then sand back to the wood to see if the pores are filled. You can spray the finish until the pores are filled, and then sand back all at once, but it's faster to do a light sanding once or twice as you progress. Once the pores are level, let the finish cure several days to give it a chance to shrink (you may need another coat or two). If you're not in a hurry, let the filled pores cure for about a week.

ADVANTAGES OF USING FINISH AS FILLER
- Avoid potential problems that may be caused by the use of a grain filler
- Wood has a beautiful, natural look and the grain is not obscured

DISADVANTAGES
- Solvent-based clear finishes can shrink, leaving pores to appear as pockmarks in the previously smooth surface

Wood Doughs and Putties

Wood doughs, putties, and catalyzed fillers used during the wood preparation stage are for repairing dents, gouges, and missing wood. As a general rule they're not used for pore filling because they dry too fast and are difficult to remove, making filling a large surface tedious. These products include older standbys such as Plastic Wood and Durham's Rock Hard Water Putty and newer waterbase acrylic wood doughs. Under solid-color finishes, catalyzed auto-body fillers like Bondo also work well.

Plastic Wood

Plastic Wood and other nitrocellulose-lacquer-based putties are fast-drying, natural wood doughs that require acetone or lacquer thinner for cleanup and thinning. They can be colored with alcohol

---

TECH TIP

You can use grain filler on bare wood—coloring the wood as well as filling it. Or, you can spray a washcoat beforehand to keep all but the pores from being colored by the filler. The darker filled pores will contrast against the lighter wood background.

and lacquer-soluble colors or UTCs. They tend to shrink more than the other putties and don't take stain when dry.

Acrylic wood putty (wood dough)

The new acrylic wood putties use water for immediate cleanup and thinning and accept water-soluble colorants wet or dry. Acetone may be needed to clean up or remove some of these putties when dry, while others remain soluble in water after drying. These fast-drying, low-shrinking, easy-to-clean-up putties are the only ones that take stain when dry and are suitable for guitar finishing with see-through finishes. They are the softest of the three putties, and therefore can't be used in areas that may be handled heavily.

Water putty

Durham's Rock Hard Water Putty is a dry powder that mixes with water, shrinks little and dries to a hard, durable fill. It uses water for cleanup, thinning, and coloring. When dry, it cannot be softened or stained to any degree.

Auto-body filler (catalyzed acrylic resin filler)

This filler, which is commonly referred to as Bondo, was one of the earliest of the catalyzed acrylic resin grain fillers. It dries fast and hard, shrinks little, sands easily, and fills large or small voids. We don't recommend it as a pore filler because it's too difficult to remove the excess and the colors are unsuitable.

Acrylic spot putty

Acrylic spot putty, another useful automotive product, is a fast-drying, noncatalyzed filler for small shallow dents. It dries upon contact with air. Spot putties are usually green, pink, grey, or white, and can be used on bare wood or directly on sealer, primer, or color coats. Spot putty was designed to fill the imperfections that are so often found after the first coat or two of finish has been applied. It's a fine pore filler under solid colors; in fact it's too bad you can't use spot putty as a pore filler under clear finishes, because it dries so fast and shrinks so little.

Grain Filler Colors

In guitar making, the most common filler colors are shades of walnut, mahogany and, on occasion, a neutral. Most building and repair shops stock a medium brown mahogany, possibly a red brown mahogany, a neutral, and the workhorse—an extra-dark-brown (burnt umber) walnut filler best for duplicating most Gibson and Martin finishes.

Neutral is a bland shade of tan that gets its color from the natural ingredients of the grain filler, whether oil or waterbased. In furniture finishing, neutral is used on light woods such as elm, oak, korina, and ash. In guitar finishing, the only common recipes that might call for a neutral filler would be ash-bodied Fender guitars finished either in natural or blonde. Even then, you must tint a neutral grain filler slightly to correctly match that used by Fender. You can add small amounts of yellow and brown pigment to neutral filler to produce a butterscotch neutral shade. Generally, though, try to use grain filler in available colors. Attempts to change a grain filler color dramatically by adding lots of pigment is rarely successful. Manufacturers add the pigment early in the manufacturing stage with high-speed mixers. When you hand mix color into filler, it is difficult to get the color to blend in. The tendency is to add too much color, which can alter the drying time, cause dry-looking chalking, and leave heavy saturations of colored pigment on the wood surface.

Filler colorants

Filler colorants, which are explained in Chapter 3, are generally pigmented (opaque) colors rather than dyes (transparent) because the pigments don't have the tendency to stain the wood surrounding the pores as dyes will. An exception to this rule would be the cherry red filler Gibson used in the 1950s and 1960s to color bare mahogany. Gibson's red filler may have had both stain and pigment added as colorants—the pigment to darken the pores, the stain to color the surrounding wood. This addition of stain would cause the finish to come to life when the lacquer solvents hit it, by drawing the stain into the clear finish.

Most of the oil-based grain fillers for guitar finishing come in satisfactory, ready to-use colors. On the rare occasion when you need added color, use artist's oil color, Japan color, a universal tinting color (UTC)—the sort of colorant paint stores use to make colors. Japan color and artist's oil colors are the best because they are oil-based products. All these colorants are described in Chapter 3. Another way of achieving a desired color is to blend two colors of grain filler together to arrive at the proper tone. Remember that an open pore casts a tiny shadow; thus pores look natural if they are filled darker than the color of the wood.

Waterbase grain fillers can be colored by mixing them together, or by adding waterbase pigments, or tinting them with liquid concentrated dye.

How to hand-mix colors

You may need to hand-mix some colors, especially if you're matching a vintage color such as the cherry red filler on the necks and bodies of Gibson SGs, Les Pauls, Hummingbirds, and J-45s of the late '50s and early '60s. Don't just stir in your pigment color. Grind the pigment into the filler using a mortar and pestle, or spread the filler on a sheet of glass and mill it in with a smooth flat piece of stone, plastic, glass, or metal. Add less color than you think necessary, and mill it into the filler slowly. It might take half an hour to do it right. If the filler seems to be drying out, add a drop of linseed oil and some naphtha or mineral spirits to moisten it.

TECH TIP

Manufacturers' colors vary, especially in neutral. We've seen some golden brown neutrals that were quite usable straight from the can.

TECH TIP

A small collection of palette knives is handy for applying the wood doughs and putties used for filling voids in the wood.

CHAPTER 3

Finish Colorants

Now comes the finish component that imparts true character to a guitar. All of the other craftsmanship that goes into a guitar certainly makes it beautiful, but the color makes it memorable. It's a rare guitar that doesn't have color sprayed, wiped, or painted on it somewhere. Even most instruments with "natural" finishes have their necks, backs, and sides stained, either for effect or simply to make the wood look more uniform.

Learning all about colors in finishes is more than academic, and not just an off-the-shelf step in guitar finishing. For most applications, you will have to make your own colorants. Why not buy them, you ask. You can buy the *materials* you need, but the finished product—colored lacquer shaders, toners, stains, and paint—are generally not available over the counter. You have to make your own.

Guitar finishers have derived innumerable effects by making variations on a few simple coloring themes. How they layer colored finishes, whether they choose a translucent or opaque color, whether they put the color on the guitar or in the finish—all this can alter the final look. Sometimes the smallest touch can make a big difference.

A Short History of Guitar Coloring

The guitar is an age-old instrument, but the 20th Century is the age of color. Here's a short history of the most significant trends and materials.

1900 to 1930

In the early 1900s, most guitars had natural-colored finishes. Their golden colors came both from the amber color of their shellac, varnish, and (after the late 1920s) lacquer, as well as from natural earth and wood-toned stains. As the wood aged, it darkened, and the colors became even more golden. Guitar makers of this era colored the necks, backs, and sides with dye stain and filled the pores of open-grain woods. Martin and Gibson both used mahogany and walnut tones; Gibson also used a purplish wine red, "Dark Mahogany," on the sides and backs of many guitar and mandolin models. Opaque black pigmented varnish is found on a number of those beautiful Gibson Style-O guitars, and black or white was used as the top color for some Gibson mandolin and guitar models.

Gibson started using sunbursts in the late teens. Martin didn't start until the 1930s, after they had begun using lacquer and spray equipment. Gibson hand-applied their early sunbursts, mostly in red tones over golden yellow, or brownish-black over golden yellow (the Lloyd Loar "Cremona Brown" sunburst was modeled after the antique look of violins). Gibson most likely used alcohol stains, although they probably dabbled in some waterbased stains. Gibson applied early sunbursts as stains on bare wood.

1930 to 1960s

The big guitar makers used the same natural-finish look into this period, but shellac and varnish gave way in the late 1920s to lacquer as a topcoat, and spray finishing replaced hand application. Sunbursts became very popular, especially at Gibson, Epiphone, and Gretsch. Martin sunbursts appear to have been sprayed with lacquer shaders, while Gibson and the others did everything from staining bare wood to spraying dye-colored and pigment-colored lacquer shaders and toners (more about shaders and toners later in the chapter). Some of the earlier 1930s Gibson sunbursts obviously had pigmented stains (especially on less expensive models) because the wood is opaque toward the edges. The more expensive models, or at least those made of figured maple such as the Nick Lucas, had finishes that were dark yet so transparent you can see all the way to the bottom of the figured maple's shimmering curls.

As the Gibson finishers were mastering spray finishing, surely they experimented and took some creative license. The results are the variety of finishes we study today. From the early 1920s onward Gibson set many of the color standards which the other manufacturers had to live up to (and for which Gibson is still top dog today). Their use of cherry red over a yellow base coat on the 1958 Les Paul Standard flamed maple top was the inspiration for many of today's modern transparent colored finishes (PRS, Hamer, Tom Anderson, Brian Moore, and Pedulla, for example). Incidentally, this famed "Cherry Sunburst" was first used on Gibson's J-35 flattop guitars from 1939.

Duplicating these inventive finishes isn't easy. Without literally digging into the layers by sanding or scraping, it's difficult to determine exactly what materials Gibson may have used and in what order. Even stripping a finish is no guarantee you'll understand how it was applied, especially with lacquer finishes. Because each successive coat of lacquer dissolves the coat below it, they become one (especially when the finish is applied thin, as on an expertly finished guitar). Besides, most of us don't strip many vintage finishes—we generally advise our customers not to do that because it diminishes a guitar's value and erases some of its valuable history. Therefore, except for occasional hearsay, and experience with badly damaged guitars, we learned much of what we know about guitar finishing history by conjecture.

From the start, besides keeping a watchful eye on each other, guitar manufacturers obviously paid attention to the furniture industry. During the 1950s, Fender's Blonde, Gibson's TV and Limed Mahogany finish, and Gretsch's Platinum Gray were exact copies of the blonde furniture and piano finishes of the era. Automotive influence is seen in metallic finishes such as Gretsch's Cadillac Green, Gibson's Les Paul Gold Top, and in all the Fender Custom Colors, including Fiesta Red, Shoreline Gold, and Lake Placid Blue.

When it came to coloring guitars, Gretsch was a leader in the 1950s. They stood alone with their use of brilliant sparkle and pearl celluloid Nitron drum covering on the faces of the Silver-Jet and Duo-Jet models. Of course some Gretsch colors would have been better left alone, such as the two-tone avocado and pea soup "Smoke Green" color of the Anniversary model. (It seems Gretsch was watching the kitchen appliance industry by mistake!)

During the early and mid 1960s the big companies made few finishing changes. Martin remained traditional, while Gretsch, Fender, and Gibson continued finishing in solid colors, metallics, stains, and sunbursts. Gibson began using the Les Paul Cherry Sunburst on acoustic models like the Hummingbird and J-45. You might not realize it, though, because ultraviolet (UV) light caused many of those early 1960s cherry sunbursts to fade to brown. All the 1966 Gibson Hummingbirds and J-45s that we have seen have lost the red from their sunbursts.

The "flower power" of the late 1960s influenced finishing into the 1970s, as Fender featured psychedelic hippie finishes of paisley or flower print, and *au naturel* electric guitars became as popular as brown rice and sandals. It wasn't uncommon to see a perfectly fine Les Paul Gold Top stripped and refinished natural. This produced a horrible appearance because wood intended to be hidden by gold paint was not necessarily good looking or well matched.

Also, by the end of the 1960s, individual guitar makers and repairmen opened up shops around the country. Mostly self-taught, these new luthiers found the woodworking aspect of guitar making to be easier than the finishing part, and few could compete with the "factory look" of Gibson and Martin. Coupled with the fact that they wanted the wood shown in its natural beauty, many of the young builders used simple oil or wax finishes. Alembic, still the leader among these builders, perfected the techniques required to make natural-finished instruments that looked and felt as good as they sounded.

1970s through the 1980s

This ten-year period saw marked changes in traditions for coloring guitars. A wild variety of high-tech polyester and polyurethane finishes became popular, inspired by Eddie Van Halen, Randy Rhoades, and other rock players. Found mostly on instruments imported from Japan and Korea, these pin-striped, paint-striped, tape-lined, fish-scaled, flip-flop finishes mimicked motorcycle and automotive trends. Because of their complex nature these finishes are beyond the scope of this book, but if you want to learn to paint guitars—not *finish* but *paint* them—hang around good motorcycle painters, tee-shirt artists, or makers of plastic and radio-control models.

1990s

With the EPA putting ever more stringent regulations on the emission of volatile organic compounds (VOCs), finish manufacturers in the 1990s began producing finishes that require little or no solvents. VOCs are the harmful hydrocarbons released into the atmosphere as solvents evaporate.

Some major guitar manufacturers switched to more efficient spraying systems and to finishes that don't require solvent (catalyzed, UV-cured, and waterborne). Small shops should keep an eye on the finishing industry and make plans to at least experiment with solvent-free finishes—especially waterborne—because they are the least toxic. The low toxicity of waterborne finishes makes them appealing to woodworkers. Although the first waterborne lacquers could not be applied, sanded, or buffed comparably to nitrocellulose, they have since improved so that the feel, look, sound quality, and ease of application are more than satisfactory to a number of better guitar makers.

A Little Bit of Color Theory

Primary, secondary, and intermediate colors

Understanding the mechanics of color will help you achieve the look you want. Color wheel basics are a good place to start. For centuries artists have used the color wheel, a method of arranging paint colors in a circle around the edge of the palette in the best order for mixing colors. The color wheel holds twelve colors: the three primary colors red, yellow, and blue are spaced equally apart on the edge of the wheel, and between them are the colors that result when they're mixed. Half of the wheel's colors, from yellow to red-violet, are considered "warm" colors; the remaining half, from green to violet, are the "cool" colors. Most paint and art supply stores sell an inexpensive cardboard artists' color wheel with which you can compare colors.

For **pigment colors**, the three primary colors of red, yellow, and blue produce all the other colors when they're mixed in different combinations and amounts. Two primary colors mixed together become the three secondary colors: orange (red and yellow), violet (blue and red), and green (yellow and blue). Primary and secondary colors together produce intermediate colors. Colors exactly opposite each other on the color wheel are complementary colors. Black is the combination of all the primary colors, whether made of stain or pigment.

The three primary colors for dye and stain are different from those for pigment, but the use of a color wheel and the results of mixing colors are similar. Light goes through dye to produce these colors; for pigments it bounces off. The three primary **dye colors** are yellow, cyan (blue-green), and magenta (purplish-pink)—the same as in photography and printing. By mixing any two of these we get the secondary dye colors: red (yellow and magenta), green (yellow and cyan), and blue (magenta and cyan), and green (yellow and cyan). Again, we obtain the intermediate colors by blending the primaries and secondaries. This difference between the pigment and stain primary colors is a subtle and technical distinction, but may explain any difficulties we might have in mixing the desired shade of each of the different types of colorants.

The **value** of a color refers to its lightness or darkness, which is controlled by adding or reducing the quantity of colorant or by adding black or white. Black darkens a color's value to create a color **shade**; white lightens a color's value to create a color **tint**. Fender's Daphne Blue and Fiesta Red are tints because white lightens the base. Dakota Red is a shade because black darkens the base. The dark burgundy or cordovan-colored cherry red used on Gibson SGs, although transparent, is a shade of red.

Chapter 3: Finish Colorants

TECH TIP

Transparent orange, green, and blue aerosol toners are used in the furniture industry to correct or shift a color which is either too warm (red) or too cool (blue). Orange kills blue, blue kills orange, and green removes red. Cyan in particular is a good corrective shade.

TECH TIP

Don MacRostie threw out the hundreds of bottles of colors he'd collected over the years, saying "I want as few colors as possible now in order to keep in practice at mixing what I need at the time." This is good advice for everyone.

Shifting a finish

When mixed, complementary colors neutralize (decrease) each others brightness. Complementary colors called blockers are used to shift the tone of a finish from being too warm or too cool.

If a finish is described as being too warm, it has too much red or orange. A too-cool finish has more blue or green than optimal. Other color problems are finishes that go too dark or are overpowered by one color, such as red. To neutralize, shift, or weaken a given color, use its complementary color on the color wheel. Orange, green, blue, and black are able to neutralize, or pull, most unwanted colors from the average guitar or furniture finish. Corrective colors are used sparingly so as not to muddy, darken, or blacken the results. Remember the ultimate end of mixing opposites is black.

Here are a few common corrective colors for guitar finishes:

- Orange warms cool colors by neutralizing blue and green (oak).
- Blue cools the darker warm colors by neutralizing the stronger reds (mahogany). Cyan is a particularly good corrective shade.
- Green neutralizes the purples and reds. A finish that is too brown can be lightened with green because it removes the red.
- Black reduces the brightness of any color, and makes brown when added to orange.

Complementary colors can be sprayed in thin transparent layers over an already-applied finish to help "pull" or "shift" an overpowering color, or they can be used to change a color before it's applied.

Dyes and pigments

All the myriad, colorful effects on guitar finishes are accomplished with a variation on one of two substances: dye or pigment. Dye will be used predominately when the wood is figured—no maker builds with high quality wood only to paint over it (although we do see occasional figured wood which was colored more than it probably should have been). Pigment is used to block or hide wood (as with painted guitars), or sometimes to highlight dyed wood (as in the case of many sunbursts). When light rays hit pigment, they're either reflected off the pigment particles or absorbed by them so that we can't see the wood at all (if it's covered adequately). The majority of pigment used on guitars, however, is either in the form of a grain wood filler colorant or a solid color (paint) like Fiesta Red.

Dye

Dye is **transparent**. Light rays pass through and reflect off the wood's surface, so that we see brightly colored wood and highlighted grain. Guitar dyes are either liquid colorants or powders that dissolve in an appropriate liquid solvent (usually alcohol or water) to produce a transparent stain that penetrates deep into the wood. When the solvent evaporates, the dissolved dye color remains in the wood. Because it penetrates the wood, dye doesn't need a binder such as lacquer or shellac to help it adhere. Dyes are used alone as stains, or they can be added into the finish to color it—producing a transparent shader or toner. You can see through a clear glass jar filled with dye stain, shader, or toner, because of their transparency.

Although PRS guitars have created a lasting demand for such diverse transparent shades as black, silver, pink, green, and blue, guitar finishers still most often use red, yellow, and brown. With these you can duplicate most sunburst, shaded, and toned finishes.

Pigment

Unlike stains that dissolve in their solvent, pigment doesn't dissolve; it suspends in solvent and binder to produce an **opaque** colorant that sits on top of the wood or in any open pore that can hold it. Pigment needs a binder for it to stick to the wood after the solvent evaporates. If pigments contained no binders, the color would return to a powder that could accidentally be wiped or blown away. Since pigment is suspended and not dissolved, it must be stirred before use and it produces opaque stains or paint. You cannot see through a clear glass jar full of well-stirred paint or pigmented binder.

There are, however, pigment stains, pigment wiping stains, and the heavier-bodied pigmented glazes, which are translucent and may only obscure the wood to a certain degree. Such pigment stains are what you will find at a hardware store when you ask for a house stain. They're prevalent in the furniture industry, but have seldom been used on musical instruments. Some of Gibson's early dark sunbursts, however, may have been pigmented stains rather than opaque nitrocellulose lacquer.

Before the 1950s, when Fender introduced automotive colors for guitars, solid pigmented finishes were mostly limited to black, white, brown, red, and shades of yellowed white and tan (like the old National Polychrome finishes). White, black, and red are still the most-used pigmented colors found in guitar shop finishing cabinets, but today, anything goes.

The Most Common Methods of Coloring Guitars

The most common methods of coloring guitars are staining, toning, shading, painting, and a combination of all these techniques. When you want the wood to show, you stain, tone, or shade it. When you want to completely obscure the wood, you paint it.

A 1960 cherry-red Gibson ES-335 was **stained** red. A 1956 blonde Fender Telecaster or Mary Kay Strat was **toned** with a see-through white. A 1956 Gibson ES-5 Switchmaster was **shaded** a tobacco sunburst. The 1958 Gretsch White Falcon was **painted** white.

Staining

Staining is the process of coloring bare wood with either a transparent dye stain or a translucent pigment stain that doesn't completely hide the wood. It is either wiped or sprayed on. Dye stain differs from toner, shader, paint, and pigment stain because it has no binder (finish) in it. Dye stain is like colored thinner or solvent—once the thinner evaporates, only the color is left behind. **Dye stain** is transparent. **Pigment stain**, which is usually oil based, is translucent or even opaque, depending on the amount of pigment used. In modern guitar finishing, most staining is done with a dye stain in either alcohol-soluble

TECH TIP

To make extra-strong shaders and toners, initially mix the dye stain used to color them by adding half or less of the recommended amount of solvent to the powdered or liquid stain. (The missing solvent can always be added later for "normal-strength"). Strong shaders and toners can be weakened, or made "normal," by adding clear lacquer or additional thinner (this is called "extending" the mix). Weaker shaders and toners—especially transparent dye-based ones with no pigment—are used to adjust an existing color or to create the vintage look of aged ambered lacquer.

or water-soluble form. Because it's transparent, dye stain colors the wood without hiding it. It's ability to penetrate gives wood a look of depth under clear finish coats.

Toning and shading

Toning is the process of spraying a transparent or translucent colored finish uniformly over the entire surface of the wood. Shading is a spray technique used to darken, highlight, sunburst, or even hide certain areas with a coat of colored finish. We refer to the finishing materials used for the two processes as toners and shaders respectively, although the two terms are actually defined by the way the finish material is used. This book's recipes refer to the use of a toner if we're toning, and a shader if we're shading or sunbursting, regardless of the transparency, strength, or opacity of the material.

What sets both toning and shading apart from staining? When staining, the color is wiped or sprayed onto bare wood without a clear finish (binder) to keep it there. For toning and shading, the color is mixed into a clear finish (binder) and applied as a coat of colored finish. Toners and shaders are clear lacquer (or other finish) to which colorant is added to produce a transparent or semi-transparent colored finishing material. Stain is in the wood, while toners and shaders sit on top of the wood. They are always sprayed, usually in thin coats. They can be applied directly on the bare wood or between coats of clear finish.

The degree of transparency, translucence, or opacity of a shader or toner depends on what it's colored with and how much colorant is used. Toners and shaders are colored with either a liquid dye (available in powder or liquid form), a pigmented grain-dispersion such as a lacquer base concentrate, or both dye and pigment together. Here's how to tell the difference in an already-mixed product: If no solids settle to the bottom of the can, the liquid is a dye stain. If there's a sediment cloud or the mixture darkens when stirred, it's a pigmented stain or a pigmented dye stain.

Toners or shaders colored with dye will be transparent (imagine looking through colored cellophane). Shaders colored with pigment will be translucent, and may border on being completely opaque. If you overdo the pigment, the toner or shader eventually becomes paint. We use extra-strong dye shaders and toners, with or without added pigment, when we want hiding power but wish to keep the overall finish thin. This is very important when touching-up areas such as broken pegheads or neck resets and there's a need to hide the repair fast, keeping finish coats to a minimum thickness.

Paint

Paint is the generic word for any opaque pigment-based finish, whether it's house paint or guitar "paint." You would rarely ever brush paint onto a guitar, though! You're spraying paint if you're using a pigment-based color to achieve a solid opaque finish like Eric Clapton's Stratocaster "Blackie," for example. The topcoats are sprayed clear, but the color coat is opaque—you cannot see the wood.

Staining, toning, shading, and painting combined

A finish may combine two or more elements of staining, toning, and shading for dramatic effects. A 1959 "three-tone" Fender Stratocaster is stained overall in yellow, and shaded in the red transitional area and on the dark edges. The entire effect is called a sunburst, and would be sealed in with coats of clear lacquer.

Sometimes a finish includes all elements. In reproducing numerous Gibson, Gretsch, and Guild sunburst finishes, we might have a **stained** base coat on the bare wood, a dark **shaded** sunburst top, and dark areas of shader highlighting the neck heel, waist, sides, and peghead. Also, we'd **paint** the peghead face black. A coat of clear amber lacquer would **tone** the entire finish and make the binding look aged, and once again we'd finish with several coats of clear.

Colorant Types Used in Guitar Finishing

The two best types of colorants for guitar finishes are transparent liquid stains and opaque liquid pigments. These bottled colors are easy to use, and they make color blending simple.

Many other colorants have been used over the years, including powdered stains, artist's oil colors, Japan colors, earth powders, and universal tinting colors (UTCs). Each is described below.

Liquid stains (transparent dyes)

Liquid stains are good transparent colorants for staining wood or coloring clear finishes. These highly concentrated, brilliantly colored dyes mix easily into water-, lacquer-, or alcohol-based finishes. They can also be used for coloring waterbase grain fillers.

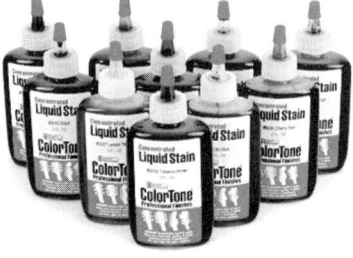

Liquid stains produce deep transparent stains, shaders, and toners. They are pure, require no straining, and definitely fall into the "extra-strong" colorant category. They have excellent resistance to fading (lightfastness).

You can make a stain solution by mixing these concentrated liquids into water, alcohol, or lacquer, but they don't mix into petroleum-based solvents such as mineral spirits or naphtha.

Mixing with water: Water-soluble stains are great for touching up dings, scratches, and sand-throughs. Because they're waterbased they don't melt into the surrounding lacquer and color it. This has advantages on difficult projects. If you foresee accidental sand-throughs in a sunburst finish, for example, start with water-soluble stain so you can touch it up more easily. Water stains can be used for staining or sunbursting the bare wood for clear beautiful colors. They barely bleed into shellac or lacquer finishes, so you won't get colored runs and sags (although any dye bleeds a little bit when it comes in contact with strong solvents). We don't recommend hand-applying waterbase stains, because wiping is likely to leave lap marks. Spraying gives the most uniform coverage.

Waterbase stains have these negative aspects:
- Water raises the wood's grain more than alcohol would. You can reduce the problem by damp-raising the grain and sanding a couple of times before using the dye.
- If you plan to use waterbase lacquer, the waterbase stain is likely to bleed into that finish when a heavy clear coat is sprayed over it. (Similarly, alcohol-based stain bleeds into lacquer or shellac).

Mixing with alcohol: Liquid stain can also be mixed into a number of alcohol solvents to produce stain. Alcohol stains are better than water stains for a wiped-on sunburst. The lap marks aren't as strong, thanks to alcohol's reluctance to penetrate too quickly and its ability to redissolve itself and "move the color around" easily.

Solvents for these mixtures include denatured alcohol, methanol, grain alcohol (ethanol), and non-grain-raising (NGR) reducer. NGR reducer is the best choice because you can use it as a wipe-on or spray-on stain, or add it directly to lacquer to make your own shader and toner.

Alcohol stains don't raise the grain, because they evaporate quickly and don't swell the wood the way water does. NGR reducer is an alcohol solvent with a glycol ether additive. The glycol ether acts as a retarder, slowing the drying time so that lap marks from wiping are less prominent. Glycol ether is a retarder in lacquer, so it will extend the drying time. It's also a **bridging solvent**, allowing two normally incompatible chemicals to blend. For this reason you can add plenty of NGR stain to lacquer to make shaders and toners, despite the great amount of alcohol in the stain (which would usually cause problems).

Stain applied to bare wood is absorbed into the wood pores. If it isn't properly sealed before the first topcoats go on, the stain will often bleed into the wet finish. This is why it's convenient to use a stain which is not soluble by the topcoat. Unfortunately, you can never seal alcohol stains entirely, but vinyl sealer, clear lacquer, or shellac do a pretty good job if sprayed quite light and dry.

Negative aspects of alcohol stains:
- Alcohol stains cannot be touched-up easily if sanded through. The alcohol solvent melts into the surrounding finish, doubling up color at the edge of the sand-through.
- Alcohol stains are redissolved by lacquer and can bleed up into the lacquer finish and onto guitar bindings (they also bleed slightly into waterbase lacquer).

Powdered stains

Before bottled liquid stains came on the scene, it was necessary to mix from dye powders to achieve their effects. These powders are still available today for making up your own liquid colors. Unlike liquid stains, they are not universal: you'll need to purchase different powders for each solvent (water, alcohol, oil/lacquer). You can combine these powdered stains to create almost any color: lower the ratio of dye to get light tones, or increase the ratio to yield a stronger stain.

Liquid pigments (opaque)

Liquid pigments are bottled colors that mix directly into the finish you're using. They're easy to use: mix them into clear lacquer to create opaque colors for many popular solidbody finishes. Use white liquid pigment in clear lacquer to create an opaque white that can be tinted to create pastel colors. Mix pigments together to create custom colors.

Liquid pigments (sometimes called "base concentrates") are available separately for waterbase or solvent-based lacquers (ColorTone Liquid Pigments for Lacquer and ColorTone Liquid Pigments for Waterbase Lacquer). Solvent-based liquid pigments work with both nitrocellulose and acrylic lacquers.

Opaque lacquers

White and black are the solid colors we use most, and they're readily available (even in spray cans). White is used as an overall finish color, and to touch up other white surfaces such as bindings. It's also a base for mixing lighter colors like Surf Green, Sonic Blue, Flamingo Pink, and Fiesta Red. Black is used as an overall finish, to color peghead faces, and to mix into other finishes to darken them.

Other opaque colors are made by adding liquid pigment to clear lacquer or by using them to alter another color such as shifting red to orange, blue to green, and so on.

UTCs (universal tinting colors)

UTC is a term that refers to a number of products. The carousel of tinting colors at your local paint store dispenses UTCs, and some bottled colors are called this, too. When a finish recipe calls for a UTC, liquid pigment is the best choice.

Speaking of paint stores: their colorants cannot be mixed with nitrocellulose lacquer. Paint store UTCs are compatible with oil-base and waterbase products only.

Automotive paints

One of the things that makes an electric guitar cool is a great color, and where could you find more or better colors than on automobiles? Automotive paints have been used in the guitar industry for decades. In the 1950s, General Motors used nitrocellulose lacquer (other car makers used enamel). Fender and Gibson began using GM lacquers for their opaque custom color guitar finishes in the late 1950s, with the convenience of being able to choose a favorite custom color lacquer right at their local auto parts store.

Acrylic resins were perfected in the 1960s. Because of their ability to withstand the elements, they replaced the resins used in automotive enamel and nitrocellulose lacquer—producing acrylic enamel and acrylic lacquer. When GM began replacing nitrocellulose lacquer with acrylic lacquer during the 1960s, Fender and Gibson were able to make the acrylic lacquer work, too—even combining it with clear nitrocellulose lacquer topcoats after a little practice.

In the late 1990s acrylic lacquer began disappearing from the shelves of a majority of your local auto stores—leaving acrylic enamel and the new urethane finishes for those wishing to use an automotive color on a guitar. The colorants used in the base coat for both of these finishes is the same—it is the other additives which make it a urethane or an enamel. These are not compatible with nitrocellulose lacquer.

If you're only spraying one instrument, or one now and then, this may not be the colorant for you. You need special, primer (sealer) and topcoat—a big investment for which you probably won't have another use.

Japan colors, and artist's oils

Japan colors and artist's oil colors are pigments ground into linseed oil that can be used to shift or tint oil-base grain wood fillers, or oil varnish, but you won't find either of them in most guitar finishers' cabinets.

Like oil-based grain filler, these products require longer drying time, although Japan color has driers added to it that make it dry faster than artist's oils. For that reason, Japan drier would be a better choice to add to an already slow-drying oil-based grain filler.

Earth colors

Earth colors ("fresco powders") are powdered pigments that come in a wide variety of reds, browns, tan, ochre, umber, and white. They can be used to great advantage with alcohol-based padding lacquers to hide or repair defects, and in some cases to color wood fillers and wood doughs.

Earth colors do not dissolve; they disperse into the film. Contrary to what some manufacturers suggest, these pigment powders will not do a good job of coloring grain wood fillers.

CHAPTER 4

Tools and Materials for Applying Finishes

Since 1930, most American guitars have been spray finished with lacquer. Certainly a number of finishes are brushed or wiped on, including waterborne finishes, shellac, polyurethanes, brushing lacquer, and catalyzed finishes—and the techniques and tools for hand-applied finishes are well covered in other books. Our emphasis, however, is on how to apply professional-looking sprayed lacquer finishes on guitars and other fretted instruments.

There are several methods you can use to apply a sprayed finish. These include aerosols, compressed-air, and turbine-driven HVLP (high volume, low pressure) spraying. Each method requires different equipment and has its own advantages and disadvantages.

Aerosol Spraying

Aerosol spraying is the easiest way to get started in spray finishing because there's virtually no setup, cleanup, or expensive equipment to buy. Aerosols produce a rougher surface than compressed-air spraying, however, and this requires more sanding to achieve a level surface. Also, because they're thinned with flow out and fisheye additives to allow for low-pressure spraying, they require more coats and extra drying time between coats to achieve a "build." When all is said and done, however, an aerosol finish is the same nitrocellulose product used on factory guitars. In fact, aerosol finishes can look excellent when properly applied. You're limited only by the finishes and colors available in cans and, of course, your skill and patience.

ADVANTAGES OF AEROSOL SPRAY FINISHING
- Inexpensive way to get started in spray finishing
- No mixing of lacquer, thinner, and additives
- No cleanup

DISADVANTAGES
- Limited colors
- Not cost effective, when spraying many instruments
- Aerosols leave a rougher surface after drying, requiring more sanding for satisfactory results

Compressed-air Spraying

Compressed-air spraying is the most popular finishing method today because it offers great flexibility in the choice of finishing materials and lays down a high quality film. Because you fill the spray gun yourself, you can mix and spray either stain or finish, or any other material desired. As an extra bonus, you have compressed air available for other uses around the shop. Compressed-air spraying requires a compressor, air lines, a regulator, a spray gun, and a filter to remove oil and moisture from the lines to prevent blushing (a haze produced when moisture is trapped under the finish).

Air compressors

Air compressors are made in tank or tankless types, but we advise you to own a 3 to 5 horsepower tank-type compressor with a 20 to 30 gallon tank. The tank is a reservoir that the compressor keeps filled with air. It acts as a buffer to maintain uniform pressure at the spray gun, thereby eliminating pulsing, the surge caused by the stroke of the compressor motor's piston(s).

Most of us started out with small, affordable 1-1/2 to 2 horsepower compressors, only to discover that we needed more volume to run pneumatic tools such as dual-action sanders, in-line sanders, rotary grinders, die grinders, and vacuum jigs. Air tools don't operate very well on compressors rated under 3 horsepower, and 4 to 5 horsepower models are best. Today, thanks to the import tool market, there are many affordable compressors in the 3 to 5 horsepower range, costing $350 to $500. This is what smaller compressors cost twenty years ago.

Air lines

Air lines can be iron, copper or flexible rubber hose. Of these, galvanized iron pipe would be our first choice for an air line material. The heat of compressing air allows it to hold more moisture than cooler air; as the compressed air cools, the moisture condenses in the tank and air lines. As the pressure is released at the gun, the air is cooled even more, further contributing to condensation. Condensation, as mentioned before, can cause blushing in a sprayed finish—so run your air lines at a slight angle to drain back toward the compressor, and include drain points with valves. Drain the tank and the drain points frequently. Also, a long run between the compressor and the spray gun is better than a short run (a 50 to 100-foot line is ideal). Don't lay flexible line on a cool concrete floor because it adds to the condensation problem.

To further improve moisture problems, install a regulator, filter, and moisture trap at the end of the air run, near the spray gun. There are a variety of setups available, including combination regulator-filter-moisture traps. The regulator adjusts the spray pressure and the filter and moisture trap removes oil and water from the air.

A truly professional setup would include an oil filter, regulator, and separate desiccant-granule moisture trap. The inexpensive desiccant granules soak up moisture. You can remove and clean them regularly and replace them when they're dirty.

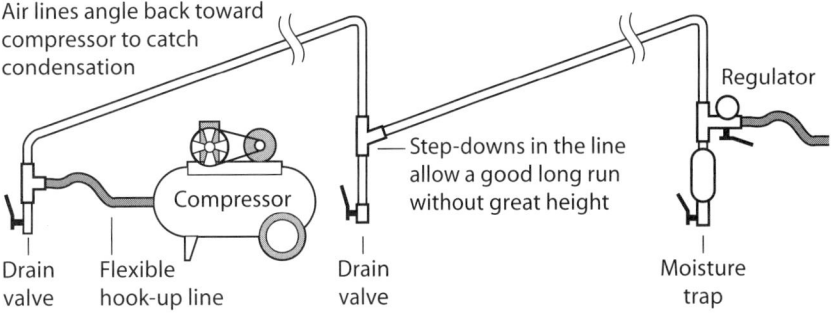

Drain valves at the bottom of each vertical pipe are for removing condensed water

Compressed-air spray guns

Compressed-air spray guns are available in three types: pressure-feed guns, siphon-feed guns, and HVLP guns (high-volume low-pressure). The pressure-feed system uses an external tank or "pressure pot" filled with fluid and pressurized with compressed air to force the fluid to the gun. The gun has no cup and is therefore lightweight and maneuverable. The pots vary from small quart-size ones to ones holding many gallons; hence with the right size pot you don't need to stop spraying to fill the cup. The pressure-feed system is geared toward high production, and is beyond the needs of most small shops.

We recommend traditional siphon-feed spray guns or the newer gravity HVLP guns for small shop guitar finishing. Siphon-feed spray guns use compressed air within the gun to create a vacuum which draws fluid from the fluid cup through a siphon tube to the nozzle. For production finishing, the fluid cup must be refilled often because of its small size (most cups hold either a quart or a pint). For small shop spraying, filling the cup is not a problem.

Compressed-air gravity feed HVLP guns are relative newcomers to the finishing business, but are finding themselves widely used in automotive body shops and furniture shops. These guns have the cup on top, so the fluid is fed by gravity into the air stream, reducing some of the gun's requirements for compressed air. The air nozzle converts compressed air to the HVLP spray. HVLP guns are highly controllable and come in a couple of sizes that can be adjusted to do anything the family of conventional guns can do (i.e. finish coats, shading, and airbrush work). They are more efficient at putting finish on the work, saving dollars of material. Their reduced tendency to over spray promotes a healthier environment and complies with environmental emissions regulations. And lower pressure in the air stream means they blow around less dust and dirt, resulting in a cleaner job with less masking required.

Single-stage guns

A single-stage, siphon-feed guns allow fluid to flow from the gun as soon as the trigger is pulled. Air brushes like Bink's "Wren" are good examples of this simple type of inexpensive, low-maintenance gun. It can produce a well-atomized, high-quality spray pattern and is easy to clean. The only disadvantage of a single-stage gun is that it doesn't allow complete control of the air and fluid mix.

Bink's "Wren" is a good example of an inexpensive, low-maintenance, single-stage gun.

Two-stage guns

Two-stage compressed-air powered-guns are by far the most popular siphon-feed models and come in the widest variety of styles. They're also available in a variety of prices, a good range of quality, and in three sizes:

- Small airbrushes for detail and touchup work
- Medium jamb guns used for spraying automotive door jams on the production line and by musical instrument finishers for shading and coloring
- Standard production guns hold one-quart or more, and are used for laying on the heavier clear coats

Chapter 4: Tools and Materials for Applying Finishes

Medium jamb gun for shading and coloring.

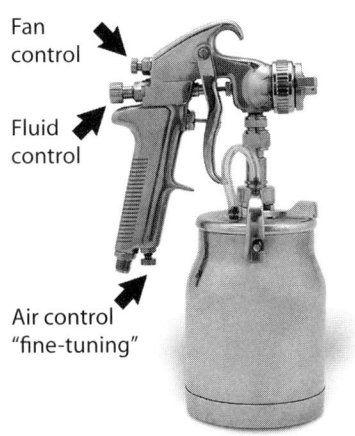

Standard production gun for spraying heavier coats.

TECH TIP

As a general rule, manufacturers recommend a .060-inch to .070-inch orifice for spraying lacquer. For spraying waterbase lacquer, a .040-inch orifice is better.

Most finishers have at least one of each of these spray guns. Two-stage guns are so named because they have "two-stage triggers," not because they have two adjustment knobs (which they do, and some guns have three knobs). The function of these adjustment knobs is explained in Chapter 7: Adjusting your spray gun.

When you press the trigger, in the first stage you'll feel it come to a rest as it releases air into the gun. The air flows around the fluid tip as it waits for the needle to pull back from the orifice. At the second stage, the trigger pulls the tip of the fluid needle from the orifice "seat" (the orifice is the small round hole in the fluid tip) and releases fluid. If it is a siphon-feed gun, the fluid is siphoned out of the cup below. If it is a gravity-feed gun, fluid flows by gravity out of the cup above to the fluid tip, is atomized by the moving air, and sprays out the air nozzle onto the work.

Finishers like two-stage guns because they lay down a high quality finish coat. That's because they give the operator thorough control of the air and fluid mix. They're also capable of handling high-volume production. You'll put in more maintenance on these guns, but that little extra time is worth it.

Controlling atomization

Atomization, or the degree to which the fluid is reduced to a spray of microscopic droplets, is controlled by air pressure, the size of the spray gun's fluid tip orifice, and the choice of fluid needle tip and air nozzle. Professional sprayers will select and adjust these elements to get optimum atomization of the material they're spraying, and then fine tune it by adjusting the air pressure at the regulator.

Air pressure alone is an adequate way to control atomization, and most hobbyists simply use the spray gun as they buy it. However, if you happen to have trouble spraying a particularly heavy or light material, or get consistently poor finishing results, take the time to contact your spray gun's manufacturer—changing tips may solve your problems. If you buy brand-name spray guns (Binks Sames™, DeVilbiss™, Sata™ etc.), you'll be able to buy interchangeable parts at your local auto-parts supplier.

ADVANTAGES OF COMPRESSED AIR SPRAYING
- It's a plus to have compressed air available for general shop uses such as blowing off dust and powering pneumatic tools
- A quality compressed air gun can lay down a beautiful finish that saves time at the sanding and polishing stage
- A wide choice of materials can be mixed and sprayed

DISADVANTAGES
- Initial cost is high (but not as high as the turbine HVLP system mentioned below)
- Unless well equipped and well handled, they can introduce moisture into the air stream

Turbine HVLP spraying

Turbine HVLP spray guns use a large amount of air (65 cubic feet per minute) at a low pressure (3 to 10 pounds per square inch), instead of a small amount of compressed air (around 10 cubic feet per minute at 25 to 50 psi) to carry the lacquer onto the work. The typical turbine HVLP system which is suitable for most small shops includes a turbine-powered air supply, a special large-diameter air-supply hose, and an HVLP gun (which is different than the normal compressed-air powered spray guns). Put simply, a turbine is a small motorized box that works and sounds like a vacuum cleaner running in reverse. A turbine supplies warm, dry filtered air to the spray gun through a large (1 to 1-1/4 inch diameter) air hose that is ribbed, flexible, and lightweight like a clothes-dryer exhaust hose.

Turbine-powered HVLP guns use a pressurized cup instead of siphon-feed to move the fluid into the air stream. Unlike compressed-air guns mentioned earlier, they must have the correct fluid tip, orifice, and air nozzle for the material being sprayed, in order to do their best work. Though fussy, HVLP guns properly set are much more efficient than compressed air guns, depositing 65% or more of the finish material onto the work, instead of into the air. In comparison, a conventional compressed-air system deposits about 30% of the material onto the work.

Turbine HVLP systems do a good job, and we see them in use by both novice and veteran finishers. If you can only pick one system, though, we still recommend compressed air because it has so many other uses around the shop.

ADVANTAGES OF TURBINE-POWERED HVLP SYSTEMS
- Warm dry air is less likely to cause blushing in the finish
- Highly efficient in transferring materials, therefore less overspray is introduced into the environment

DISADVANTAGES
- The initial investment is substantial—costing nearly the price of a compressed air system without offering the benefit of compressed air for other uses
- Turbine HVLP systems use only large finish-coat spray guns; airbrushes and mid-sized "sunburst" guns are not yet available for them
- Large turbine hose makes spraying a little awkward

Spray Booths

Except on certain perfect spraying days, of which everyone gets several each year (in the Midwest they're usually in the spring and fall), you must spray indoors if you want enough protection from the elements to apply a quality finish in a safe environment.

When spraying inside, you should have some form of spray booth, either homemade or commercial. Lacquer vapors can build up to an explosive level whenever a lot of spraying is taking place and air movement is not sufficient to evacuate the fumes. If this happens, a spark from an electrical or mechanical source can ignite the fumes, causing an explosion. Fresh air intake is a must because atomized lacquer and the vapors of curing finishes are highly toxic. A simple, modest spray booth with an explosion-proof fan and lights and a respirator mask approved for organic vapors are the minimum you'll need to ensure your safety.

We won't describe commercially available booths except to say that besides being large, they're expensive when new; used ones can be found quite inexpensively though. To build your own spray booth, designate a corner or room of your shop for that purpose. It will need an explosion-proof exhaust fan, explosion-proof lights and switches, fresh air intake (filtered to keep out dust), and a filtered air line for the spray gun.

One of the nicer homemade booths we've seen has walls and a ceiling made of 5/8-inch gypsum board. Within the spray area, the walls and ceiling are lined with galvanized sheet steel to fireproof them. The sheet steel makes the walls smooth so that built-up spray residue comes off easily (dried spray buildup is highly flammable). Check with your local fire department and code office for your area's specifications.

If you don't do enough spraying each year to warrant dedicating an entire room as a spray booth, you'll probably end up spraying out the window. If so, at least make it safe and sensible by fireproofing the area and using an explosion-proof fan and fixtures.

We made a knockdown spray booth that fastens around the window frame—and can be removed—in minutes. Three pieces of drywall painted white to augment the light for visibility form a square-shaped tapered funnel. The funnel directs the air flow and spray pattern toward the explosion-proof fan at the small end, and of course the finisher sprays at the large end. The funnel shape eliminates dead corners, where vapors can accumulate, and generally makes for an efficient air flow (opening a window across the room lets in fresh air).

Whether your spray booth is a permanent walled structure of drywall and sheet steel or a knockdown, half-funnel version for occasional use, the interior walls should be smooth and slick so that you can easily remove built-up over spray residue. If you can't clean walls frequently, then you'll have to replace them frequently because spray buildup is highly flammable.

Explosion-proof fans

An explosion-proof fan must have a totally enclosed, fan-cooled motor with waterproof electrical connections and a nonsparking aluminum blade and shroud. Most electrical supply houses have vendors that can supply a variety of fans, motors, pulleys, enclosures, shutters, and lights that meet spray booth safety requirements (in this country, the Grainger Company is a good source).

The fan blades should be set five feet or more away from the sprayer's position. Install a baffle of some type of loose-mesh filter to keep finish exhaust from collecting on the fan blades. Furnace filters (the kind in loose rolls or sheets, not the stamped-hole cardboard type) make a good over spray collector.

Filtered air intake hole

What goes out must come in, so the door to your booth should have a large filtered air intake hole to keep the air moving. Serious

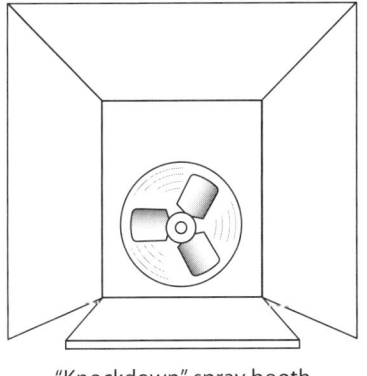

"Knockdown" spray booth

booth builders run air replacement duct from outside (sometimes it's heated) directly into the spray room. This replacement air must be forced in at a rate equal to, or greater than, the amount of air that the exhaust fan is evacuating. You can accomplish this by mounting a squirrel cage fan in the ducting. This causes the spray room's air pressure to equalize or pressurize, respectively. A pressurized spray room also pushes air out of the room when the entrance door is open so that dirty woodshop air and sawdust will not rush in. The best spray booths even have a double-doored entrance leading into the spray room, similar to a decompression chamber used by deep sea divers.

If you're spraying in a room that also serves as a woodshop, it's a good idea to dust and vacuum the walls, ceiling, and floors and then damp-mop the floor to keep dust down.

Lighting

Good lighting is essential for observing how the wet coats of finish are laying on the guitar and to help you detect any problems with coverage, coat thickness, and flow-out properties. Position lights on each side of your work area or booth as well as behind you. A mix of incandescent and fluorescent lighting—rather than just one or the other—is helpful when you're making color judgements in paint or stain. Natural light is always great when you can get it, and so is full-spectrum lighting. Colors look *vastly* different under the different light spectra, that's for sure.

Explosion-proofing is just as important for lights and lighting as it for fans and ventilation. The simplest safe lighting solution is to install the sealed, gasketed, weatherproof octagon boxes made for outdoor floodlights. Equip the boxes with hazardous-area light bulb receptacles and glass safety dust domes. The thick glass protects a light bulb from shattering if accidentally bumped and keeps vapors from coming in contact with the hot bulbs or electrical contacts. These domes are used in farm silos and in many underground situations where flammable dust, particulate, and vapors may be present.

Devices for Holding the Work

To free up your hands for the precise art of spraying, you'll need a good way to hold the piece being sprayed. Holding devices can't get in the way of the spray, they must be comfortable and manageable if you're hand-holding the work, and they mustn't touch the piece (at least not where it's wet). It's worth spending the time to make good holding devices. There are so many ways to hold instruments for spraying that we can only give you some ideas here. For most instruments there are any number of ways to make do.

Guitars and other instruments with glued on necks (as opposed to bolted on necks) have their own built in spray "handle" in the neck itself. Many finishers use this to advantage by spraying the neck and body separately, letting each part dry thoroughly before using it as a handle for spraying the other part. (The C. F. Martin Company finishes

Chapter 4: Tools and Materials for Applying Finishes

the neck and body separately before gluing them together). The only "equipment" you need is your own hands and occasionally a vice.

Hooks and hangers

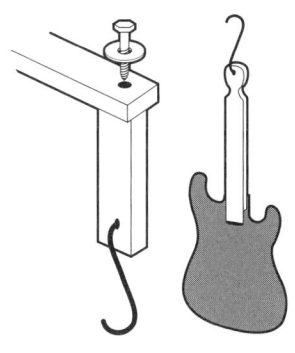

Hooks and hangers allow you to have both hands free while you spray, and they can be used for hanging and drying a guitar as well. You can bend a 3/16-inch drill rod (old truss rods work great) into large loops that will thread through a tuner hole quickly and without touching anything so that you can turn the work while spraying, some form of ceiling-mounted swivel is necessary to hook the hanger into. A swivel hanger is a good way to finish spraying the mid-point of a neck.

An eye-screw threaded into the strap button hole on the butt end is perfect for hanging or spraying the guitar upside-down.

Guitars with bolted on necks are a different story. Because the neck and body aren't combined, the neck doesn't act as a "handle" for spraying the body, and vice versa. The most professional way of spraying bolt-on neck bodies is on a spray carousel.

Spray carousels

Rotation pin at center keeps turntable on benchtop (mount wheels well in from the edge)

Body up on nails sits on "spraying board"

Spray carousels, or turntables, are common in the furniture industry. The version shown is copied from the one used by Fender up until the early '60s. The circular plywood carousel has three wheels, rests on any work surface, and can be pinned in the center to the table. The circular shape allows the operator to turn the table easily with a free hand without needing to look away from the work while spraying. Fender rested the body being sprayed on the carousel using small nails as legs, or stands.

Nail-stands

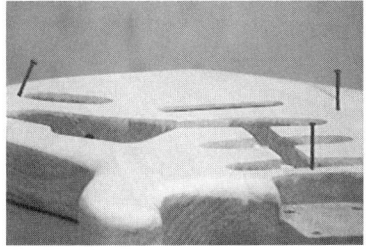

Before about 1962 or 1963, Fender drove three nails, placed at strategic points, into the face of the guitar as a makeshift stand to support the wet body on the carousel. The finishers could then turn the guitar over onto its face for spraying the back and part of the sides. They drove a nail at a 60-degree angle into the side wall of the jack cup hole (they drove it at an angle to avoid splitting the wood at the hole's edge). A second nail, driven between the neck pocket and front pickup hole, did occasionally split the wood. The third nail hole was located under the pick guard near the bass side front edge of the bridge.

Pipe stand with tube handle

Sometime after 1962, Fender began using the right-angle stand in conjunction with a hollow-tube spray handle screwed into the neck pocket. The handle initially served to store the bodies for drying—allowing them to be hung on a "tree." At some point, someone must have looked at the hollow-tube hangers and thought up the clever hanger-carousel combination.

You can make a stand from two pieces of 3/4-inch plumbing pipe, an elbow, and a flange to mount it to the edge of the carousel table. The body holder is a one-inch electrical conduit pipe flattened on one end with holes drilled through the flat area for screwing it to the body cavity. The handle fastens into two neck-mounting holes on the bass side of the neck pocket using two sheet-metal screws. Only enough of the sharp sheet metal screw thread cuts into the walls of the hole to hold it, and no sign is left when it's removed. The tube slides onto the stand and becomes a self-supporting rotating handle for spraying. Combined with the revolving carousel, it allows the finisher complete mastery over the work.

Between 1962 and 1964, the two holding techniques overlapped, with both nails and a "handle" being used. If you look at a Tele you'll see a similar thing. The hole is either beside the screw hole (which can and often does cause splitting there) or on the wall of the control cavity, which is probably a better location. Speaking of Teles, a round, tight-fitting "stick-handle" can be shoved into the side-mount jack hole—yet another way of holding a body!

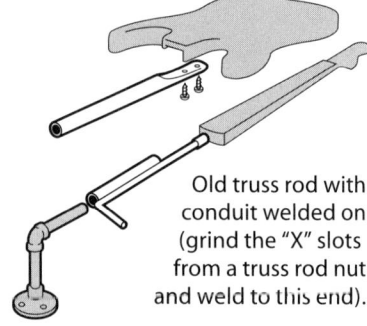

1" electrical conduit flattened on end (sheet metal screws fasten to neck mount holes).

Old truss rod with conduit welded on (grind the "X" slots from a truss rod nut and weld to this end).

The plumbing pipe and the elecrical conduit are two slightly different sizes, allowing one to slide over the other.

Handle for necks

You can take the handle trick one step further by using it to hold necks, too. Take a piece of the 1-inch tubing, weld or tape a piece of 3/8-inch steel rod or a Fender truss-rod nut to the outside, and thread one end to fit the 10-32 (or whatever size you need) truss rod thread. Bend the other end into a hook. Now you can slide the neck handle onto the hanger and use the spray carousel for careful neck spraying. It offers especially good control for tinting a neck with a vintage color or for general spraying, and the hook lets you hang the neck out of the way for drying. When spraying a clear finish, leave the neck on the hanger so it remains level while the finish sets up, to allow the lacquer to flow out level without sagging. Turning it once or twice further avoids any sags.

Simple wood handle

Bandsaw any 3/4-inch scrap wood to a basic handle shape and fasten it into the bottom of the neck pocket. Many finishers use standard neck mounting screws through the body from the rear to hold the handle. The screws must be alternated if you want lacquer to cover evenly, however. Plus, they get in the way when you're sanding between coats. We prefer to mount the handle by choosing mounting screws large enough to bite into the clearance holes in the neck pocket. Two screws are plenty.

Masking Supplies

Masking-off, or protecting certain areas from stain and finish, is a big part of finishing. The right masking supplies can make the job easy. Bargain-basement masking tape is never a bargain!

Masking tape

Masking tape should be fresh and not too sticky. When tape is old or low grade, the adhesive becomes too tacky and may pull off wood fibers, color, or finish. Also, bad adhesive contains strong chemicals that can cause the finish under or near it to lift and wrinkle. Art supply and auto stores usually have the freshest and best masking tapes, including draftsman's tape which is ideal in many situations because it has a low "tack" but good adherence. Depending on the masked area, you'll need tape from 1/8 inch to 1 inch in width.

Pin striping guide tape

An important specialty tape is the light green latex pin striping guide tape (also Fine Line tape) sold at automotive supply stores. We use the 1/8-inch and 1/4-inch most often. Without wrinkling, buckling, or lifting, pin striping guide tape can follow the tightest curves and prevent finish or color from running underneath. It's very gentle on finish, too.

Electrician's tape

Black plastic electrician's tape is handy too, especially for super glue repairs during a finishing schedule. It does the best job of taping off when you want to use water-thin super glue next to it. The glue won't wick underneath the tape. This tape is also excellent for taping off bindings during the color stages.

Sign painter's tape

The most revolutionary masking tool in our shop is sign painter's tape (like TransferRite). It has a treated paper surface backed with a delicate latex adhesive. Available in many widths, it's great for taping off large or small areas without the hassle of using paper and masking tape. Roll the tape across the surface, trim it with a sharp knife, and you're done—it's a great time-saver. It won't pull off vintage finishes, and anyone who tries this product will find many uses for it.

Paper for masking

Clean paper is a must-have in a finishing shop. Newspaper's not the best choice because of the ink, but blank newsprint paper is good (our local newspaper doesn't mind saving the end rolls of newsprint, which have a good deal of paper left on them). A local motorcycle paint shop sells rolls of a 24-inch wide smooth, crisp, green paper it uses—the type auto-body shops use to mask off windows. It seems almost like butcher's paper. We use the green paper to mask off large areas by trimming it close to shape with a knife and then taping along the edge. It also makes a good removable surface to protect the workbench while you perform messy tasks such as stripping, staining, and grain filling.

Miscellaneous Tools and Supplies

Numerous items—both hardware-store and finish specialty tools—come in handy around the spray booth:
- Glass turkey baster with rubber bulb for transferring liquids
- Rubber squeegee
- Rubber kitchen spatula (for cleaning out containers)
- Hobby knife (X-Acto's inexpensive slim-handled aluminum body with the number eleven blade is our favorite)
- Single-edged razor blades

- Three pairs of scissors with different colored handles: one for sandpaper, one for cloth, one for paper
- Glass microscope slides (which make excellent scrapers)
- Used silk-screen material for straining
- Pipe cleaners
- Soft absorbent rags
- Paper towels
- Long handled cotton swabs
- Clean glass jars with lids
- Pipettes
- Glass measuring cups, small and large
- Measuring spoons
- A gram scale (our digital scale cost $150, and was worth it, but a diet scale would do)
- Short lengths of guitar strings, both wound and unwound (appropriate gauges fit and clean the many different sized holes in a spray gun; a ball of solder tinned onto the end makes a good handle)
- Metal trash container with lid
- Spraygun wrench
- Screwdriver or other lid-prying tool
- Used empty metal spray cans–quarts and gallons—to hold junk thinner and other throw-away solvents, etc. (mark these with an "X"!)
- Good selection of bristle brushes, including specialty brushes made for cleaning siphon tubes

CHAPTER 5

Abrasives and Smoothing Tools

Wood preparation is probably the most important step in getting a professional-looking finish. If the surface of the instrument has been brought to a uniform, flawless state, the finish can be applied evenly and effortlessly, and repair work during finishing won't be required to correct defects missed at the wood prep stage. Even on new instruments, finish repairs and touchups not only take far more time than wood preparation done properly in the first place, but they usually result in visible flaws in the final finish.

The prep work necessary for the best guitar finish is generally more demanding than that needed for the average piece of furniture, and certainly eclipses anything needed for household finishing projects such as floors and window trim. Most of these projects don't require pore filling, seldom have decorative inlays and marquetry, and rarely use three or more different woods or materials on the same piece.

Sandpapers

There's a dizzying array of abrasives—the industry's term for sandpaper—on the market. Sandpapers differ in grit type (silicon-carbide, aluminum-oxide, garnet, etc.), backing (paper, cloth, and Mylar of different weights), bond (adhesives used to keep the grit on the backing), and grit size. Here's all the information needed to choose the right sandpaper for your job:

Sandpapers for guitar finishing are no different than those for general wood finishing, although we instrument finishers are more likely to progress to finer grits, and less likely to skip a grit along the way. Also, since most guitar finishes are rubbed to a high gloss, guitar finishers almost always progress to a final wet-sanding in preparation for the buffing stage. (Furniture finishers often quit after a 320- to 400-grit dry-sanding, and get a final low gloss sheen with 0000 steel wool and wax).

Sandpaper grading scales

All grits are not created equal. Sandpapers are manufactured under one of four major grading scales for abrasive grit size and shape: The North American CAMI scale; the Japanese JIS-scale; the European P-scale; and the Micron scale. You can usually tell what type of sandpaper you have by the markings on the sandpaper backing. CAMI-scale papers have just a number. P-scale papers have the letter P before the number. Micron-scale papers are identified by the Greek letter mu, as in 80μ. JIS-scale papers generally have Japanese characters on the back. With the exception of Micron papers, however, higher numbers mean finer sandpaper, lower means coarser (micron grading is the opposite).

P-scale and JIS-scale abrasives are quite similar and both are graded to much finer tolerances than the CAMI-scale; Micron-grading tolerances are even finer. Therefore P, JIS, and Micron-graded sandpaper

Abrasive Grading System
for Aluminum-oxide, Silicon-carbide, and Garnet

Micron grade	USA CAMI grade	European P-grade	Japanese JIS	Coarseness description
1	2000		8000	Micro fine
2			6000	
3	1500		4000	
4				
5			3000	
6				
6.3			2500	
6.5				
7.6	1200*		2000*	
9				
9.2	1000*			
10			1500*	
12				
12.2	800*			Ultra fine
13			1200*	
15				
16	600	P1200*	1000*	
19.7	500	P1000*		
20			800*	
23.6	400*	P800*	700	Super fine
25				
28.8	360**	P600	600	
30				
		P500*		
36	320**	P400	500*	Extra fine
40			400	
		P360		
44	280**			
45		P320		
48			360	
53.5	240**	P280		Very fine
55				
57		P240	320	
60				
66	220**	P220	280	
78	180**	P180	240	
93	150**	P150		
116	120**	P120		Fine
141	100**			
		P100		
192	80**	P80		Medium
268	60**	P60		
		P50		Coarse

This chart compares the different grits of the Abrasive Grading System.

* Papers meant only for wet-sanding
**Papers meant only for dry-sanding
(Many papers can be used for either wet or dry.)

Grits from 120 to 220 are the most useful in instrument shops for sanding wood; (60-, 80-, and 100-grit papers are for the rough-shaping and initial smoothing of wood). Grits from 220 through 400 are great for dry-sanding finish during the build stages. Grits from 500 to 2000 are the most useful for wet-sanding finishes. Unless specified otherwise, as in the case of P-graded or JIS sandpapers, the grit-numbers recommended in this book are for CAMI-graded papers.

have more uniform grits than CAMI-graded paper, and are less likely to scratch because of a stray oversize grit particle. Also, grit for grit, they cut faster and more aggressively than a CAMI paper. They are higher priced accordingly but worth it to finishers who use orbital sanders for their final sanding, especially for catalyzed, high-tech polyesters and UV-cured finishes (more on these later).

Another type of sandpaper, which uses it's own grading scale that does not compare to the scales mentioned above, is the Micro-Mesh brand. Their brand-specific grading ranges all the way up to 12,000-grit. Micro-Mesh offers the finest-grit papers available. If you're trying to wet-sand a small touchup on a thin, old vintage finish, you can't afford to make scratches that can't be removed. Micro-Mesh" sandpapers are great for such extreme polishing and for vintage repairs.

The coarse grits (100- to 320-grit) of the less expensive CAMI-graded papers work perfectly well for sanding wood and for dry scuff-sanding the finish between coats ("scuff-sanding" is a light, dry-sanding of the finish to remove obvious high spots and dust specks). The finer JIS-scale and P-graded (and sometimes Micron-graded) papers are much better for the fine, wet-sanding stage of finishing.

Loading versus nonloading papers

Standard sandpapers load, meaning they get clogged by swarf, the dusty residue created by sanding. Nonloading papers are available with either a powdered stearate lubricant or else a special coating over the abrasive to help shed swarf. Called "open coat" or "no-load," and found under trademark names such as Carborundum Dry-lube and 3M Fre-Cut, these sandpapers come in both disc and sheet form. They're becoming increasingly available in hardware stores everywhere. Though they still cost a little more than conventional papers, we feel they are a good value.

No-load sandpapers range in grits from 60 to P1200. Grits as fine as 320 and 400 are available in both pressure-sensitive adhesive and "hook and loop" form—the two popular ways of instantly attaching sandpaper to the electric hand-held random-orbit sanders that we've all become so fond of. Hook and loop sandpaper uses a Velcro-type fastener; pressure-sensitive papers are coated with an adhesive. (We recommend an electric random-orbit sander for the small shop, by the way, and describe them in more detail later in this chapter.)

Stearated no-load sandpapers are usually bluish-white, light cocoa, or light grey. The powdered stearate coating applied to the surface of the abrasive sheds during sanding, taking paper-clogging sawdust or powdered finish with it. The paper wears out as the stearate sheds and the grit becomes dull.

Nonstearated, coated, no-load papers (3M's gold-colored P-scale 216-U is a good one), are more efficient than the stearated variety. They cut more aggressively and don't break down as fast, allowing them to last longer (but they're more expensive, too). These coated papers were developed for use with waterbase finishing systems because stearate residue can cause fisheye problems on wood later sprayed with waterborne lacquer. Stearate-caused fisheyes are similar to the oil and silicone-caused fisheye problems in solvent lacquer finishing. We choose the nonstearated papers for sanding waterbase finishes.

Grit composition

The materials used on sandpapers for the most common guitar finishing jobs (and for all woodworking and wood finishing) are garnet, aluminum-oxide, and silicon-carbide. The manufacturing codes on a paper's backing normally indicates what kind of grit is used. For example, with 3M papers (we're most familiar with 3M sandpapers), the first digit of the number on a CAMI-scale sandpaper usually indicates the grit type. Garnet starts with 1, aluminum-oxide starts with 2 or 3; and silicon-carbide starts with 4. Carborundum, Norton, and other manufacturers use similar systems, and surely they'd be glad to help you decode them if you're interested.

Garnet sandpaper

The traditional standby for sanding wood is garnet paper. Golden orange in color, garnet paper is widely available and is sold in sheets in a good range of grits. No-load versions are scarce. Garnet is a good choice for hand sanding, but is not as good for power sanding because it has a softer grit than the other papers. It tends to wear out quickly from the friction and heat of power sanders during medium to heavy cutting. Garnet loads quickly, too.

Garnet is an excellent choice for final sanding end grain, or blotch-prone woods like spruce, alder, mahogany and others, because of its peculiar tendency to burnish wood and close off the pores. This allows stain to penetrate more evenly (though less deeply) for a uniform color.

When it's sharp, garnet paper removes wood quickly and removing scratches well. It can be used with waterborne finishes, is relatively inexpensive, and is softer and more gentle to the wood than aluminum oxide.

Aluminum-oxide sandpaper

Aluminum-oxide sandpapers are designed for wood, but they work well on finishes, too. White, yellow, gold, or brown, aluminum-oxide sandpapers are a woodworking mainstay. They have a tougher grit than garnet paper, with points that don't round over as easily, and therefore tend to scratch more. But they're also longer lasting and have more aggressive cutting action (therefore, they're more economical).

No-load aluminum-oxide papers are available both with and without stearates. Price not withstanding, P-scale no-load aluminum-oxide papers are probably the best all-around choice for sanding wood or finishes. However you might choose aluminum-oxide in the earlier wood prep stages and then end with a garnet paper for the final sanding if you're staining the wood (especially if it's blotch-prone, as mentioned earlier).

Aluminum-oxide papers often get a bad rap because there are lots of cheap, crude versions on the market (those horrible dark brown ones you see at discount-marts). Don't judge them all by those bar-

---

TECH TIP

If you suspect you may have a stearate problem, wipe the surface of the wood or the finish with a rag damp (not wet) with mineral spirits. The mineral spirits will cause the stearate to "let go" and it will collect onto the rag. Another good stearate remover is a household glass cleaner such as Windex.

Chapter 5: Abrasives, Power Sanders, and Smoothing Tools   47

TECH TIP

Although the manufacturers don't recommended wet-sanding with aluminum oxide paper, we've found that 3M's gold colored P-scale no-load can be used for up to two hours before becoming waterlogged.

gain-basement varieties. If you try aluminum-oxide and don't like it, keep your eye out for better quality papers and try again.

Silicon-carbide sandpapers

Silicon-carbide sandpapers are designed for sanding steel and hard-finish coatings, but some varieties work great for sanding wood and finishes, too. In fact, one of the sandpapers instrument finishers use most on wood or for dry-sanding lacquer finishes is the no-load, stearated, silicon-carbide type mentioned earlier—the standard white, or bluish-gray "hardware store" variety. These papers shed sawdust well because of the stearate, and they're available in more sizes and grits than other papers for random-orbit sanders. (The stearates will cause fisheyes in waterborne lacquer, however.)

For years the most-used sandpaper for final-sanding finishes was 3M's Wet-or-Dry, the black or greenish-black silicon-carbide CAMI-scale wet-sanding paper. This type of sandpaper is not available in the no-load variety per se, but when it's used with water, as it usually is, it is nonloading. These days P-scale and JIS-scale wet-sanding papers outperform the traditional CAMI-grade Wet-or-Dry mentioned above because they leave fewer scratches and cut more aggressively. (Since these papers must be used wet to avoid loading, they aren't very effective for sanding wood.)

3M's Imperial is a popular version of a P-scale, silicon-carbide wet-sanding paper. It cuts so well that you can go too far if you're not careful. This is because the bonding method holds the mineral very rigid so that it cuts like a planer. It cuts deeper, which makes for better stock removal, but it also leaves a coarser scratch pattern, grit for grit, when compared to the gold P-scale alumium-oxide papers mentioned earlier. (You would probably need Imperial P1000 or P1200 to get a smoothness equal to a finish sanded with P800 aluminum oxide.)

Dry-sanding a finish

All finish sanding up to the final coat is done dry (without water or other wet-sanding lubricants) using 220 to 320-grit no-load sandpaper. Scuff-sanding is a quick light sanding that cuts down any high spots in the finish but that normally doesn't remove the majority of the shiny low spots. Level-sanding is not usually done until several coats have built up enough material so that the surface can be sanded close to level or flat without risking a sand-through. A level-sanding does remove the low "shiny spots" (more on sanding a finish in Chapter 8).

Dry-sanding Fre-Cut papers are available in grits finer than 320, but the finish (especially lacquer) can clog, or "corn," the paper enough to make dry-sanding with finer grits painstaking because you'll constantly have to change to fresh paper. Corns are buildups of small hard lumps of finish that can scratch a well-earned finish.

Some finishers use 400-grit during the finish building stage, though we think that's overkill. A 220- to 320-grit sanding adequately levels lacquer coats faster, and the sanding scratches will melt in and disappear when you spray successive coats. If you want to sand finer than 320, the best sandpapers to use are the P-graded, nonstearated, gold-coated aluminum-oxide type because they'll clog less.

You can dry-sand at any stage by hand, using a sanding block or with an electric random-orbit sander. If you use the random-orbit, try substituting 280- or 320-grit where you would normally use 220, because power sanding is more aggressive than hand sanding.

Level-sanding typically would be done two or three times (but there are no hard and fast rules): we sometimes level-sand halfway through the build coats, we always level-sand just before the final wet flow coat, and we always level-sand after the last coat has cured (before rubbing out the finish). Scuff-sanding, and the first two level-sandings, are usually done with 220- to 320-grit, and any sanding scratches melt in when sprayed with a coat of lacquer (some finishers use 320-grit on the level-sanding before and after spraying the final coat, however).

A finish which is about to receive color should always be level-sanded with 320-grit because colored finish needs a smoother surface in order to flow out more evenly and cover with fewer coats to keep the overall finish thin. (It's especially important to keep a color coat thin because the pigment in it makes it soft. Soft finishes are not desirable because they scratch and mar too easily).

Wet-sanding a finish

Although you'll do most sanding with regular paper, wet-sanding will always have its place. Most finishers switch to wet-sanding with super fine-grit (or finer) wet-sanding papers once the final coats have cured. For one thing, even high quality, very fine dry papers will corn with small lumps of finish than can scratch a finish you've just managed to get perfect. Water serves as a lubricant and a coolant to wash out any grit-clogging particles and reduce the heat of sanding. Wet-sanding gives the most glass-like, scratch-free finish. This is because dry-sanding scratches are deeper and have more-vertical sidewalls than wet-sanding scratches. Wet-sanding scratches may be as deep, but they're not as obvious because the edges of the scratch are more rounded. Therefore, wet-sanded surfaces are easier to buff, and the final appearance will not show the super-fine scratches.

Many instrument makers prefer P-graded and JIS-graded papers over the CAMI-grades because as noted earlier, CAMI-graded papers can have the occasional oversized grit particle, which can cause a nasty scratch just when you've gotten your finish near perfect. At this point you're looking for smoothing power, not cutting power.

Wet-sanding papers are available in grits ranging from 220 to 2000. Some finishers stop well short of 1000-grit, some go beyond, some use all the grits, and others skip as many as two grits at a time. The sandpaper grits you choose depend upon the smoothness of the final coat and how you plan to buff it out. With power buffing you can remove coarser scratches than you can with hand rubbing; therefore, a P800-grit wet-sanding may be all you need before buffing. If you're hand rubbing, go to at least 1000, and perhaps as high as 1200 or 1500. Only experience on your particular finish can guide you.

Power Sanders

Power sanders fill an important role in sanding. In a skilled finisher's hands, they speed up wood preparation as well as finishing and take much of the drudgery out of finishing a guitar. When used improperly however, they can ruin a finish. Instrument finishers use orbital and random-orbit sanders most commonly in their work, although a number of professionals with sufficiently large air compressors will use the air-powered DA sanders as well.

Power sanders speed up the sanding of large flat areas but can be too aggressive if proper care is not taken, and can easily remove more material than necessary. Orbital sanders leave more visible marks than random-orbit models. The random-orbit sander leaves almost undetectable marks, removing scratches and machine marks quickly, and making a coarse grit paper act like a fine grit. Dual Action (DA) sanders leave even fewer marks and are more powerful.

Orbital sanders

Orbital sanders were among the first generation of vibrator, or "jitterbug," sanders. They have an eccentric weight on the shaft of the motor, which causes the pad to travel in small circles, and a counterbalance built into the motor to reduce vibration. The sanding pad is either square or rectangular and does not rotate. Sandpaper, cushioned with a rubber pad, is clipped onto the bottom.

Random-orbit sanders

For musical instrument work, random-orbit sanders are a quantum leap above the plain orbital sander. Still new to many woodworkers, random-orbit sanders are electric woodworking counterpart to the dual-action (DA) air-powered sanders used for decades by automotive finishers. Like orbital sanders, random-orbit sanders also sand in a small orbital pattern; but the circular sanding pad makes a constant slow rotation—removing the circular marks made by the faster orbital action, thereby leaving fewer visible marks. A brake mechanism keeps the pad from rotating too fast because slow rotation is an integral part of its action.

The paper is attached either by pressure-sensitive adhesive, or by hook and loop (Velcro), and some models have built in dust collection. We recommend an electric random-orbit sander for the small shop.

DA sanders

Like random-orbit sanders, DA sanders can be held almost flat to the work and therefore do a good job of sanding flat surfaces. DA sanders are variable speed and maintain power whether running slow or fast. At the higher speeds they're more aggressive than random-orbit sanders, so if you need to remove some wood—smooth a rough-carved top for instance—a DA sander will have its place in your shop.

These sanders probably were the inspiration for the random-orbit sanders because they work much the same. The drawback to DA sanders, and the reason that you don't see more of them in woodworking shops is that they require a good deal of air to operate (a minimum of a 3-horsepower compressor). Even an adequate compressor will run constantly in order to keep up with a DA sander if you're doing much sanding—something to think about in the typical small shop with the compressor mounted close by (compressor noise can be unbearable).

Scrapers

Scrapers are hardened pieces of thin flat steel in any shape, 1/32-inch to 1/16-inch thick. Historically, scrapers preceded sandpaper, and have been a major woodworking tool for centuries. Their edges are specially sharpened and shaped to scrape the wood's surface smooth and perfect to accept the level finish we're all looking for in guitar finishing.

Anything with a sharp edge can act as a scraper, such as a broken piece of glass, pocket knife, chisel, single-edge razor blade, or the blade of an X-Acto knife. These do not have the curled edge of a properly sharpened steel scraper, and work better on plastics and finish than wood, but can serve a useful purpose on harder woods. The negative hook angle, or "rake," of these makeshift scrapers exerts a shearing (scraping) action, while the hook-edge scraper has a positive rake and cuts like a plane. The negative rake is good for hardwoods while the positive rake is better for softwoods.

TECH TIP

Make a great instant scraper in seconds by drawing the edge of a fresh single-edge razor blade along a piece of steel (the edge of a table saw or a band saw table, for example). One careful "draw" of the blade against the steel curls the edge into a tremendous throw-away scraper.

Scrapers excel at removing sanding scratches on any woods, but especially hardwoods with pronounced grain and end grain areas (cutaways, roundovers of solidbody guitars, or sculpted areas such as the heel of a mahogany guitar neck). You can enhance the grain in areas like these by using finer-grit sandpapers but scrapers will do it better and more quickly. They cut off the wood rather than scratching it off as sandpaper does, giving the wood a cleaner look.

Scrapers are also the best tools for trimming binding flush with the wood surface. They play an important part in most Gibson-style finishes. The factory avoids time-consuming masking procedures by purposely applying some stains, filler, or finish directly over the binding, then scraping the areas clean afterward.

Use a scraper for smoothing and leveling high spots on flat surfaces, large or small: the face of a newly bound peghead, plastic components, wood inlays, and all the narrow sides of the peghead. Scrapers smooth the latter without removing the crisp, sharp edges (unlike sandpaper, which has a tendency to round over a sharp edge). Scrapers are also the best at removing the small, dirty smudges and sanding scratches that often show up on clean white binding after the final sanding.

Single-edged razor blades make good light-duty scrapers for small areas on wood and plastic bindings and for levelling finish repairs. Draw the entire edge of the razor blade at an angle along a piece of hard steel to curl its edge into a burr. You'll be impressed by how well it works. When the edge is dull, throw the blade away and make another when you need it.

Quickly and adequately sharpen a scraper by simply clamping the flat steel into a vise and filing the thin edge sharp and square with a smooth mill file. Several strokes will give a usable edge for most

Chapter 5: Abrasives, Power Sanders, and Smoothing Tools

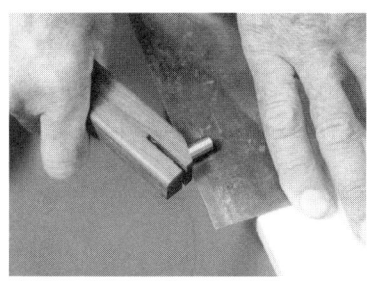

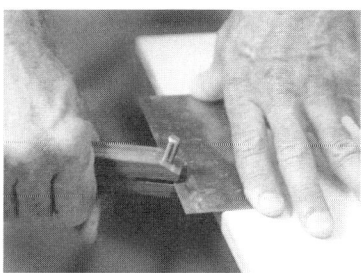

TECH TIP

To sharpen a scraper, first sharpen and square its thin edge with files and stones. Draw a hardened steel burnisher along the scraper's flat side to "draw out a burr" (top photo). Next, work the burnisher along the thin edge (middle and lower photos) to "turn the hook" of the burr. This turns the burr upward and creates the scraping edge. The burnishing tool shown here is slotted to hold the steel rod at the perfect angle for turning the hook.

scraping needs, although the edge may need to be resharpened more often than if it were finely honed.

Other Tools

Scotch-Brite flexible abrasive pads

Scotch-Brite is 3M's trademarked name for the flexible abrasive pads that some call synthetic steel wool. They're made by gluing an abrasive to a nonmetallic, fibrous material that makes up the pad. Unlike steel wool, Scotch-Brite does *not* shed zillions of tiny metal hairs all over our shops that stick to magnetic pickups, rust under waterbase finishes, imbed in *any* finish, and leave traces of oil on whatever they touch. For these reasons many of us no longer care to have steel wool around—at least not in the finishing area. Steel wool, especially the non-oily variety which some abrasive suppliers offer, is still a useful tool in other areas of a shop however.

Flexible abrasive pads are available in several grits—medium (red), fine (gray), and ultrafine (white)—and can be used wet or dry in any situation calling for steel wool. On bare wood the pads remove hard sharp edges and corners and produce a smooth patina on both flat and rounded surfaces. On finish, flexible abrasives reduce the sheen of gloss lacquer, remove the dust specks or nibs raised in the early stages of finishing, and do an excellent job of light scuff-sanding between coats.

Flexible abrasive pads are great for working with grain wood fillers too. The medium (gray) grit is perfect for burnishing and cleaning off residue from dried oil-base or waterbase filler before spraying a wash coat, and it's great for removing waterbase filler residue because it can be used wet (with, or in place of, a sponge).

Soldering iron

A soldering gun or soldering pencil is very useful in the wood preparation stage. A 25- to 40-watt hobby soldering pencil provides enough heat to steam out crushed spots that can happen during the construction phase.

Sanding blocks

Sanding blocks, or backing blocks for hand sanding, are another valuable wood prep tool. Commercially made types are available with spring-loaded grippers that hold sandpaper firm, however most of us use home-made blocks of wood because we can cut and shape them in sizes to suit the task.

A sanding block should fit not only the job at hand but your hand as well, and should have no sharp corners. Bevel or round the top edges for a comfortable feel, and pad the bottom with a thin layer of leather, felt, styrofoam, or hard and soft rubber.

Sanding table

A large flat surface of perhaps 24 inches square, with anywhere from P50- to P150-grit aluminum-oxide sandpaper fastened to it with double-stick tape makes a great "leveling table." By gently lapping the front and back on the flat surface, you can use it to remove imperfections or warp from solid-bodies about to be refinished. As the surface nears flatness, progress to finer grits, sand with the grain, and switch to a random-orbit to finish the job.

CHAPTER 6

Materials and Tools for Buffing

A professional-quality musical instrument finish is one that is applied thick enough to be sanded flat and buffed to a high gloss but remains thin enough to give the instrument good tone. A finish of between .004 inches and .009 inches is a good goal for both acoustic and electric instruments (especially acoustics). That's why good wood preparation and correct finish application are so important. Surely any successful guitar finisher reading this book would admit that getting the factory look, that perfect gloss, is the hardest part of the finishing process to master.

Buffing, or rubbing out, is the final stage of making ever-finer scratches until the unaided eye sees a smooth surface (under high magnification and brilliant lighting, even the most perfect-looking surfaces have a scratchy tale to tell). Buffing materials and tools include a variety of compounds, polishes, pads, bonnets, buffs, and power tools for this final stage of finishing.

Compound and Polish Types

Buffing compounds and polishes are micro-fine abrasives suspended in liquid, paste, or solid bars of emollients. All three compound types are available in grits ranging from coarse to extra fine and beyond. In guitar finishing, we want compounds that will eliminate the scratches left by the final sandpaper grit. Starting with too coarse or too fine a grit is a waste of time. Only experience will help you know just what grit to use and when to change—practice on scrap!

Some finishers switch from sanding to buffing at an earlier stage than others; you can stop sanding and begin buffing any time after a 500- or 600-grit wet-sanding. The final finish will not look as good as one that was sanded finer, but it will be adequate unless you're hand buffing.

Buffing compounds come in grits, graded coarse, medium, and fine. **Coarse compound** (brown) is used to follow a 500-grit wet-sanding. It must be followed with medium (tan) compound to get the best look. **Medium compound** (tan) is used to follow an 800- to 1200-grit wet-sanding and will often produce an acceptable finish. **Fine compound** (white) is used to improve the look of the medium compound. You don't have to use it, but the final gloss will be better.

Liquid compound

Liquid compound is formulated for hand rubbing. This is the safest polishing method because it avoids the damaging heat buildup that power buffing can produce. Liquid compound cools the surface and lubricates the polishing pad as you work but it's really the elbow grease that's most important.

Hand-application is easy, safe, doesn't generate heat, and won't drag the finish. It's an inexpensive way to get started. Don't expect to get the "factory look" of machine buffing, however. You'll see a powdery residue in nooks and crannies and nowhere near the glassy finish of commercial guitars.

Paste compound

Paste compound is formulated for hand-held electric polishers but it can be hand applied. Power buffing is often combined with paste hand rubbing to get those hard-to-reach areas that the stationary buffer cannot reach, such as around F-holes, on elevated fingerboard extensions, and on fancy peghead shapes. On these hard-to-get areas, we use pastes of the same grit and brand as the bar compounds used on the larger machine-buffed areas. Unlike liquid compound, paste leaves little or no residue.

Bar compound

Bar compound (rouge) is used for power buffing on a pedestal buffer. The compounds have the consistency of heavy, cold modeling clay. This is the product to use when you want a factory look. You have to practice power buffing with bar compounds, though. They can heat a finish, causing uneven areas (drags), and even can rub through to the wood. The compound is held against the rotating buffing wheel until the heat of friction softens it and the wheel picks it up (called loading). Rouge cools and feels stiff when the wheel's not in use, but each time you buff, it resoftens and does its job.

Cloths, pads, and buffs

Cloth is the only material appropriate for hand polishing with liquid compound. Choose clean, lint-free, well-used cotton such as diapers, tee-shirts, or old flannel shirts.

For hand-held machine buffing using paste compound you can choose among foam pads, lambs wool "bonnets," and both hook and loop cotton or foam pads. The plastic-backed foam pads have a 1/4-inch arbor that fits into your electric hand drill. Wool bonnets usually are mounted on flexible rubber discs that also have 1/4-inch arbors to fit an electric hand drill. The foam pads, and the wool-rubber disc combinations, are available at most hardware stores and automotive supply stores. Hook and loop pads of soft cotton or foam work on random-orbit sanders to buff delicate areas such as F-holes on arch top instruments or for buffing an entire instrument.

Buffs used on pedestal buffers

With pedestal buffers, we recommend Canton flannel cotton buffs exclusively—the ventilated, pleated style with metal centers. The cotton on this type of buff is cut on the bias, or at 45 degrees, and wrapped around the center. The bias cut minimizes those long strands that separate as the weave breaks down. Long strands exposed along the outside of the buffing wheel are apt to flap around and scratch your finish. It's a good idea to give newly mounted buffs a "haircut," however, trimming exposed threads to keep them from scratching. Follow up with periodic trimming if you're seeing any fine unexplainable scratches in the final gloss.

TECH TIP

To avoid scratching a finish with a cold wheel, buff a scrap piece of hardwood first, to warm the wheel.

Chapter 6: Materials and Tools for Buffing   55

TECH TIP

Once you use a particular compound on a pad or bonnet, dedicate that pad or bonnet to that particular compound—use a separate pad for each compound grit.

Tools Used for Buffing

Anyone who has ever rubbed out a finish more than a time or two discovers the true meaning of elbow grease, and begins to dream of an easier way: power-buffing.

The time saved by the use of power polishing tools makes them affordable to anyone doing much finish work. Whether you're using a simple electric drill and wool bonnet or a double-wheel pedestal buffer, the task goes faster. You will have to learn the right technique because *too much speed creates friction and heat that will soften and drag the finish right off the guitar!* It may take some practicing on wood scraps for awhile before you're ready to tackle a cherished instrument but it's worth the learning curve.

Electric hand drills

Most early-stage guitar finishers start out with a variable speed electric hand drill with either a rubber disc pad and wool bonnet or a foam Unigrit pad. It's not at all a bad place to begin. With a hand drill, you can do an adequate job of imitating the results of the professional rotating hand-held buffers used in factories. You have the speed control necessary to keep from overheating and dragging the finish, although the angle of a hand drill makes it somewhat awkward to hold. Also, controlling the torque and keeping the face of the pad square to the work can be tricky.

Random-orbit sander/polishers

A random-orbit sander with the appropriate polishing attachments, makes a good hand-held buffer for a small shop (see the Power Sanders section in Chapter 5). Even if you don't have a pedestal buffer, you can do fine work. They're easy to hold with one hand and don't build up as much heat as an electric drill with a buffing attachment would. Use a random-orbit polisher with the hook and loop foam pads and both medium and fine compound.

Even with the pedestal buffer available, we still use a random-orbit buffer for the area around F-holes on archtop instruments. The foam pad floats over the hole and doesn't have a tendency to catch on the points of the hole.

Pedestal buffers

Pedestal buffers are the fastest way to get a professional look. And there's nothing but your work to hold so the technique is easy on the operator. They're a godsend for polishing pickguards, bone nuts, wooden bridges, frets, and other metal parts. We like double-ended buffers—ones with a wheel intended for a different grit on each end—because we can go directly from one grade compound to another (usually from tan to white) without changing buffs. Finishers who sand with a fairly coarse grit like 500 or 600 will keep the coarse (brown) and medium (tan) compounds on their wheels. If they sand with 800- or 1000-grit, then the choice is medium (tan) and fine (white).

Dedicate your buffer to two compound grades, and leave the buffs on. A buff breaks in, and does the best job if it's not constantly removed and alternated with another wheel.

Industrial pedestal buffers are heavy cast-iron double-ended machines with a whopping 1-1/4 inch diameter spindle, 14-inch to 16-inch diameter buffing pads, powered by 5 horsepower to 7 horsepower motors. The smaller versions most of us use work almost as well, and the principle is the same.

For powering the smaller buffers, a 1/2 horsepower 1725 rpm motor works great, but any 1725 rpm motor ranging from 1/3 horsepower to 3/4 horsepower with a 2-inch motor pulley is fine. Anything bigger than 3/4 horsepower is simply overkill. The small double-ended buffer most of us use has a three-step V-belt pulley on the shaft, which gives a good range of adjustment. A 2-inch motor pulley combined with the large 4-inch end of the step pulley will give the relatively safe speed of 850 rpm to 900 rpm that we recommend. This is a good speed at which to start a 12-inch diameter buffing pad.

Have on hand a rake, a metal-toothed comb with a wooden handle, to clean old or dirty compound periodically from the wheel's surface. The rake will also pull out uneven strands of fabric; trim them with scissors before buffing again.

Industrial right-angle polishers

The traditional professional hand-held right-angle polisher, not to be confused with a right-angle grinder, is a powerful heavy-duty machine with an 8-inch to 12-inch cloth or wool-faced disc that rotates no faster than 1600 rpm or 1700 rpm. Good ones are as expensive as many pedestal buffers and are quite heavy. At Fender, for example, hand-held buffers are supported by chain hoists and counterbalances so they float as the operators guide them. Martin buffs with smaller hand-held polishers than Fender but they're still expensive heavy machines that require an experienced, strong, and tireless operator! The novice, hobbyist, or small shop should probably consider the other tools described above, rather than a heavy-duty professional hand-held machine.

TECH TIP

Whether you're hand-buffing or machine-buffing, your cloth, pad, or buff will not be completely coated with abrasive, so it must not contain any scratch-producing material.

Finish Recipes: **Example Guitars**

A gallery of guitars from our finishing recipes

Our Finishing Recipes section (Chapter 10) is a step-by-step guide to matching the look of famous finishes. To help you picture the finishes, here are color close-ups of many of the instruments that inspired our recipes.

Recipe 3: Blackened peghead face — 1960 Gibson Les Paul Special

Recipe 5: Fender's Sonic Blue — 1972 Fender Stratocaster

Recipe 6: Fender's Fiesta Red — 1966 Fender Stratocaster

Recipe 9: Fender's Lake Placid Blue metallic — 1981 Fender Precision Bass

Recipe 10: Gibson's Gold Top metallic — 1969 Gibson Les Paul

Recipe 12 and 13: Basic Martin-style finish — 1968 Martin 000-18

Recipe 14: Gibson's Tobacco Sunburst — 1954 Gibson ES-125

Guitar Finishing Step-By-Step

Recipe 15: Modern factory color job

Recipe 16: Top of the line shaded finish

Recipe 17: Vintage sunburst with Loar-style quick blends (colors: tobacco/red mahogany/amber)

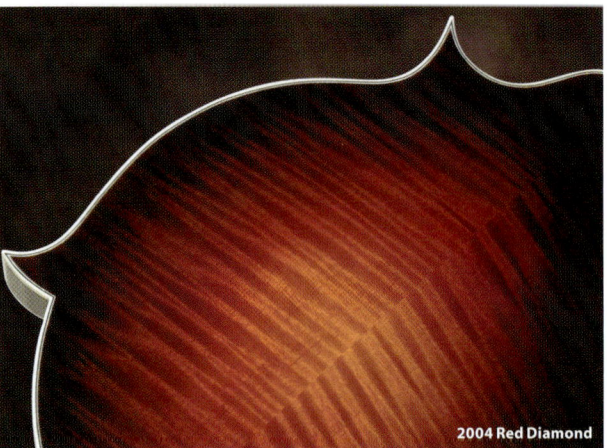

Recipe 17: Vintage sunburst with gradual blends that bring out the red (same colors as example at left)

Recipe 18 & 25: Cherry Red grain filler, before and after fading (revealed by removing the pickguard)

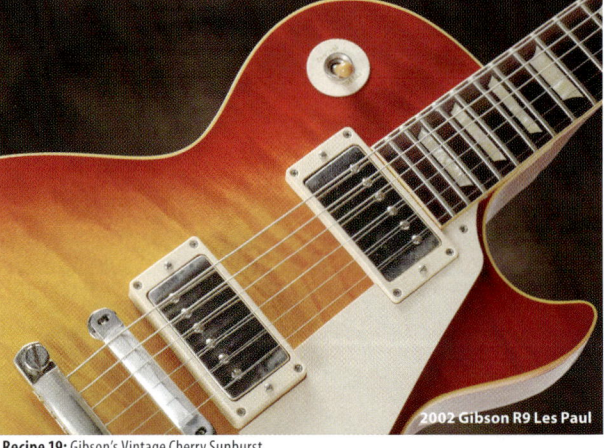

Recipe 19: Gibson's Vintage Cherry Sunburst

Recipe 20: Gibson's Cherry Red 335

Recipe 26: Gibson's TV Yellow

Finish Recipes: Example Guitars

1958 Fender Telecaster
Recipe 28: This good looking old blond shows the original white, without yellowing

1973 Fender Telecaster Custom
Recipe 28: This old blond has yellowed with age (our recipe simulates this using yellow and brown)

1959 Fender Stratocaster
Recipe 32: Pre-'56 two-tone sunburst on ash

1959 Fender Stratocaster
Recipe 33: Post-'56 two-tone sunburst on alder

1959 Fender Stratocaster
Recipe 33: Pre-'64 Fender three-tone sunburst on alder

1966 Fender Jazzmaster
Recipe 34: Post-'64 Fender three-tone sunburst on alder

1959 Fender Stratocaster
Recipe 35: It's taken since 1959 to get this aged look, but you can get it with a bit of amber stain

1970 Gretsch Tennessean
Recipe 36: One of Gretsch's flagship finishes

Guitar Finishing Step-By-Step

Two-color blends with liquid stains

Each row mixes two ColorTone Concentrated Liquid Stains to create new colors. Ratios are marked in percentages. Note that small changes in ratio are usually easier to see when mixing lighter colors. These samples are on light maple, and show stain only—no clear topcoat has been added. When a topcoat is applied, the stain colors will become more vivid.

Numbers shown are percentages of:
Lemon Yellow
Vintage Amber
Cherry Red
Red Mahogany
Medium Brown

Stain Mixing Chart: Two-color Blends

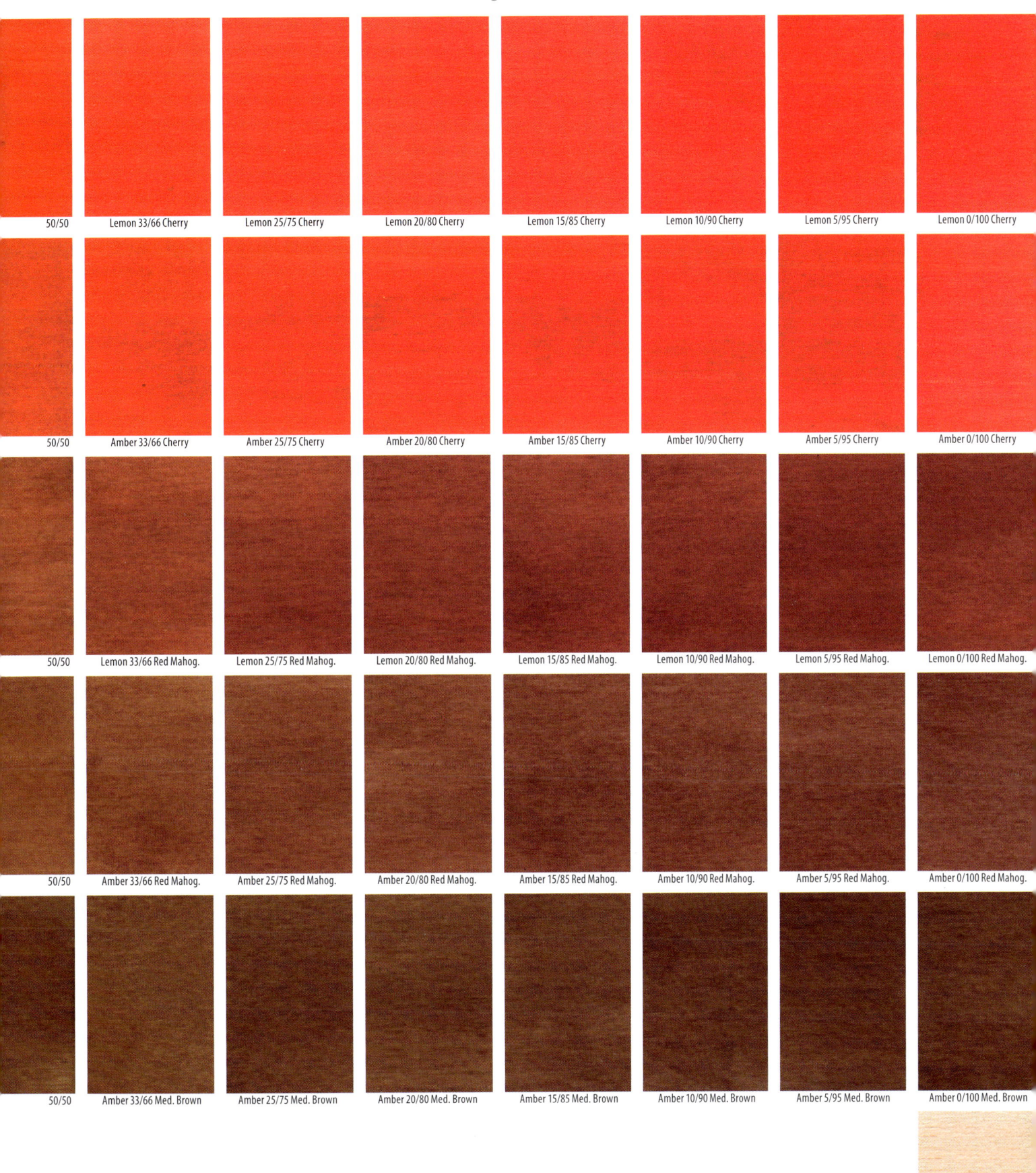

Guitar Finishing Step-By-Step

Two-color blends with liquid stains

Each row mixes two ColorTone Concentrated Liquid Stains to create new colors. Ratios are marked in percentages. Note that small changes in ratio are usually easier to see when mixing lighter colors. These samples are on light maple, and show stain only—no clear topcoat has been added. When a topcoat is applied, the stain colors will become more vivid.

Numbers shown are percentages of:
Tobacco Brown
Medium Brown
Red Mahogany
Blue
Cherry Red

Guitar Finishing Step-By-Step

1 part recommended mix + 8 parts thinner	1 part recommended mix + 8 parts thinner	1 part recommended mix + 8 parts thinner	1 part recommended mix + 8 parts thinner	1 part recommended mix + 8 parts thinner
1 part recommended mix + 2 parts thinner	1 part recommended mix + 2 parts thinner	1 part recommended mix + 2 parts thinner	1 part recommended mix + 2 parts thinner	1 part recommended mix + 2 parts thinner
Lemon Yellow, recommended mix	**Vintage Amber**, recommended mix	**Orange**, recommended mix	**Cherry Red**, recommended mix	**Red Mahogany**, recommended mix
3 times more stain than recommended	3 times more stain than recommended	3 times more stain than recommended	3 times more stain than recommended	3 times more stain than recommended
9 times more stain than recommended	9 times more stain than recommended	9 times more stain than recommended	9 times more stain than recommended	9 times more stain than recommended

Stain color density: thinned-down or concentrated

Compare the ten ColorTone Concentrated Liquid Stains at the strength recommended on the bottle (middle row), to the same colors at thin dilutions or extra-strong mixes. These samples are on light maple, and show stain only— no clear topcoat has been added. When a topcoat is applied, the stain colors will become more vivid.

10 Colors:
Lemon Yellow
Vintage Amber
Orange
Cherry Red
Red Mahogany
Medium Brown
Tobacco Brown
Black
Blue
Bright Green

An 8-day schedule for creating a Martin-style finish using waterbase lacquer

Here's Dan Erlewine in his shop, finishing a 000-style guitar with spruce top, mahogany neck, and rosewood back and sides. We generally followed Recipe 13: Basic Martin-Style Finish Using Waterbase Lacquer, a popular finish for flattops. These color closeups let you see the work and watch the changes as the finish progresses. Dan's using ColorTone's line of professional waterbase finishes: grain filler, sanding sealer and clear gloss topcoat.

DAY 1: START WITH THE NECK AND BODY CLEAN, SANDED AND READY TO FINISH

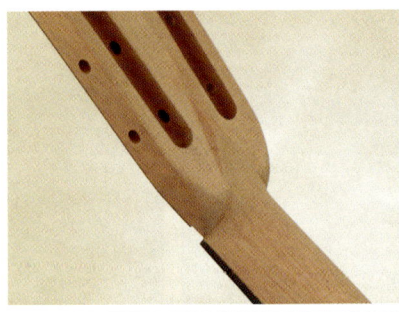 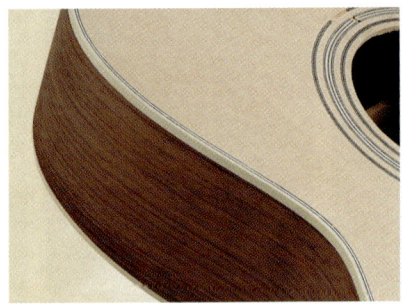 

Mask off the back and sides with paper and tape, leaving the top bare and ready to stain. You can leave the spruce top natural, which will be very white, or you can spray a bit of amber stain on it for a more vintage look. We stained the top using ColorTone Vintage Amber stain, mixed 4 oz. water to 1/8 oz. stain. That was far more stain than we needed for the top, but it filled our pint-size spray gun deep enough to keep the gun from sputtering. Spray stain on the top at 60 psi with the fluid needle nearly closed. You want a fine mist that's not too wet. After spraying the top stain, let dry at least 4 hours before continuing with the body.

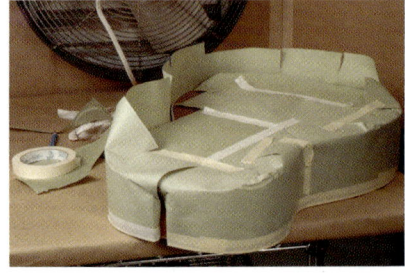

If you plan to use stain on either the neck or body, mix that now. We masked and stained the mahogany neck with a mixture of 5 parts Tobacco Brown and 1 part Red Mahogany ColorTone stain (80 drops of Tobacco Brown, and 16 drops of Red Mahogany in 4 oz. water), to resemble our rosewood sides and back. Let it dry 4 hours.

Remove the masking paper and tape from the body (leave the mask on the neck). Seal the wood (top, back, sides and neck) with 2 wash coats, sprayed 2 to 3 hours apart. A wash coat is made of an equal mix of sanding sealer and water.

8-Day Schedule: **Martin-style Finish**

DAY 2: FILL THE BACK, SIDES, AND NECK

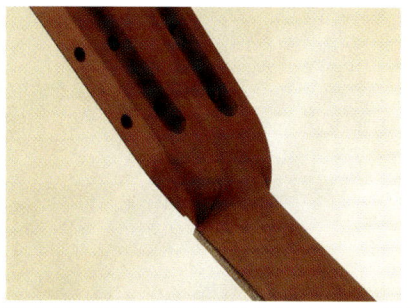

Mask off the top, leaving the back and sides exposed. Fill the neck, back and sides with ColorTone Grain Filler. We mixed 1 part black filler with 9 parts brown. We chose not to use any stain on the bare wood, letting the filler color the wood.

Work small, 6-inch square sections at a time, because the filler dries fast. Work the filler into the wood pores with a rag or brush, and remove the excess going across, or at an angle, to the grain with a flat squeegee or credit card. Remove any excess filler with grey Scotch-brite (medium-coarse grit).

Find an empty plastic household cleaner bottle with a spritzer top, wash it well, and fill it with warm or hot water. Lightly spritz the Scotch-brite, and use it to soften and rejuvenate the drying filler so that you can wipe it off more easily. You can also spritz the filled wood if necessary. Do not "over-wet." This could cause the removal of filler from the pores. The goal is to get the filler off the surface and leave it only in the open pores.

An experienced finisher can remove the filler without leaving smudgey streaks on the surface that will show later. It's not easy, however. Expect to sand the filled wood with 320-grit Fre-Cut gold sandpaper wrapped around a sanding block. Sand lightly to avoid sanding through the wash coats! If you sand through to bare wood, spray only that area with a light wash coat, and with the spray gun closed down to a small pattern, little fluid, and using a lower air pressure (20 psi).

Let the filler dry four hours, then reapply a lighter second coat of filler just as above. Let the filler dry overnight.

Guitar Finishing Step-By-Step

DAY 3: SEALER COATS

When using waterbase lacquer products, 65-75% of your final finish thickness will be sanding sealer. This is an important point that will seem odd to finishers experienced with nitrocellulose. Sanding sealer straight from the can gives the best results. Add waterbase retarder or water to reduce viscosity, or when hot or dry climate conditions cause the finish to dry too fast.

Spray 12 to 16 coats of sanding sealer, 3 or 4 coats a day, leaving 2 or 3 hours between coats (we use 50 psi). You may find that, unlike nitrocellulose lacquer, waterbase sealer coats don't look glossy and wet as you're spraying—but then they start to look wet about 30 seconds after the last pass of the spray gun. Don't lay it on thick, looking for glossy wetness. Hang the guitar up after spraying a coat and watch: waterbase goes on dull and dry looking, then looks wet about 30 seconds after, then dries down to a smooth, satin surface.

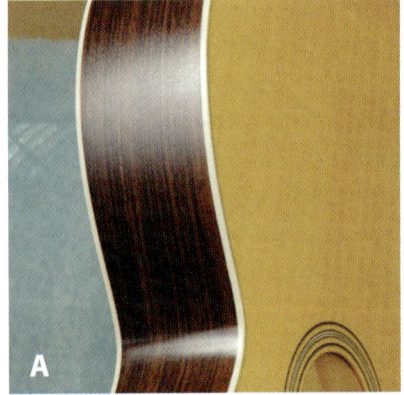
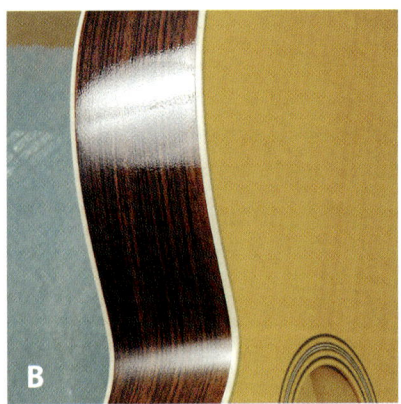
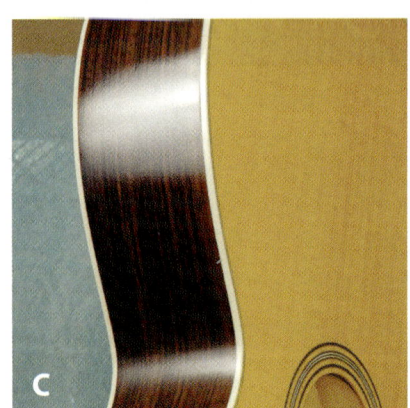

A. This newly-sprayed coat is wet, but it looks dry and pebbly (like orange peel)
B. Moments later, it turns wet and glossy
C. When finally dry, it turns satin-smooth

Without a wet gloss, there's no shine to help you see your spray pattern as you work. Good lighting becomes very important: spraying outdoors provides plenty of light on "good lacquer days." Spray light coats, and carefully overlap your spray pattern by 1/3 to 1/2 for coverage with uniform thickness.

The sealer has a 48-hour "burn-in" window; successive coats will bond best when applied within 48 hours of each other. When this time is exceeded, sanding with 320-grit paper is required to roughen the surface for good adhesion of the coats to follow. Begin following a daily spray schedule as indicated at right.

Day 3 spray schedule:

8:00 AM: Spray one coat
11:00 AM: Spray one coat
2:00 PM: Spray one coat
5:00 PM: Spray one coat
(4 sealer coats so far)

Clean your gun after every coat!

8-Day Schedule: Martin-style Finish

DAY 4: SEALER COATS

Day 4 spray schedule:

8:00 AM: Spray one coat
11:00 AM: Spray one coat
2:00 PM: Spray one coat
5:00 PM: Spray one coat
(8 sealer coats so far)

DAY 5: SCUFF-SANDING, THEN THE REMAINING SEALER COATS

Day 5 spray schedule:

Before spraying: scuff-sand with 320- or 400-grit

8:00 AM: Spray one coat
11:00 AM: Spray one coat
2:00 PM: Spray one coat
5:00 PM: Spray one coat
(12 or more sealer coats total)

We recommend 12 - 16 coats of sealer. We used 12. The number depends on the wood surface and how heavily you've sprayed. The goal is to build the finish to the point that you'll be able to sand it smooth without sanding to the wood.

Scuff-sand with 320- or 400-grit dry Fre-Cut on a small rubber backing pad. You are only knocking off high spots and dust specks, not trying to level "sinks" and low spots below the surface. If you see shiny spots, these are areas that aren't being scuffed by the sandpaper. Don't try to sand down and get them; instead, these are a sign that you need to add another coat of sealer.

Dust and small high spots to be sanded

Scuff-sanding leaves a dull surface. Low spots show up as shiny (unsanded).

Guitar Finishing Step-By-Step

DAY 6: THE FIRST TOPCOATS

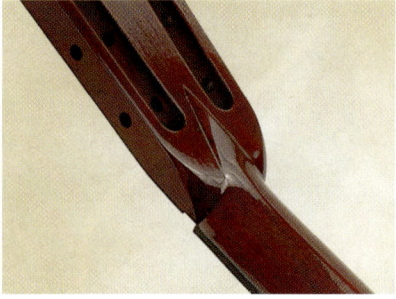  

The sealer coats built up the finish; now it's time for the topcoats. These hard glossy coats don't just lay on top of each other, they melt, or "burn in" to create one contiguous coat that will buff out nicely without sand-throughs. Use 9 to 12 coats.

Before spraying, level-sand the sealer with 320- or 400-grit Fre-Cut dry sandpaper. You should be free of all shiny spots, or "sinks," at this point.

Day 6 spray schedule:
Before spraying: scuff-sand with 320- or 400-grit

8:00 AM: Spray one coat (the first gloss coat)
11:00 AM: Spray one coat
2:00 PM: Spray one coat
5:00 PM: Spray one coat
(4 gloss coats so far)

DAY 7: DROP-FILL TOUCHUPS AND MORE TOPCOATS

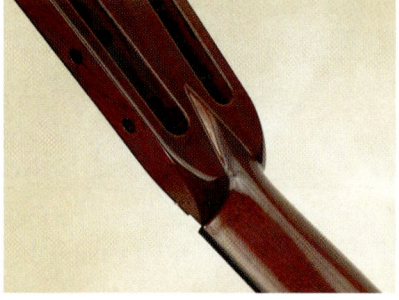  

Use a tiny artist's brush to "drop-fill" topcoat into any small craters or sinks below the surface. Tomorrow, after the drop has dried, you can level it with a thin strip of 320-grit paper pulled under light pressure from your fingertip.

Day 7 spray schedule:
Before spraying: drop-fill touchups

8:00 AM: Spray one coat
11:00 AM: Spray one coat
2:00 PM: Spray one coat
5:00 PM: Spray one coat
(8 gloss coats so far)

Drop-fill tip: a single-edge razor blade makes a good scraper for leveling a tiny drop-fill after it dries. Wrap transparent tape on each end, leaving the center of the blade exposed. This center part scrapes the drop down while the tape protects the surrounding finish.

8-Day Schedule: **Martin-style Finish**

DAY 8: FINAL TOPCOAT

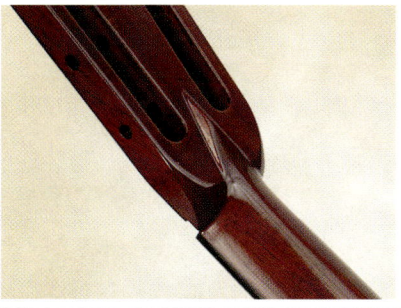  

Day 8 spray schedule:

Before spraying: last call for drop-fills!

Today: Spray one final gloss coat
(9 or more gloss coats total)

Let the neck and body dry for a week.

This morning your finish is close to being done. It should be a matte (satin) finish, like the ones you see on many non-glossy instruments. You could quit right now for that type of look. The photo below shows a closeup of the matte finish, using a strong light to emphasize the texture of the surface at this stage. This texture will disappear when you wet-sand and buff the guitar.

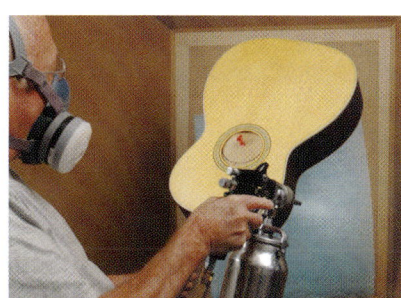

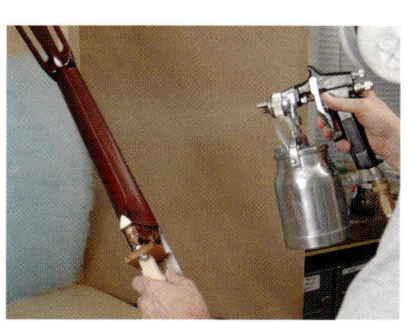 

If necessary, lightly sand any raised drop-filled spots using the strip-sanding technique. Drop-fill any remaining shallow spots. Spray one final coat and let it dry for a week.

Guitar Finishing Step-By-Step

AFTER DRYING: WET-SANDING AND BUFFING

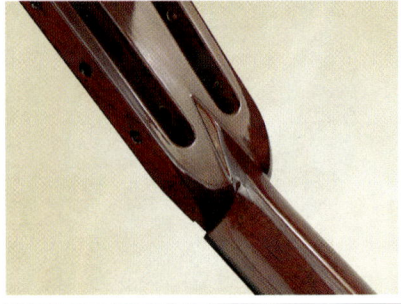

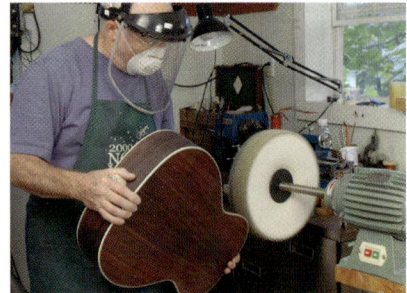

After your final topcoat has dried for a week, it's time for wet-sanding and buffing. Use 1200-grit wet-sanding paper. Soak the paper in water overnight before use.

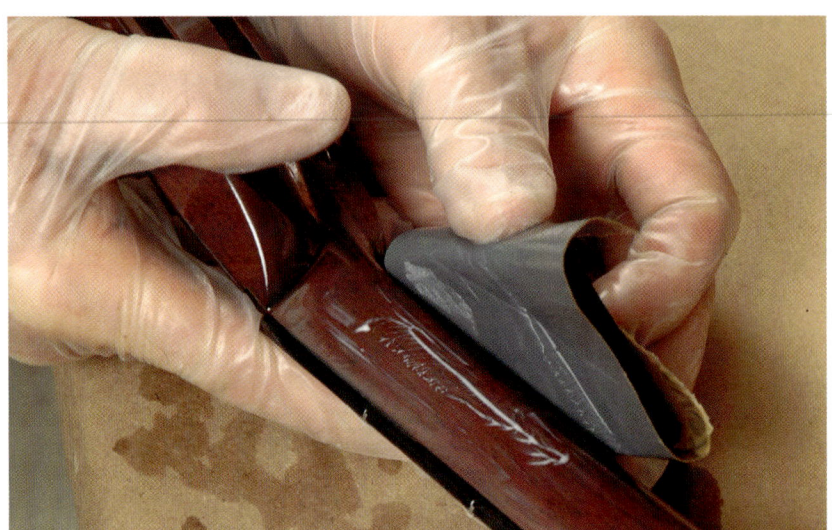

Finally it's time for the payoff to all your hard work: the buffing wheel brings out the gloss you've been picturing since Day 1!

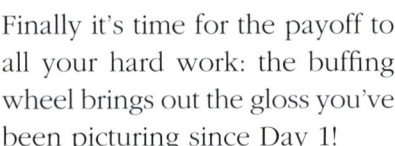

LET'S GET STARTED!

It's time to quit theorizing and get to work. If we were you, we'd be dying to get to the hands-on part! Let's start with the basics of spraying—once you master this art, you're three-quarters of the way to professional-looking guitar finishing. We'll then move on to sanding and buffing—the essential companions to spray finishing. Finally, we'll add some helpful tips in Chapter 9: Basic Finishing Steps. By then you'll be more than ready for the finishing recipes that follow!

CHAPTER 7

Spraying Basics

Everything we know about spraying we learned the hard way (hopefully you won't have to). Trial and error is a slow way to learn how to thin lacquer, use spray equipment, and troubleshoot the myriad pitfalls that come with the territory of finishing. You don't even *want* to know about silicone-caused "fisheye" problems either (actually, you do, and we tell you how to properly remove the contaminants that can cause fisheyes); and we've never met a guitar finisher yet that didn't say "what psi do *you* spray at?" This chapter tells all.

Thinning Lacquer

Solvent-based finish generally works best if you add thinner before spraying it through average siphon-feed equipment (unlike pressure-pot and heated systems used in factories that can spray unthinned lacquer). Many over-the-counter (hardware store) products such as polyurethane, ready-to-spray guitar lacquer, and waterbase finish come in the right viscosity to use and require no thinning (although at times you may thin those products, too). As you gain finishing experience, you'll develop your own formulas for thinning.

To build up enough clear coats of finish to properly sand and buff out is time consuming, so it's fastest to spray the lacquer as thick as possible. However thick lacquer is subject to problems such as sags (ridges of built-up lacquer on corners and sharp edges) and has a tendency to trap air bubbles. Trapped air bubbles usually show up in corners and are especially noticeable in cutaways, neck pockets, along frets on finished maple fingerboards, neck-to-body joints—any place air becomes trapped by the sprayed lacquer. Blushing can also be a problem.

If you have the proper equipment and the skill to spray thick lacquer, by all means do so (by this we mean large compressors, pressure-feed equipment, and even heated systems). With high-viscosity lacquer the build is quicker, so fewer coats and less thinner is required. This saves money and time and is better for the environment. (Fewer coats mean less sanding too, thankfully).

Although more coats will be necessary, requiring more spraying and sanding, and runs may occur more easily, beginners are probably safer to begin spraying lacquer a little on the thin side to avoid the above-mentioned problems. For instance, most experienced guitar finishers would rather see a run caused by a too-thin finish than the air bubbles which may occur when air is trapped by too-thick lacquer. When dry, runs can be sanded out, but air bubbles must be dissolved and "floated out" with solvent or chipped out with sharp tools. There's another advantage to thinning lacquer too, a smaller compressor can be used (thick lacquer will not spray well with compressors under 5 horsepower). Finally, we add thinner (especially retarder-thinner) to keep the lacquer from skinning over on the surface too quickly, trapping those air bubbles and moisture.

Temperature has everything to do with a lacquer's viscosity, and determines how much it will need to be thinned, and how well it will spray. As the ambient room temperature rises, the lacquer warms up, and you'll need less thinner to maintain a sprayable viscosity. It's best to keep the lacquer and the work area at 75°F or higher (or at least as warm as you'd like to be) before, during, and after spraying.

The type of lacquer you use will affect the ratios of thinner to lacquer. Colored lacquer (pigmented solid-color lacquer, as opposed to transparent colored lacquer), requires more thinner than clear lacquer—usually either the 1:4 or 1:3 ratios (see next section). Also, you'll want to shake or stir opaque colored lacquers often to keep the pigments from settling to the bottom, thereby keeping the color consistent.

Common ratios for thinning lacquers

These are general thinning ratios, and are subject to adjustment depending upon the solids content of a given formulation. These specs are for mix-it-yourself, standard, commercial lacquer, not the so-called "ready-to-spray" lacquers (which we sometimes thin 2:1 because we feel they can be a little heavy as they come from the can). The first number indicates lacquer, and the second number is thinner.

Very thin (1:4) is a thinning ratio that can be used as a light washcoat in the early stages of finishing, before grain filler, but you have to be careful to avoid runs—especially on color. We use this mix more often as a "flash" coat to melt in the scratches left from leveling the final coat. Flash coats are a nice touch if you have the time to spare.

Quite thin (1:3) is our preferred wash coat consistency, but it has too much lacquer to be a flash coat.

Thin (1:2) is still a thinner-than-normal mix (not for build coats), and could be considered yet another wash coat consistency.

Light (1:1) is what some refer to as 100%, and others call fifty-fifty. We call it, simply, one-to-one, and this is our preferred build coat using a standard lacquer. It's the most common thinning ratio for many lacquers when spraying in the 25 psi to 45 psi range, which most of us use. To get a nice, smooth, flowed-out coat with some lacquers, you must use this ratio.

Medium (1.5:1) is a good thinning ratio for beginners. It gives a little extra thickness over the 1:1 ratio so that you'll get a faster finish build without trapping air bubbles.

Thick (2:1) is another common ratio. This is the mix many finishers prefer to spray because it means applying fewer coats. Manufacturers suggest spraying this mix at 50 psi to 55 psi in a warm finishing room, but 35 psi will work well on most equipment.

Very thick (3:1) is rarely used in small shops. Experienced sprayers with compressors of 5 horsepower and up can spray lacquer this heavy, but it's not for most of us. Thick lacquer is generally heated in temperature-controlled industrial spray outfits before it will spray a uniform coat, and even then the sprayers must be experienced enough to avoid the areas that trap air or are susceptible to sags and runs.

Avoiding blushing

Retarder and retarder-thinner (Butyl Cellosolve is a strong retarder) are used to keep lacquer from blushing in hot, humid conditions or when moisture has been introduced through your spray equipment. Blushing occurs when moisture gets trapped in the lacquer and causes a bluish-white haze to cloud the finish. Retarder slows lacquer drying and permits moisture to escape. Retarder-thinner, which has the retarder already mixed in, is recommended.

Lacquer manufacturers suggest adding retarder to the thinner before using it to thin lacquer or sanding sealer. Retarder can also be used to fix a blush that has already occurred. Spray the blushed area with a light coat of retarder containing a small amount of lacquer to give it a little body. The retarder softens the lacquer enough to let the moisture escape.

Add up to 10% retarder to the thinner (creating your own retarder-thinner), and then use the thinner in your normal ratios for lacquer or sanding sealer. To make sure your ratios are right, test the drying time on scrap wood. You'll probably need from four to eight hours drying time between coats, if not overnight, before the lacquer is dry enough to sand.

Waterbase lacquer seldom blushes, and when it does the blush goes away quickly on its own without the need for retarder. Retarder is used only to extend its drying time.

Air Pressure

Getting the right air pressure is important for proper atomization. **Higher air pressures** (50 psi to 60 psi) atomize whatever you're spraying onto the guitar to a finer degree than low air pressures do. High air pressure is better for spraying thin media like stain than for high-viscosity films like lacquer. Lacquer can be over-atomized, drying before it reaches the object; this is called frosting, or dry-spray. Also, with a thicker finish such as lacquer, a high-pressure air stream can act like wind on water: it pushes the lacquer into ridges or ripples that can remain when the finish dries. An exception to this rule is waterbase lacquer, which unlike nitrocellulose lacquer, sprays best at higher pressure.

Lower air pressure (15 psi to 25 psi) is for airbrushing and touchup work. You also can spray topcoats with lower pressures, although most professionals don't. Try spraying lacquer at low pressure and see if you like the results, which can be quite good depending upon the brand of lacquer and its viscosity. Some likely unwanted results caused by under-atomization at low pressure are the famous "orange peel" look, finish buildup on the spray tip, spitting, splattering, and a weak pear-shaped spray fan pattern.

We recommend 35 psi for spraying topcoats, and 50 psi to 60 psi with the fluid needle closed down for spraying stains. Beginners should start out spraying *everything* at 35 psi. A general rule of spraying is to spray at the lowest pressure necessary to atomize the finish and have it flow out. So start low, and if you see orange peel (a pebbly look), increase the pressure.

Spray Gun Maintenance

Cleaning and setup

When you purchase a new spray gun, you should clean it thoroughly before using it. Also, you'll need to purchase the correct male air hose coupling to fit your compressor's air hose (mentioned later in "NPT Quick-Connector").

Anti-corrosion oil is used to protect the gun during warehousing and shipping. Clean it thoroughly. First, remove the air nozzle, put it in your "used thinner" jar, and flush it with thinner. (If you don't have a jar of used thinner, start one now—by re-using thinner for cleaning you will waste far less material and be environmentally conscious). Carefully clean both the male and female threads of the air nozzle to remove any grease or metal residue, which may be present from manufacture.

Fill the cup half full of warm soapy water, fasten the gun to the cup, and then shake the cup vigorously to clean the cup and underside of the gun. Next, follow the instructions given below (see "Using The Controls") to spray the soapy mixture through the siphon tube, fluid tip, and air cap. This will de-grease and remove most of the oily residue used for shipping and storage.

Then, wearing protective gloves, a respirator, and working in a well-ventilated area (or outdoors), clean the gun with lacquer thinner and/or denatured alcohol as a degreaser, to remove what the soapy water couldn't.

Experienced finishers try hard to use the least possible amount of thinner or solvent containing VOCs and other chemicals when they clean a spray gun—this applies to both nitrocellulose lacquer as well as waterbase. As little as 1 ounce of lacquer thinner or water will clean a quart-size gun if you are prudent, and 2 ounces will do the job for sure—especially if the air hose is disconnected and you are not spraying to clean the gun. Instead, use a bulb-type meat baster (or, for small amounts of thinner, a plastic "pipette" with its small tip cut off to enlarge the opening) filled with either warm water or lacquer thinner to flush out the gun, siphon tube, fluid nozzle and air nozzle. Hold the spray gun head with the siphon tube pointing upward and the spray nozzle held over the cup. Squirt the water through the siphon while squeezing the trigger. It will flow out the tip in a stream—right into the cup.

Repeat this process with lacquer thinner or denatured alcohol. Use only a small amount of thinner at a time. When done cleaning, pour the thinner into a lidded jar labeled "For Cleaning," and use it until it's dirty enough to evaporate outside. Never pour lacquer, shellac, or waterbase lacquer and dirty solvent into the sink or onto the ground—save it in a lidded-can and dispose of it yearly at an approved chemical waste disposal center. (Many small shops, that use small quantities of finish and solvent, simply pour it into a flat open container to evaporate out of doors). Wipe the gun and cup dry.

Remove the gun from the cup, and the air nozzle as well, then blow-off (or hand-dry) all the gun parts well. Set the parts to dry on a newspaper.

NPT quick-connector

You will need the proper connector to fasten onto the threaded air inlet of your spray gun. Automotive supplies, and many hardware stores, stock a variety of NPT (National Pipe Thread) quick-connectors. Buy one that is compatible with the size/style of the female quick-connect fitting installed on your compressor air line hose. The most common sizes are 1/4-inch and 3/8-inch. Wrap Teflon tape around the threaded portion of the air inlet before attaching your NPT quick-connect.

If there is no female quick-connect fitting on your air hose, and only the open end of hose, use a ribbed brass connector—a basic plumbing fitting—pressed into the air hose and secured with a small radiator hose clamp.

The most common sizes for air hose inner diameters (ID) are 5/16- and 3/8-inch. For hoses 15 feet to 25 feet long choose 5/16-inch ID; for 50 foot hose a 3/8-inch ID is preferred.

Hook the gun up to an air hose and adjust the compressor regulator to the following pressures, based on hose length.

Hoses up to 15 feet: Spray at 30 psi

Hoses up to 25 feet: Spray at 35 psi

Hoses up to 50 feet: Spray at 40 psi

For more precise regulation, you can purchase a mini-gun regulator, which installs to the air inlet of the gun. This is recommended for long hose runs over 25 feet.

Adjusting your spray gun

If you learn to spray with a two-stage gun, you'll be able to use any other style, because using a spray gun is just not that difficult in the first place.

The **fan control knob** on top of the gun controls the shape of the fan pattern. Closed down, the setting produces a narrow, round fan, ideal for small or narrow areas like sides, necks, and peg head edges; a wide-open setting produces a wide, more oval-shaped fan, better for spraying large areas such as the front, back, and sides of guitar bodies.

The amount of fluid you spray is controlled by the **fluid control knob**. Open it (counterclockwise) to get more fluid, close it for a dryer lighter application. Where you set this knob depends on your spraying technique—that is, how fast you move the gun across the surface of the guitar. If you move slowly you'll want this closed down a little so you don't get runs and sags by spraying more lacquer than will hold to the surface. Practice on cardboard or scrap wood before spraying an instrument.

The fluid control knob's setting and the fan control knob's setting need to be coordinated. Increase the air pressure at the regulator to

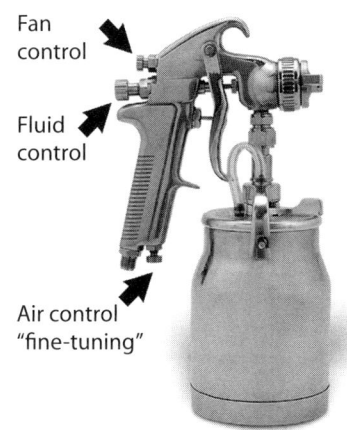

Fan control

Fluid control

Air control "fine-tuning"

get better atomization and more air flow. When spraying thinner materials, such as stains, the valve should be more closed than open and the air pressure set high to get a fine mist of highly atomized fluid. To get a heavy, soft, wet spray of finish, open up the fluid valve and reduce the air pressure. Try spraying at 25 psi to 30 psi. This is good for laying down a soft wet coat of lacquer.

Air control knob

A number of production guns have a third knob–located at the bottom of the gun handle–that controls the air pressure at the gun, instead of only at the air regulator. Turning this knob into the body completely (clockwise) closes down the air entirely. Start opening it up and air returns to the gun gradually. This is a fine-tuning knob.

Coordinating knobs

Learn how a two-knob gun works by starting with both knobs in the closed position and the air pressure regulator set at 30 psi. With the top (fan) knob closed, open the bottom (fluid) knob just slightly. Begin spraying across the work piece, and continue opening up the fluid valve until you get the spray coverage you want (wet-looking for nitrocellulose lacquer, dry-looking for waterbase lacquer). Open the fluid valve a little more while you continue balancing the fan and fluid until you get an oval fan pattern, and the type of coat you're after (dry or wet). The spray pattern should never be irregular. Use a wide pattern for spraying large areas, and a narrow pattern for small parts. If you increase the fan width, you may also need to open up the fluid delivery. You can change to a horizontal fan pattern by rotating the air cap 90 degrees after loosening the retaining ring. By going through this exercise you will become familiar with the controls on your spray gun, and learn what it can do.

A three-knob gun adjusts the same as a two-knob gun, but has the additional benefit of fine-tuning the air pressure at the gun.

Gun cleanup and maintenance

Some guitar finishers that use solvent finish (nitrocellulose lacquer most often) give their guns a complete cleaning daily, rinsing with solvent, soaking the removable parts, and then drying each part for storage. You don't have to go that far, but give your gun a quick cleaning every time you use it, and periodically clean it thoroughly. Solvent finishes redissolve in the proper solvent, so even dried lacquer finish will soften and clean up. This is not so with reactive and coalescing finishes because once they dry they can't be redissolved

Emptying and cleaning a spray gun after use

Here's how to thoroughly clean a spray gun using only a small amount of thinner:

Solvent Finishes (nitrocellulose lacquer or shellac): The air passage of the spray gun is not user serviceable, and should require no cleaning if you use dry, filtered air at all times. But any parts that come in contact with finish should at least be rinsed with solvent. Unplug the air hose from the gun, then loosen the gun lid and raise

TECH TIP

A good way to transfer all liquid in a can without mess is to stand the dripping can on end for a minute as shown, then flip the can over so any drips will fall into the cup — keeping the rim of the can clean.

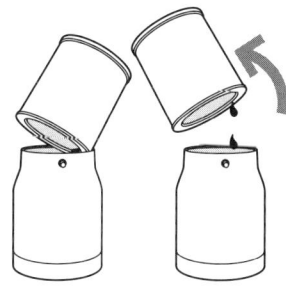

TECH TIP

An option to returning the finish to its can is to put a lid on the spray gun container to keep the finish from evaporating and thickening. Cup lids are available at automotive supply stores. Or, the lid from a quart-size finish can makes a good cup lid — file two round grooves in its lip to clear the two studs on the spray cup, and place waxed paper in-between as you press the lid down.

the spray gun up over the can while triggering to let all the fluid drip out of the siphon tube and into the can. Wipe the siphon tube with paper towel, and inside the can as well if you can get your hand inside (wear protective gloves). Pour just enough thinner in the cup to spray, replace and tighten the spray gun head, and shake the gun to clean its interior. Spray some thinner to flush out the siphon tube and nozzle, then leave the thinner in the can until your next spray session. Discard any solvent-soaked rags outdoors to dry, then rinse them with water and put them in the trash.

Waterbase Lacquer: Don't leave waterbase lacquer in the can for more than two or three spray sessions (approximately 6 hours). Then, after following the above instructions for letting the finish drip out of the siphon tube, pour the finish from the cup back into its can.

Waterbase lacquer cleans off easily before it dries. A deep sink is the best place to clean the gun. Rinse out the cup with water (preferably hot) and rinse the gun on all surfaces. Turn the spray gun upside down, with the siphon tube facing up, and run a stream of water into the tube while pulling the trigger until a steady stream of clean water flows. Pour some water into the cup, assemble the gun, and spray some water onto a paper towel until the water is clear. It's clean enough by now to spray it directly onto your open hand—you will see when the stream is no longer "milky". Rinse the gun and can one more time, remove the air cap and nozzle, and set the loose parts aside to dry.

Never leave water in the gun or cup, which often contain aluminum parts. Water reacts with aluminum and pits it, creating uncleanable pockets that retain stain and other finishing residue.

The parts that require attention are:

Air cap. Immerse in thinner for several hours to remove finish.

Fluid nozzle. Unscrew and immerse in thinner until any finish is dissolved.

Fluid needle. Unscrew the valve and the needle will pull out, allowing you to immerse it in thinner until any finish is dissolved.

Fluid needle packing and adjusting nut. The fluid needle of a two-stage gun has a packing seal and adjustable packing nut that fit around the needle's smooth shaft, forming a flexible seal that lubricates the needle and keeps it from drying out and sticking. This seal lets the needle move back and forth with little resistance, but keeps air from being sucked in around it (which would interrupt the fluid flow and cause sputtering). Tighten the nut occasionally to keep compression on the seal, and put a drop of lightweight household oil, or sewing machine oil, on the needle. If the packing seal in front of the trigger gets hard and brittle, replace it. It is common to replace the packing once or twice a year, depending on how frequently you spray. To prevent drying, put a drop of the same lightweight oil on the seal once in awhile to keep it supple.

Cup, lid, and gasket. Clean them regularly.

Spraying Techniques

Many builders finish the neck and body separately using shop-made fixtures for holding the work. Necks, being small, are easy to handle and spray. A guitar body, however is a bit more difficult to spray. A good approach is a handle in the neck pocket, which holds the body with the neck joint end toward the floor, butt end up. Start spraying on the sides at the butt end, coming along the bass side to the neck joint. Stop spraying and return to the butt end to make the same pass on the treble side. For side coverage you can turn the nozzle so that the fan pattern is horizontal, or you can use a vertical pattern. For tops and backs, however, the vertical fan pattern is recommended

On the top or back start at the butt end and spray across the surface from left to right, then with an overlapping spray from right to left, then left to right again, and so forth. Continue until the entire top or back is coated down to the neck-joint end. (If you start spraying at the top of your project and move downward, the wet spray dissolves any dry over-spray. If you start at the bottom and work up, you may end up with dry, over-sprayed coverage.

When working on vertical parts, move the gun fast enough to avoid sagging. Avoid over-thinning. Rotating the air from vertical to horizontal, allows you to spray vertical parts without tilting the gun.

Good finishing takes practice. Time spent perfecting your technique will keep you from spending more time undoing mistakes. Set up your work, then relax and concentrate on refining the air pressure, viscosity, fluid level, fan pattern, and other peripherals—all of which happen at once. Your goal is to develop a robotic consistent spraying technique. Here are some tips to guide you:

- **Keep the gun at 90 degrees** to the work at all times, without tipping or swinging it. This is difficult to do but pay close attention to position until it becomes second nature. To spray around the sides, you might need to coordinate the movement of both the instrument and the spray gun to keep the spray square (90°) to the surface of the guitar.
- Keep the spray gun at a **constant distance** (about 8 inches) from the guitar at all times.
- Move the spray gun at a **constant speed** (about the speed of painting with a paint brush).
- Move the gun in a **straight line** and **overlap** each pass by one-third to one-half its width when you make the next pass.
- To eliminate spattering, **start and stop spraying off to the side** of the instrument. Begin moving the spray before the finish hits the instrument, and wait until the spray is completely off the instrument before releasing the trigger.

TECH TIP

Before spraying a project, clean the spray area, room, or booth until it is free from dust. It's a good idea to damp mop the floor, walls, and ceiling just before spraying and to blow down your body, gloves, respirator, and clothing. Otherwise, when spraying with an air compressor, the back-pressure will pick up lint from your hair and clothing and lay it right into the finish.

TECH TIP

Most of us use the orifice supplied with our spray gun. However any orifice from .050 to .080-inch seems to work well for us with either nitrocellulose or waterbase lacquer. Each may need a slightly different air pressure, but that will come easily with a little experience.

Right way

Distance from work stays the same, coverage is consistant

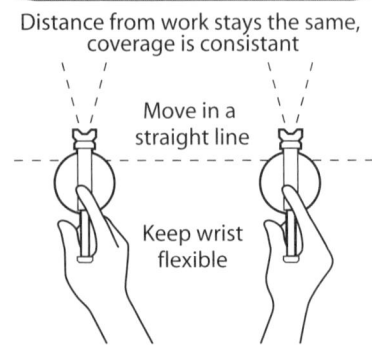

Wrong way

Arcing motion produces heavier coverage at the center

Wrist is too stiff

TECH TIP

If you plan to spray indoors—even with aerosol cans—an exhaust fan/spray booth is necessary to evacuate fumes. Of course you need an organic vapors mask to reduce health risks. Don't underestimate the value of a good spray mask. Several prominent builders have been forced into early retirement from luthiery due to overexposure to lacquer fumes.

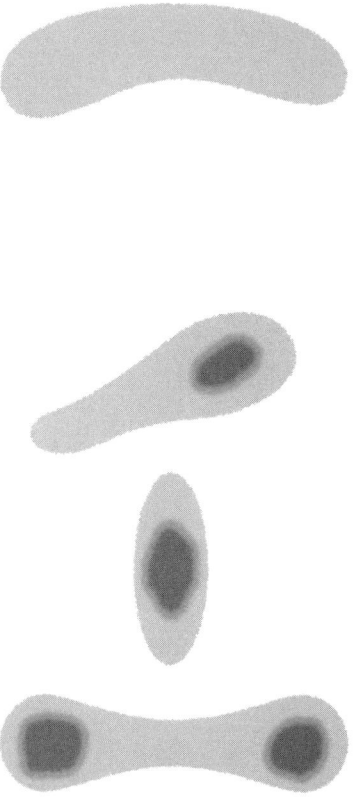

Troubleshooting

Most spraying problems are the result of finish building up at the air nozzle or because a fitting is loose. If your gun won't spray correctly, here are some likely causes and solutions.

- **Problem:** A dry coat, spitting, or no spray at all.
  Cause/solution: Blocked air vent hole in the cup lid. The Production Gun has a neoprene anti-drip hose connected to the vent hole, while the Touchup Gun has an open vent. The open vent needs to be cleaned constantly; the anti-drip hose and nipples it connects to also need cleaning, but far less often. Use a toothpick or small brush to remove any dried finish. Soak the lid and anti-drip hose in solvent if necessary.
- **Problem:** Finish bubbles inside the cup, or spits around the air nozzle-retaining ring.
  Cause/solution: Air leaks. Usually an air leak simply means the air nozzle is loose—tighten its retaining ring. Air leaks also occur if threaded connections are loose. Use Teflon tape on the gun's threaded air input before fastening your hose connector and on the threaded coupling between the gun body and the fluid nipple. Finally, the needle-packing washer may be dry and worn, or the hex-nut cap that tightens the packing may be loose.
- **Problem:** Spray pattern is curved into a sausage shape.
  Cause/solution: Material buildup on the air nozzle. One of the side-port holes is blocked, so air is coming only from the opposite (clean) port. This forces the fan pattern in the direction of the blocked horn. This problem may also be caused by a partially-plugged fluid nozzle.

  Remove the air nozzle and soak it in thinner. Squirt thinner through the blocked side-port holes until they are clean. You may need to poke a toothpick or broom straw into the holes to clear them, but never use a metal object to clean them.
- **Problem:** Pattern is heavy and wet toward one end.
  Cause/solution: Material buildup around the outside of the fluid nozzle orifice, or a partially-plugged fluid nozzle orifice. A loose air nozzle may also be the cause. Remove the air nozzle, soak it in thinner, wipe it clean, and be sure to keep it tight.
- **Problem:** Spray wet and heavy in the center.
  Cause/solution: Too much material, or the material is too thick. Reduce the air pressure, or increase the material flow. Thin the material.
- **Problem:** Spray is split, or heavy and wet on the ends of the fan pattern and weak and dry in the middle.
  Cause/solution: Air pressure is too high and you're not spraying enough material. Or, you may be spraying a thin material and attempting to get a fan pattern that is too wide for thin material. Reduce the air pressure, or increase the material flow. Also, with the fluid needle wide open you can reduce the spray pattern size by turning the fan control valve inward clockwise. Perhaps you should stop and start over, adjusting the spray gun from ground zero.

- **Problem:** Spray fan is intermittent and pulsating.
  Cause/solution: There may not be enough material in the cup, and if you tip the gun excessively, the siphon tube sucks in air and causes sputtering. The material may be too heavy for the gun. Look for an obstruction of dried finish somewhere. Check for a loose fluid nozzle, or a damaged or dirty fluid nozzle seat. A loose or cracked siphon tube may be the culprit. Look for a dried needle packing, or perhaps a loose or defective swivel hex-nut that connects the gun body to the cup.

  Fill the cup 1/2 to 2/3 full, and don't over-tip the gun. Back out the needle packing hex-nut and put a drop or two of light oil on the packing (or replace the packing if it can no longer make a seal). Tighten the fluid nozzle, or remove it to clean the contact areas with thinner. Thin material that is too heavy to spray.
  Note: The factory seats the fluid nozzle very tightly. When removing the fluid needle for the first time, hold the gun in a padded vise and use either a metric open-end wrench or an adjustable crescent wrench to loosen it. When you reinstall the tip, apply just enough torque to snug it. However, the fluid nozzle seldom needs to be removed for cleaning if you are conscientious about cleaning the gun regularly.

- **Problem:** When triggered, fluid needle moves sluggishly or not at all.
  Cause/solution: Finish buildup between fluid nozzle orifice and needle—sealing them together; dirty, gummy needle shaft or packing. Remove the air nozzle and submerse the fluid nozzle portion of the gun in thinner until the hardened finish softens. Then back out the needle packing hex-nut; if the needle is stuck in the packing, squirt some thinner into the packing to loosen it (otherwise you can't remove the needle).

  To remove the needle, back out the fluid adjustment valve all the way and remove the compression spring. Pull out the needle, and clean it with thinner. Sight through the needle passageway and out through the fluid tip—if it's blocked, clean the passage using a thinner-drenched pipe cleaner. Clean or replace the needle packing before reinstalling it, and put a drop or two of light oil in the packing hole.

Fixing finish contamination

Some of the problems you encounter in spraying have nothing to do with your technique or your equipment. They are the result of something in the spraying environment that shouldn't be there. Your best bet is to thoroughly clean your work area and the work piece before you begin spraying. We give some tips below for that. If contamination problems occur anyway, despite your best efforts, we also give some tips for undoing the damage.

Fisheyes are irregular craters that can occur in your finish when grease, oil, wax, or especially any lubricant containing silicone is present on the wood or the finish. These contaminants can be introduced by guitar case cleaners, polishes, and even sandpaper, or they can migrate from oiled tool surfaces. Any of these substances can make the surface tension uneven, causing irregular flow-out. Silicone contamination looks like little fisheyes or craters; wax deposits cause the lacquer to stay wet and shiny in patches; oil contamination is similar. Human sebaceous oil, such as that on your nose and face, doesn't seem to cause reactive problems with finish, but we still don't recommend that you rub your face and then touch a surface about to be sprayed.

The best solution to these problems is to avoid silicone oil or wax in the first place, but if they're present, wipe down the guitar before you spray finish on it. Use separate clean rags refolded often to expose a fresh surface. Dampen the rags in the following order:

Step 1: Naphtha removes wax, but not silicone. If silicone is present naphtha reacts to it by cratering just as lacquer would. If that happens, use mineral spirits. If you know that you only have wax contamination, you could stop cleaning here.

Step 2: Mineral spirits removes silicone by dissolving it and drawing it from the wood. This puts it in a solution that can be mopped up with rags. You're moving the silicone around on the surface though, and a slight residue will remain.

Step 3: Ammonia and water removes the last bit of remaining silicone. Ammonia actually releases the silicone from whatever it's clinging to. We don't use it first, because the mineral spirits are necessary to draw silicone out of the wood. This gets it into a solution that can then be mopped up with rags and cleaned in the last step with ammonia.

You've cleaned everything (you think) to perfection, you spray your piece and despite everything, craters pop up. What do you do? If proper cleaning doesn't eliminate fisheye, which will be evidenced by the continuance of craters, your best solution is to seal the wood with a wash coat of fresh-mixed shellac. Because shellac is the very best sealer for locking in silicones, it's not a bad idea to use it even if you think you have removed all contaminants by cleaning.

An alternative to cleaning, but one we don't recommend, is to add **fisheye eliminator** (a silicone additive) to your lacquer. By "fighting fire with fire," so to speak, the whole finish becomes one big fisheye. Some of us used this stuff when we first started out, (because it was available and we thought we were supposed to), but wished we never had. If you use it in one coat, you have to add it to every coat. Then it starts getting around the spray booth, the fan, the shop, and of course the spray gun, and soon you can't spray without using it. Fisheye eliminator is messy, not good stuff to handle, a pain to use, and it changes the gloss and hardness of the final coat.

CHAPTER 8

Sanding and Buffing Techniques

Here are some tips on sanding wood and finish, and for buffing the final coat. Sanding and buffing require patience and an attention to detail that separates the amateurs from the pros in a highly visible way, so this chapter bothers with such subtleties as how to hold your sandpaper or when to start and stop your sander. Chapter 5: Abrasives and Smoothing Tools should be reviewed before this chapter.

Techniques for Sanding Wood

A truly good finish begins at the bottom layer: the wood. Proper and thorough sanding of the wood will translate into a finer finish with less time and effort. Most sanding techniques are the same for finish as for wood, but here are some rules that apply only to sanding wood:

Sand with the grain

Sanding in the direction of the grain is just common sense. If you've ever put stain on wood that's been sanded across the grain you will see why. On wood, marks left by hand sanding across the grain, or swirl marks left by random-orbital sanders, become particularly evident with stain and transparent or translucent finish over them. Try cross-grain sanding on scrap wood and then stain the piece. Any cross-grain scratches will stand out immediately, while those same scratches with the grain will not be noticeable at all.

It's OK to hand sand at a long angle across the grain. In fact, sanding this way is faster than just sanding with the grain. Sand slightly to the right and left of center but *not at right angles*. Afterwards, be sure you finish by sanding with the grain to remove any angled scratches.

Use power effectively

Electric hand sanders, and random-orbital sanders in particular, are great timesavers that can be used on wood or finish. Random-orbital sanders leave fewer and smaller swirl marks than their predecessors, the orbital or "oscillating" pad sanders. However, even random-orbit marks are visible if you look closely. Keep swirl marks to a minimum by using fresh, sharp paper of the proper grit and grit order and by sanding at the proper speed. Most novice finishers move electric sanders too quickly and end up with unnecessary swirl marks. Read the manufacturer's suggestion for the correct operating speed.

Never start or stop a power sander on the guitar, or you could leave deep, orbital swirl marks that take considerable sanding to remove. Start it before approaching the work, glide the running machine onto the work at a shallow angle, do your sanding, and then glide back off before turning off the motor. After turning off your sander, make a habit of not setting it down until it stops moving completely—it will last longer.

Also, attend to sander maintenance. Random-orbit sanders have a built-in brake that keeps the pad from revolving too fast. The brake, which wears in time, is replaceable in minutes, and the part is only a few dollars from a manufacturer's service center. You'll know the brake is wearing when the pad doesn't slow enough as you glide the running tool onto the work—causing a dig or gouge in the wood. If that happens, it may be time to replace the brake.

Electric sanders get you where you want to go in a hurry, but a quick hand sanding is usually needed afterward for a perfect finish. Follow electric sanding with block sanding by hand, moving with the grain to remove any swirl marks.

Pick the right grit

Chapter 5 explains how to choose the right sandpaper. At the finish stage you'll want to pick a fine enough grit to avoid *creating* scratches that are difficult to remove. No matter what, don't start sanding with anything coarser than 120-grit.

Most guitar woods are ready to spray after a careful sanding that ends between 180- and 220-grit. This holds true for mahogany, rosewood, walnut, maple and the other woods used for necks, backs, and sides. For top woods such as spruce, cedar, and redwood, 220 is most common, and some might sand as fine as 280- and 320-grit—but no finer! We've seen finishers sand wood up to 600-grit, thinking that it will look better. They're polishing the wood, not sanding it, and lacquer can actually have trouble adhering to wood that's been sanded *too* smooth!

Breaking edges

Finish clings better to curves than sharp angles. To lessen the chance of sanding through the finish, especially during the early stages of building, gently round all sharp edges of the raw wood by hand. Smooth the edges of pickup cavities, control cavities, peghead edges, and other angled parts with 180- or 220-grit using a backing of cloth or foam rubber to soften the bite of the paper. Sometimes we roll the sandpaper into a tube so that only a small pinpoint area contacts the wood at any one time, turning the tube constantly to expose fresh grit. If you can avoid it, don't sand any edges once you've begun finishing until you reach the wet-sanding stage. If you have not built up the finish extra thick in these areas, you can easily burn through the edges during the rub-out.

Raise the grain

Between each sanding stage, lightly dampen the entire surface with a clean rag soaked in water but *squeeze it out well*. This dampening causes the wood fibers to swell and raise or "fur up", making it easy for the sandpaper to cut them off after they have dried thoroughly—leaving a smooth level surface. Don't sand too hard or you'll go right through the raised fibers and into new wood; you'll have to redampen the wood and do it again! Use this damp sanding at every stage of wood prepping for the smoothest possible surface. This technique results in wood that won't swell much when color and finish are applied.

If you're sanding a gentle concavity like the recurve of an archtop guitar, use a sanding block with give. Felt is the best but soft cork works, too. In tighter curves such as a guitar's waist or in a cutaway, use a flexible rubber backing pad. Because these areas are narrow, you could also carefully sand without a pad.

Techniques for Sanding the Finish

You can use the same techniques, sandpaper types, and tools for sanding finishes that you use for sanding wood—just don't use as coarse a grit. For sanding wood we use 120- to 220-grit. For sanding finish we start at 220-grit and go up from there. In general, if we choose to use a random-orbital sander (though understand that you do not have to power sand), it is only for dry-sanding during the earlier stages of finishing. The final wet-sanding before buffing should be done by hand. Wet sanding with electric sanders—even a random-orbital sander using a fine grit—leaves scratches in the finish. Power sanders move too fast and the finish builds up instantly, causing mounded clumps of hardened finish (corns) that can make deep scratches.

Dry sanding with random-orbit sanders using hook-and-loop Fre-Cut sandpaper in 220-, 280-, and 320-grit paper can level a coat of finish in a hurry. Blow off or vacuum the powdered lacquer dust often and change the paper frequently.

Scuff sanding

The term scuff sanding is used throughout the industry to describe a quick, light dry-sanding on a finish to remove the nibs (the small hard specks in the finish caused by raised wood fibers, trapped air, or dust). We usually scuff sand lightly after the first couple of coats of sealer or wash coat are down and before coloring or top coating. We may scuff sand again in between the third and fourth coats of a six- to eight clear-coat finishing schedule. Also, we scuff sand any over-sprayed or touched-up areas along the way to blend them into the surrounding finish before top coating continues. Scratches from a 220- to 320-grit scuff sanding will melt in when successive lacquer coats are sprayed and are invisible in the final rub out. Don't scuff sand after the last coat because no more coats follow, those scratches will show in the final rub-out.

Scuff sanding is not level sanding but if the finish coat has enough build, sometimes a more aggressive scuff sanding will break the finish surface (helping solvent to escape) and to level most of the high spots. It won't necessarily remove the shiny *low* spots in a finish. You may also choose to scuff sand a grain-filled surface once it has dried, but take care not to sand through the wash coat below!

Level sanding

Unlike scuff sanding, level sanding removes finish and evens the surface—including the low, shiny spots of lacquer that may have shrunken over a filled pore. We usually level-sand dry with 220- or 320-grit Fre-Cut paper, but the fine-grit wet-sanding, which comes before buffing, also produces a level surface. You can't level sand

TECH TIP

For areas you sand by hand—generally larger flat surfaces or long, gentle curves—use a sanding block, which spreads out the sanding pressure and prevents the roundness of your fingers from causing slight hollows in the surface. On all flat surfaces—wood or lacquer—choose a wood, felt, foam-rubber, or styrofoam block with a flat bottom, wrapping the sandpaper around it.

until there's enough finish build-up to sand, of course. Typically that would be after four clear coats, but will depend upon the solids content and viscosity of the finish. A level sanding, wet or dry, might be used at the following stages:

- After at least four clear coats are down so that they can be well leveled to receive color or sunburst coats. Dry sand with 220- to 320-grit.
- After the last "build" coat of a six-to-eight coat schedule and before a flow coat, which is a final, well-thinned coat (or sometimes two) sprayed to melt in any scratches and flow out the finish. Dry sanding here would usually be done with no less than 320-grit, and might be as fine as 600-grit. Often, a flow coat is so perfect that you don't need to wet sand it, and you can go directly to buffing.
- After the final coats are cured. Wet sand with 600-grit or finer (study the benefits of various grit and particle type), using water as a lubricant.

Wipe-sanding and color-sanding

"Wipe-sanding" is our name for what car painters call "color-sanding," or the process of knocking off only the dust specks, overspray, and pebbly bumps that result from spraying a coat of finish onto a smooth surface. This is accomplished by using very fine sandpapers (500-grit and above), and wiping lightly, *one time* across the finish (or just one area of the finish). Often we'll use a round-edge sanding block of rubber, cork, felt, or padded wood as a backer for the sandpaper. Wipe-sanding's usually done on the color coats because we worry more about disturbing them, but the technique can be used anytime during finishing.

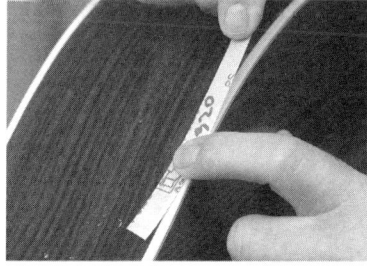

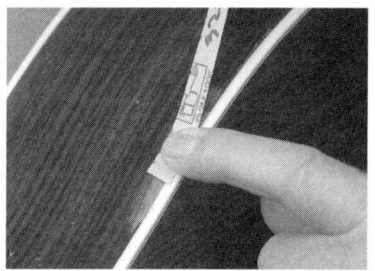

Strip-sanding

Strip-sanding—pulling strips of Fre-Cut sandpaper across areas of raised finish defects such as runs, sags, and drop-fills—is the best way to pinpoint one area. The size of the sandpaper strips depends on the size of the defect; usually the strips are 1/4 to 3/8-inch wide x 6-inch long, and range from 220-grit to 600-grit (320-grit is used most often). Hold the edge or corner of a small rubber sanding block (or use your finger) over the defect and apply pressure only on the raised area as you pull the strip across only the defect. You may benefit by pulling/sanding in several directions. Stop when you start to get close, and switch grits. (You needn't go finer than 320-grit if you will be spraying more coats over the area).

Wet-sanding

After the final gloss lacquer coat has cured at least a week (two to three weeks is even better) the instrument is ready to be wet sanded to a smooth, dull, satiny patina before being rubbed, buffed, or polished. The best clue for determining if a solvent-based finish is ready for final sanding is when you can no longer smell any solvent. For waterborne finishes, wait as long as the manufacturer recommends, and then wait a bit longer! The harder the finish, the easier and better looking the rub-out will be.

We recommended avoiding CAMI-grade papers for wet-sanding because you can easily put scratches in the finish, requiring additional sanding and buffing. Washing your wet-sanding paper often also helps avoid scratches. In a worst-case scenario you'll have to go back and spray more lacquer to melt in any scratches that do occur and to ensure that the finish is still thick enough to buff. If this happens, sand with a *minimum* of 600-grit if you're using traditional 3M silicon-carbide wet-or-dry sandpaper. Start with an even finer grit if you're using P-graded papers.

Before you wet sand, you may want to soak your paper (preferably overnight) in water or lubricant such as naphtha or mineral spirits. The wetter it is the better it will perform. It won't load up and particles will wash out more easily as you go. While sanding, wash out the built up particles at least once every 30 seconds in a deep bowl filled with warm water (add a little soap if you like), and change the water in your bowl often. Hold the paper against your fingers and brush the particles off with your thumb.

We recommend wet-sanding with water because of the obvious fire hazard, toxicity, and unpleasant smell of petroleum-base solvents. Water lubricates the paper and washes out any finish that may be clogged between the grit particles. The reason some finishers prefer naphtha or mineral spirits instead of water (it's common in furniture finishing), is that naphtha evaporates the fastest. Consequently, it's least likely to lift the finish in unprotected areas like tuner holes, pickup routs, and other areas where water could get under the finish, swell the wood, and cause the finish to crack. That won't happen however, if you protect all the instrument openings and sand cautiously in areas where moisture can get under the finish.

In the final wet-sanding before buffing (Chapter 9, Step 10: Final sanding and rubbing out) you can add a little liquid soap, like Murphy's Oil Soap, to increase the lubrication. Don't use soap if you intend to follow the sanding with more finish, though.

Don't forget scrapers

Scrapers, described in Chapter 5, can be as important as sandpaper in many finishing situations. Not only can scrapers leave the surface and grain of *wood* clean, perfect, and free of abrasions, they can smooth a finish too. They remove high spots, raised fibers, or dust specks from the surface of thin wash coats—especially shellac.

Generally hold a scraper almost perpendicular to the surface (about 70-90 degrees). Hold it with both hands, bending it into a slight curve, then pull or push to remove wood. The amount of curve bent into the scraper and the angle at which it's held control the amount of contact it will have with the wood—taking a wide or narrow cut.

In guitar finishing more than furniture finishing, because of binding, marquetry, pearl inlay, and the smaller flat and curved surfaces, scrapers are often held with one hand and used in a more delicate manner than they might be on furniture.

Scrapers can level fills, runs, and sags. Use files and sandpaper (with a backer block) for the *initial* leveling of finish drop-fills, runs, sags,

TECH TIP

Wet sanding papers are designed to be soaked in water overnight before being used. They will work right out of the package, simply dipped in water. However, if you let them get really wet you won't believe the difference in performance. They won't load up, and the particles will wash out much more easily. In the hands of an experienced sander, one 4-inch square of well-soaked 800-grit wet-or-dry paper can sand an entire guitar.

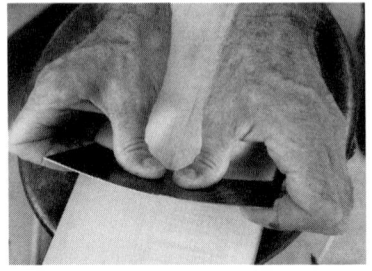

Chapter 8: Sanding and Buffing Techniques

TECH TIP

Wrap transparent tape around each end of a razor-blade to expose only the center for cutting, and then use it to level a fill or a high spot—especially runs and sags once they're hard and dry. You'll be able to get as close to the surface as the thickness of the tape without unwanted scratches.

A utility knife blade notched into a wooden dowel makes a good binding scraper.

and for patches of all types of filler. Then try *completing* the leveling task with a scraper. Used carefully, a scraper will level a finish repair exactly flush with the surface, without leaving scratches around the area, as sandpaper and files will.

- A throw-away razor-blade scraper is great for leveling finish repairs. Both sharp ends have been stoned to dull them.
- A utility knife blade notched into a wooden dowel makes a good binding scraper.

Techniques for Buffing the Finish

Nothing's more frustrating than not being able to rub out the finish so that it looks as good as what you've been imagining all along. I would not have said this a few years ago to small shop finishers, but if you want the best-looking finish possible, invest in a pedestal buffer. Most of us who started out hand rubbing, then polishing with every electric sander and polisher known to man, would have started pedestal buffing years ago if reasonably priced ones had been within our reach, as they are now.

There's still a place for other types of buffing. Hand buffing and buffing with various hand-held power tools are economical and practical for people who are starting out or who cannot invest in a shop full of finishing tools. Also, certain situations call for these techniques.

No matter how you buff, starting with the correct grit is important. If you start too fine you'll never get the coarser scratches out. Starting with a compound that's too coarse will merely duplicate what was accomplished with wet-sanding. Buff in several directions, especially on a wheel, so that grooves won't develop.

Hand rubbing

Hand rubbing with buffing compound on a soft cloth, such as a clean diaper, can provide an excellent look. Prepare a suitable size pad by folding the corners of the cloth into your palm to show a smooth face. Lay a line of liquid compound a half-inch wide and three or four inches long onto the instrument, and pick it up with the pad as you rub. Polish in a circular motion. As the pad becomes conditioned with use it will polish better and faster. Rub across the grain, with the grain, and even in figure-eights. By combining all these motions, you can successfully rub out even difficult areas.

Don't overdo the compound by continuously adding it when it's not needed. A cloth or pad that's properly charged with compound should be damp, not wet. After a few minutes of polishing the rag will be warm and may even feel dry, but if it's producing a shine, don't add more compound. Around F-holes, in cutaways, and on peghead edges, try rubbing with a smaller, thinner section of cloth backed by your fingertips. Don't rub one area too long; even hand rubbing can build up heat, which may soften and drag the finish.

Buffing with an electric drill or random-orbit sander

A variable-speed electric hand drill equipped with a flexible 5-inch to 6-inch rubber pad and lambs wool "bonnet" or a plastic-backed foam pad can give good results. Whichever you choose, dedicate a separate pad for each compound grit, and don't mix grits.

As with hand-polishing, lay the compound on the finish surface, but pick it up with the tool running very slowly! Paste is best, but you can use liquid if you don't mind a little splatter. Pick up the compound a little at a time until the pad absorbs it all, then increase your speed and downward pressure at the same time. Hold the drill with both hands for good control, and move with a slow, regular, circular motion. Use the variable-speed trigger to keep the pad from going too fast and burning through the finish.

Pedestal buffing

The best way to produce a "factory finish" look using a stationary buffer is using flannel buffing pads and bar compound. Expect to add compound several times while buffing an entire guitar. Whenever you aren't getting good results, stop the wheel and look it over as well as feel it. Soon you'll know whether the buffs are loaded with compound or not, which they should be to work correctly. Novice polishers have the best chance for safe buffing if they use a 12-inch buff and keep the wheel speed below 1,000 rpm. Always buff a scrap piece of hardwood to get the wheel warm, and avoid scratching a finish with a cold wheel!

There are two dangers to avoid in machine buffing. One is hurting yourself by allowing the wheel to catch an object and throw it at you. The other is harming the finish by burning it.

To avoid injury, it's a good idea to wear a clear face shield. At least wear safety glasses! Approach the wheel when it's not running and practice your positions. You should know which way to buff the various parts without sticking a part or edge into the spinning buff and having it caught and thrown at you, or at the floor.

Hold the guitar firmly and *concentrate*. Buffing is not a time to let your mind wander! On short, double-ended buffers (where the wheels are close together) keep your eye on both wheels at once. If you're buffing the body on the right-hand wheel, make sure you don't catch the neck or peghead on the left-hand wheel. Never, ever, buff an instrument that has strings installed—especially loose strings hanging from the peghead.

The buff rotates downward, toward the floor. You should start buffing on the main surface and move toward the lower edge. When you get to the edge, pull the work away. This will keep the buffer from grabbing your instrument and throwing it. You shouldn't buff on the edges anyway, because that's where you'll burn through. If you buff the main finish surfaces, the edges will take care of themselves.

The other danger with machine buffing is that the finish can be dragged right off the guitar as it softens under the heat of polishing. This is a particular problem at the edges, and especially on new finishes that soften and melt at relatively low temperatures. Everyone who has ever machine-buffed a guitar has buffed through the finish at least once, but the quality of a machine-buffed finish and the time

TECH TIP

It's okay to buff lightly on the large round-overs of a Stratocaster, but not on the harder edges of a Telecaster, Les Paul, or ES-335—you easily can cut right through, even to bare wood!

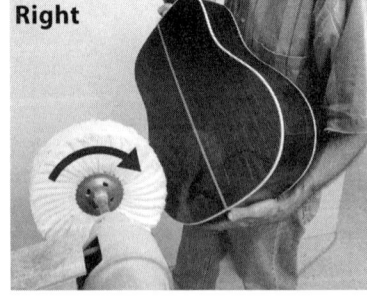

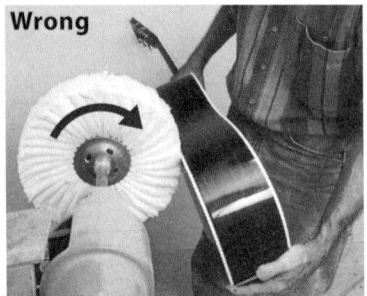

"Coming on to an edge" with a buffer is trouble: don't approach the wheel with the edge of the workpiece. Allow the wheel's motion to move off the edge rather than onto it.

you'll save are well worth the risk and the time spent mastering the pedestal buffer.

Sanding Schedule Example

This sanding and finishing schedule uses a hypothetical instrument: a solid-body mahogany guitar, finished in transparent cherry red like a Gibson SG. Notice that the grit chosen for power sanding is slightly finer than for hand sanding. This is because power sanding is more aggressive, especially with a random-orbital sander.

Step	Suggested grit
Sand all wood	180-220 Fre-Cut (or power sand with 240 Fre-Cut)
Break sharp edges (control cavities, pickup routs, etc.)	180 Fre-Cut
Sand edges off fingerboard, especially plastic binding and end of nut	180 Fre-Cut (or power sand with 240-280 Fre-Cut)
Apply walnut brown grain filler to bare wood, wipe clean, allow to dry	
Scuff-sand grain filler residue if necessary	220 Fre-Cut
Spray one coat vinyl sealer (dry 15-30 minutes)	
Spray second coat vinyl sealer (dry 15-30 minutes)	
Scuff-sand lightly	220 Fre-Cut
Spray one coat cherry lacquer toner (dry 15-30 minutes)	
Spray one coat cherry lacquer toner (dry 15-30 minutes)	
Spray one coat clear lacquer to lock in color, then scrape binding within 20 minutes, handle the finish carefully (dry 30 minutes)	
Spray one coat clear lacquer over entire instrument (dry overnight)	
Scuff-sand lightly only if necessary	220 Fre-Cut
Spray 6 to 8 coats clear lacquer (spaced evenly through the day, dry overnight)	
Level-sand entire finish	320-600 Fre-Cut
Spray two thin flash coats (let dry a week)	
Final-sand entire instrument	800 or finer
Hand-held buffer:	**Buffing wheel:**
Repeat previous two steps, flash coats and final-sanding with 1200-grit.	May continue final-sanding by hand to 1200-grit, this is more handwork, but will make buffing faster.
Buff with hand-held buffer and medium compound. Progress to fine compound if necessary.	Buff with coarse compound (if you final-sanded to 1200-grit, start with medium compound). Progress to medium, then fine if necessary.

WATERBASE FINISHING IN A NUTSHELL

Wood preparation
Clean surface and sand to 220-grit

↓

Stain (optional)
Liquid stain dissolved in water or alcohol

↓   ↓

Non-porous wood
Maple, spruce, basswood, alder, poplar, ebony, etc.

Porous wood
Rosewood, mahogany, ash, koa, walnut, etc.

↓

Wash coat (optional)
1-2 coats • 1-2 hours apart
Thin down sanding sealer by mixing it 50/50 with water

↓

Grain filler
Natural for light woods, medium-brown for dark

↓

Sanding sealer
Build level surface, about 65-75% of your final finish thickness • 12-16 coats • 3-4 coats per day • 2-3 hours apart

↓

Color coats (optional)
Stains or pigments can be added to sealer or lacquer steps • 1-3 coats • 2-3 coats per day • 2 hours apart

↓

Clear topcoats
9-12 coats • 3-4 coats per day • 2-3 hours apart • Allow to cure for one week prior to sanding and buffing

↓

Wet sand and buff
Wet sand with 1200-grit and finer, buff to high-gloss

Chapter 9

Ten Basic Finishing Steps

Here are the ten basic steps to follow for producing any guitar finish in this book. Certain finishes won't require every step, but all stringed instrument finishing will follow the order of these steps. We must emphasize the virtue of patience in wood finishing. Hurrying or skipping steps produces a poor finish.

NITROCELLULOSE FINISHING IN A NUTSHELL

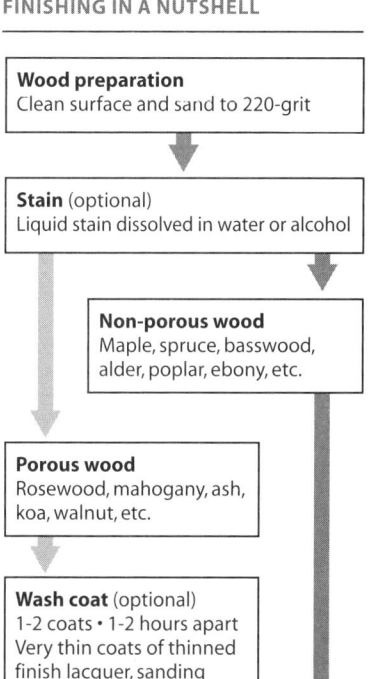

Step 1: Wood Preparation

Wood preparation is the most important step in finishing, and the key to professional results. We stated this more than once already but it still bears repeating. It's the *last* step of the manufacturing process and the *first* step of the finishing process. Wood prep is much the same for both new work and for refinishing. For refinishing, you'll have a few extra preparation steps, such as stripping an old finish, but after that it's the same: properly sand the instrument, see that all binding is smooth and flush, install the string nut if appropriate, bevel and shape the fret ends, remove all surface glue residue, and clean off any dust or residue.

Unless you're in production and have worked out all the bugs of manufacturing, it's a good idea to string an instrument to pitch and test-fit all the parts. Assemble the instrument as if the finish had already been applied (except for electrical wiring, of course). Some builders don't install the nut until after finishing, but you won't get that perfect factory look without finishing over the ends of the nut. Resist the temptation to play your guitar, though; you could get dirt and grime on the wood that might never come out! Stages of wood preparation are:

- Cleaning
- A close inspection for imperfections
- Repair of any major imperfections
- Initial sanding and scraping to remove slight imperfections and to bring the entire instrument to a uniform surface
- Dampening the wood to raise the grain
- Final sanding
- Final inspection, cleaning and degreasing
- Masking off

Clean off contaminants

Clean the wood surface before beginning the wood prep stage, especially if you're refinishing old work, if the instrument has been handled much, or if you know there's silicone, waxes or oils loose in your shop. If you're building, and the new wood was planed to thickness, there's always the possibility that the saws, jointers, planer beds, knives and cutters used to surface the wood were sprayed with wax or silicone lubricants at the lumbermill. Or something in your shop may have transferred contaminants.

When **cleaning new wood**, wipe the surfaces with three separate clean rags, dampened (but not dripping wet) with the following cleaners in order: (1) naphtha to remove waxes; (2) mineral spirits to remove silicone; and (3) ammonia and water (1/4 cup household ammonia in a quart of warm water) to remove any mineral spirits and silicone left on the surface. Clean the wood in that order, and you'll probably never have fisheyes or poor finish adhesion.

If you are **cleaning refinished wood** (you've chemically stripped a guitar) wipe the surfaces using five separate clean rags dampened with these cleaners in order: (1) warm water to wash up general residue and stripper sludge and to help stop the stripper's action; (2) lacquer thinner (or other appropriate solvent) to remove finish residue; (3) alcohol to help remove any shellac or alcohol-soluble dyes; (4) mineral spirits to help eliminate silicones; and (5) the ammonia/water mixture mentioned above.

Performing a close inspection

A close inspection involves looking for areas needing special sanding attention, and for major imperfections such as chips, dents, dings, scratches, binding problems, tear-out, and glue smears. Be honest with yourself about what you see; any imperfections you skip over now will look worse later.

Wet the wood to make irregularities easier to spot. Use a rag dampened in water or naphtha (naphtha won't raise the grain) to highlight any glue squeeze-out, spills, or smears which usually aren't visible unless the wood is wet. If you don't find them until the final stages of wood prep, you'll have to go back through the grits to get rid of them.

Repairing imperfections

This step might seem unnecessary on new work, but it's tough to build anything without making a stray mark or leaving some unwanted residue behind. You shouldn't find much. Refinish work is another story; it often needs extensive repair work.

Start by removing any surface glue residue. Wet it with the appropriate solvent, let the glue soften, and scrape, wash, or wipe it off (once cured, epoxy can only be removed by scraping or sanding). Your thumbnail or fingernails are just about the best glue removers around.

Glue to be removed	Solvent	Tip
White polyvinyl (Elmer's or yellow aliphatic resin such as Titebond	Hot water, acetone	If water won't soften the glue, use acetone or lacquer thinner to do the initial softening; follow with hot water
Animal hide glue	Hot water	
Super glue (cyanoacrylate)	Acetone	
Epoxy, uncured	Acetone	
Epoxy, cured	None	Use abrasive tools, scrapers, and elbow-grease

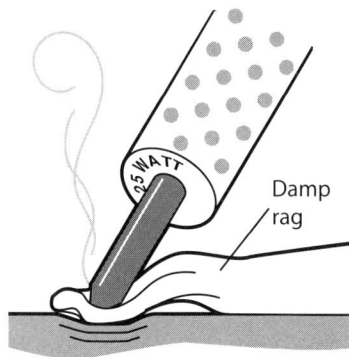

Next, repair imperfections. Before resorting to fillers, consider the **steam technique**. Steam will swell out most dents and slight scratches. Often the crushed wood is not missing, it's simply compressed. All you need is a 25- to 40-watt soldering iron and a clean, wet cotton rag, which will protect the wood from being scorched by the iron and add moisture for the steaming process. First, dampen the wound with clean water. Next, rest a small area of the wet cotton rag on the dent to keep the soldering iron tip from contacting the wood and burning it as you steam. Don't lay the rag on the wood surrounding the dent or you'll steam more than just the dent, and the results may show later. Two or three attempts will usually give great results.

Another trick is to place only a small *piece* of the wet rag directly on the dent—this pinpoints only the dent and guarantees that you won't steam more than you intended. Heating a small scrap of clean, ink-free, wet cardboard will do a good dent-steaming job, too.

Fill any holes, tear-outs, and chips...anything you can't steam out. The specific filler to choose depends on whether the top finish is clear or opaque. Common filling materials are described in Chapter 2.

Wood dough and putty are the most popular fill materials for small and even medium-sized dents. Fill them with several layers of dough; each coat should dry before the next coat is added. If you intend to stain the section, be sure to use wood fillers or doughs that will accept the specific stain. Practice on scrap.

For professional results, you can etch simulated wood grain lines into the filled area, and then treat these etched lines as if they were real wood pores—filling them with a colored grain filler to imitate the surrounding finish. Also, to overlap and hide the fill line, you can paint grain on rather than etching it in.

If the finish will be clear, and you don't want a repaired fill to show under clear finish, inlay it with a matching **wood patch**. It shrinks and expands with the surrounding wood, making it a top choice. Wood can be inlaid a variety of ways, but it takes practice to get professional results. Elliptical or diamond shapes make small patches less obvious. When a patch is close to a "trim line" such as a pickguard, bridge, or an instrument's edge, run the patch right to it or under it to hide the glue joint, and run patches along a grain line wherever possible. Picking the right glue for a wood patch is very important. Using hot hide glue results in the most invisible glue line.

Clear fillers, epoxy, super glue, fiberglass resin, or the finish you're using can be used for minor repairs in natural-finished unstained woods or under colored topcoats that are separated from the wood by a clear sealer coat. Known as drop fills, these can become invisible once the finish is applied, or in some cases will show boldly. Their visibility depends upon the wood's color and grain structure, the extent of the damage, and your skill and prior experience. (Nothing beats knowing what a specific wood's reaction will be when it's introduced to different drop fill materials). When you add color to the scenario, especially if it's colored bare wood, clear fills really start to show; the color soaks into the fractured grain of the damaged area at different rates, causing uneven staining.

Clear drop-fills which are intended to be covered later with dark transparent colored lacquer shaders *can* be hidden quite well, because these shaders have good hiding power. Practice executing clear fills on separate matching pieces of wood before attempting an actual repair. If you're happy with the results, carry on.

With solid-colored (painted) finishes, filled repairs won't show unless they shrink excessively and leave a telltale mark. A glued-in matching wood plug, which shrinks and expands with the surrounding wood, is still the best fill material, but auto-body filler, spot-putty, and epoxy or fiberglass resins work well for large holes. Mix auto-body filler according to the instructions provided, and pack it into the spot to be filled. Allow it to harden completely before leveling it; the important thing here is to fill the void completely and for the filler to bond well to the defect's walls.

Fix gaps around bindings. Like bumpers on a car, decorative bindings protect wood edges from damage. Because they are glued into a channel, bindings have long contiguous glue lines that can easily separate from the wood. Even a slight gap will draw in the finish and result in a sunken line. All of these gaps need to be filled and are among the easiest repairs to make.

Acrylic wood dough is a good filler for gaps between binding and wood, regardless of whether the binding is plastic or wood. These gaps are usually very narrow and acrylic wood dough fills are very difficult to find, especially when both the gap and fill are kept clean. Super glue is great for filling small gaps in wood bindings but you must not let it leach into nearby wood, especially spruce and other light woods, because it can make staining impossible. Use super glue only to fix bindings on dark woods, under painted finishes, or in areas that absolutely require its structural strength.

Melt binding scraps to fix plastic binding imperfections. You can dissolve exact-matching binding in acetone for a fill material (not all bindings will dissolve well in acetone—vinyl, for example will not). This mix can patch joints that are less than perfect, or even build up worn or missing areas. Butt joints that don't quite meet will disappear if you wipe a smear of "binding melt" into them. Be sure the joint is clean and free of dirt. If dirt has penetrated a joint, chisel or scrape it out before applying the fill.

Sanding and scraping

Wood preparation sanding need not be taken any finer than 180- to 220-grit. Sand with the grain and be sure to remove any cross grain scratches from coarser grits used earlier and any cutter marks from woodworking machines like routers and saws. Refer to Chapters 5 and 8 for tips on sanding materials and techniques.

As we already said, scrapers are especially useful for removing scratches in end grain and side grain, for leveling high spots in flat surfaces such as the face or rear of a peghead, and for cleaning up cutaway areas where normal sanding is awkward.

If you're finishing an instrument that has a bolt-on neck, double check the neck's fit to the body, and adjust to allow for the thickness

---

TECH TIP

Avoid using super glue, which is often touted as a great drop-fill for bare wood. In reality, it's a poor choice because of its tendency to run and wick into the surrounding bare wood. It seals the wood so that it will neither take a stain nor look like the surrounding wood under a finish (unless the finish is opaque, of course).

of the finish on both parts. The neck finish, in lacquer, will measure around .006 inch to .008 inch, and the finish rollover into the neck pocket will be about the same. The finish feathers out to a bit less down the side walls of the neck pocket—probably .002 inch to .004 inch. Both sides of the neck plus both sides of the pocket combine for a total of .025 inch to .030 inch, or the thickness of two or three business cards. Be sure to allow for that or the parts won't go together after finishing.

Grain raising

In this step you wet the wood to swell the wood fibers and, after drying, lightly sand away the raised fibers as described in Chapter 8. On finely figured woods to be colored later, you can combine grain raising with *grain enhancement* by using a water-soluble stain instead of just plain water. After final sanding in the next step some of the color will remain deep in the wood, enhancing the wood grain. This grain enhancing technique is described in detail in "Vintage-style Sunburst on Figured Maple and Spruce" recipe in Chapter 10.

Final sanding

Read over the sanding tips in Chapter 8, and then final sand with either 180- or 220-grit paper (280- or 320-grit on spruce or cedar tops) in the direction of the grain. Use compressed air to blow off any sawdust and sandpaper residue. If you use a shop vacuum, be careful not to let the hose touch or mark the wood!

Final inspection, cleaning, and degreasing

The final inspection won't take long if you've done your work properly. Be critical, and look for anything else that will cause you problems as the finish goes on. Complete the inspection by degreasing the entire instrument with a light wipe, using a rag dampened with naphtha. Some finishers use a tack cloth, which has a sticky coating that picks up dust particles. Tack rags are fine if you don't press them against the wood too hard, but they can leave residue if you're not careful.

A clean paint brush will remove most sawdust trapped in open-pore woods, but compressed air works best. Once the piece is clean, never handle it without gloves unless you have scrubbed your hands. If you scratch your nose or face, wash the oil off your hand. If you're in the finishing mode, degrease door handles, telephone receivers, lamps, and anything that you might touch after someone touched it who just ate a hamburger and a bag of chips before dropping by to visit—or even worse, used Armor All on their guitar case.

Masking off the instrument

Masking is the last step of wood prep. Areas that aren't to receive color in Step 2 should be masked off now (an instrument receiving an all-natural finish needs little masking—perhaps only the nut and fretboard). Some production finishers—most notably Gibson—do not mask plastic bindings, preferring to scrape the color off afterward (and, of course, a little plastic with it). This accounts for the famous "ledge" of clear-lacquered binding that almost all Gibson instruments have (except for some early Gibson mandolin finishes, which look as if there's *no finish* at all on the binding—as if scraping the binding was the last step performed). Heavy scraping is acceptable for new work but perhaps not on a refinishing job where the binding's been scraped already and there may not be much plastic left. Most small-shop finishers take the time to mask carefully.

Cover the large areas—tops, backs, necks, and sides—with clean paper (newsprint will smudge clean wood) and use tape only at the edges. Avoid putting strong tapes on bare, unsealed spruce and similar woods because the tape will tear out the wood when you remove it —seal spruce and similar woods first!

We usually tape off the wide exposed side of bindings, but not the thin top edge (it's easy to scrape). Wide, multiple-bindings are a different story; these can be "double-taped." Run 1/8-inch or 1/4-inch latex tape on the top surface first, following the curves and working the tape tight to the surface with a fingertip and edge of your thumb. Next run the side tape and fold it over the top edge onto the other tape.

As a rule, when you mask binding which will have a strong dark color next to it, leave a small amount of binding showing (untaped) so that color overlaps it intentionally. Then when you scrape, if there are any irregularities in the binding height, or if you slip with the scraper, you won't scrape into the bare wood—there will always be dark color to scrape into. Bare wood scraped by mistake loses color instantly and must be touched up—avoid this if you can.

"Quick-mask" refers to a fast, low-tack, temporary masking of an isolated area. When quick-masking we often press tape against our clothing to lessen the tack. Wider tapes such as a two-inch masking tape or sign painter's tape are good for quick-masking because they cover a lot of area at once. You needn't be too careful when quick-masking, except to see that the leading edge is straight and clean along joints and binding. An example of a quick-masking would be lightly taping the peghead edges while spraying black lacquer.

If you plan to use color in later steps, these same masking techniques apply. On any given project, you might choose to mask the following areas, using the materials described in Chapter 4 under "Masking Supplies".

- **Peghead overlays:** Protect natural wood veneers from stain or paint. When you're painting the peghead face black, tape off everything except the peghead face.
- **Peghead inlays:** Some of us prefer to tape off inlays rather than scrape color from them, and sometimes we'll use a combination. If we were painting a Gibson peghead, we wouldn't tape off the word "Gibson"—that's too tedious—we'd scrape it. But we probably would tape off a simple crown inlay.
- **Instrument top, or face:** Whenever the top is a different wood than the back and sides, mask it off, along with the binding, while you stain, color, or grain-fill the body.

TECH TIP

A piece from a gallon-size plastic milk carton can be cut to shape and used in place of cardboard to block a soundhole. Blow up a balloon and then maneuver the reusable plastic into position. The inflated balloon acts like a spring to hold the plastic against the underside of the top. Another good reusable soundhole blocker is a piece of car inner tube—the rubber's smooth surface allows the built-up lacquer to be peeled off when heated with a hair dryer and accurately measured to determine the thickness of the lacquer.

- **Fretboard and fretboard edges:** Always mask off the fretboard and the fretboard binding.
- **F-holes and F-hole binding:** These can be tough to scrape, so masking's a good idea. Also, masking keeps the spray from entering the body through the F-holes.
- **Soundhole:** Always protect the instrument's interior from lacquer spray. Mask the interior of the guitar by stuffing newspaper into the body, being sure to tuck it completely into the soundhole. For a more professional seal, prepare a 4-5/16-inch diameter cardboard disk, hinged in the middle with tape, and insert it into the soundhole. Hold it in place against the inside edge of the soundhole with an inflated rubber balloon.

Step 2: Transparent Stains on Bare Wood

Transparent dye stain can be applied now, or later on in Step 8. Top-of-the-line instruments with figured wood may be partially colored now, either by hand-wiping or by spraying stain on the areas that are to receive color. In Step 8 you can apply additional color, in the form of a lacquer shader or toner, to augment and complete a stained sunburst applied now. This highlights the beauty of the wood and adds depth because some of the color goes into the grain and some of the color suspends in the finish.

When color is applied at the bare wood stage, it's a labor of love: although it might seem obvious to stain the bare wood, it's not easy, time-saving, or foolproof. If you're skilled enough to stain the bare wood without producing a blotchy uneven look, however, you'll realize a number of benefits.

For one thing, staining bare wood means your final finish will be thinner. This is definitely a plus for an acoustic instrument but just as important for solid-body finishes (Les Paul players appreciate good tone, too). For another thing, stain applied to bare wood imparts the greatest clarity, color depth, and brilliance. Stain can make even mediocre woods look gorgeous. Finally, staining bare curly maple and other highly figured woods accentuates their beautiful patterns unbelievably.

On the downside, imperfections, especially fills and glue residue, show up instantly on bare-stained wood. Also, water stain takes hours to dry compared to colored lacquer shader, which dries instantly and can be applied in multiple coats of color one right after another to build color in successive layers and without soaking the wood. Soaking the wood, even with lacquer thinner or alcohol (but particularly with water), is a potential problem for the glue used in veneered tops, backs, and sides.

Alcohol stain is the most suitable where wetness and grain raising are insurmountable problems. For example, when refinishing a plywood-laminate Gibson ES-335, where the outermost layer of wood has already been sanded thin at the factory. Alcohol stains aren't as likely to delaminate the thin plys because they don't wet the wood in the same way as water does.

Of course alcohol stains have their own problems, too, which we've detailed in Chapter 3. They're soluble in the lacquer topcoats, which means they may bleed out of the wood and float up into the lacquer, even onto bindings. Once finish has been applied, mistakes in alcohol stained wood can't be touched up as easily as water stained wood can because the alcohol colors the surrounding finish along with the wood. Still, they have a strong place in bare wood staining—especially in production shops—because they dry fast and don't raise wood grain as much as water stains do. Alcohol stains work well on hand-wiped, old-style sunbursts too, but more often than not they're sprayed on.

Some typical situations in which bare wood might be stained:

- **Coloring the neck, back, and sides of a mahogany-bodied guitar.** If the top is spruce and meant to be natural (as they often are), tape it off carefully because you won't be able to remove stain that inadvertently touches the spruce.
- **Highlighting and coloring figured woods,** especially maple, and particularly in carved areas, because the stain soaks into the absorbent end grain, building contrast in the figure of the wood.
- **Staining a one-color instrument** such as an orange Gretsch 6120 or a cherry-red Gibson ES-335. These initial stains may be the only color an instrument gets when using clear finish for successive coats. It can make the color richer, too, if color is sealed in under clear coats and then more color is applied later by shading or toning (Step 8).
- **Applying a yellow base coat** or "ground coat" for underneath subsequent darker sunburst colors. It can be applied directly to the bare wood by spraying or wiping on a waterbase or alcohol-base stain.
- **Sunbursting** in shades of red, yellow, gold, brown, and black, even on bare spruce. Check out the many sunbursting recipes in Chapter 10.
- **Sap staining** light wood, especially maple, so that any dark sapwood streaks blend in with the stain. This is especially common when maple is used as a neck wood on an instrument with mahogany back and sides to make the maple look like mahogany to begin with (before toning over it with perhaps a cherry red toner as is common on many 1980s Gibson Les Pauls).

Hand staining

Despite its down side, hand staining, usually wiping with a rag, is the preferred way to duplicate the traditional Gibson sunbursts of the 1920s. It's also an easy way to lay down a yellow base coat to be followed with a sprayed-on sunburst. The yellow is light and the darker sunburst colors will hide any blotches or lap marks on the end grain or edges of the instrument. Lap marks occur when you stop wiping for a second, when you overlap a stroke more aggressively (or wetter) than the one before it, or as your rag comes on and off the instrument. Blotches can occur when part of the grain structure—especially end grain—soaks up more or less than the surrounding grain structure.

The trick to minimize this problem is to wipe straight water or alcohol solvent (whichever solubility is needed for the stain) onto the end grain to pre-soak it. It consequently won't absorb as much stain.

Remember that water stains are harder to apply by hand because the lap marks will be stronger. Some furniture finishers disagree, but as a general rule in guitar finishing, lap marks are worse with water stain than with alcohol stain. The wood has a greater affinity for water, and water feels the same about wood. Because of this, hand-applied sunbursts are most easily done with alcohol stains, which are less invasive.

Spraying stain

For almost all other types of guitar finishing, spraying is our preferred way of staining. More than at any other stage of finishing, when you're staining bare wood you must practice on scrap! There's no sealer coat to protect the wood from your experiments, and no amount of solvent—water or alcohol—will ever draw all the color from stain mistakes on bare wood, especially maple and spruce. When we spray stain onto bare wood we generally use two or three light coats to reach the final shade.

Because it's simply colored solvent without body, stain atomizes well and sprays best in the 50 to 60 psi range. Experiment with spraying stains unthinned and thinned to get a feel for coverage.

Color matching with stains

Whether you're coloring a new instrument to match a vintage look, or touching up a repaired area on a guitar that still retains much of its original color, there will be countless times when you'll want to achieve a color that's not readily available in stock colors. There are ten or twelve stains we commonly use: red, orange, yellow, green, blue, black, honey amber, golden brown, medium brown, red brown, dark walnut, and dark mission brown. In factory guitar finishes these colors often are mixed to achieve a tint, shade, or special look. If you're splitting hairs, expect to do some mixing and experimenting. However, the stock colors by themselves are often right for the job, and all you need to know is how strong to use a particular stain. We make up sample boards, for color and strength, of any stain we use.

Step 3: Wash Coating (optional)

According to the *Coatings Encyclopedic Dictionary*, a reference work offered by The Federation of Societies for Coatings Technology, a wash coat is "a wood furniture coating which is applied after the body stain that seals the wood surface and stiffens the wood fibers for subsequent sanding."

In everyday use a wash coat seems to refer to any well-thinned finish serving a variety of purposes. It primes the wood to keep it from absorbing an excess amount of whatever finish follows it; stiffens the wood fibers for subsequent sanding; promotes good adhesion for successive coats; seals the wood from direct contact with grain filler or colorant to follow; seals in contaminants such as silicone or oil that may have inadvertently come in contact with the wood; separates one finishing step from another, and; late in the finishing schedule, melts-in sanding scratches and smooths out final topcoats before buffing. Still, a wash coat's biggest use is to lock in stain and to seal the wood before grain filler is used.

Skip the wash coat step and go on to the next appropriate step if any of the following apply: if you don't intend to use grain filler; if your recipe calls for grain filling the bare unstained wood (many reproduction vintage Gibson finish recipes call for filling the bare wood first); if your finish is intended to be completely natural without grain filler or colorant; or if you know that contaminants aren't present.

Even if you don't apply a washcoat now, when you begin applying finish at a later stage the first coat should be wet and thin for good penetration.

Here in Step 3, a wash coat assumes its most common role—separating one step from another by keeping the pigment of any grain filler (Step 4) from muddying the look of the wood. If separation is your only goal, use a well-thinned coat of your intended finish as the wash coat (just plain lacquer for example); you won't need a barrier wash coat here. Consider using a barrier wash coat here if there are any suspected contaminants in the wood. (We've described the many ways contaminants creep onto a project. Here's another: playing the instrument prior to finishing!)

Any finish that is well-thinned becomes a wash coat, and thus must be sprayed lightly to avoid runs. Its low viscosity lets it follow the contours of the wood's surface exactly, coating open pores with finish but not filling them. The pores remain open to accept the grain filler. A proper wash coat adds little to the thickness of the final finish. Because it is thin and has low solids, it helps avoid pinholes caused by air bubbles or solvent trapped under a thick finish.

A barrier coat is a material that has lower solubility in the solvents of the coats applied above it. In guitar finishing, the best barrier wash coats for bare wood or stained wood that is to receive lacquer topcoats are fresh shellac or the vinyl-modified lacquers sold as vinyl sealer and vinyl wash coat (these are described in Chapter 1). Shellac adds a beautiful golden hue to wood, and it's the best for sealing over suspected silicone troubles. Most guitar finishers use vinyl wash coats though, because they're more convenient, easier to use, are a great moisture barrier, and do an adequate job of sealing silicones. Along with its barrier-coat properties, vinyl sealer also promotes good topcoat adhesion and imparts a neutral tone to the finish. Most manufacturers recommend it under today's popular ready-to-spray, guitar lacquer topcoats.

Shellac, on the other hand, must be mixed fresh, and it can pool—leaving an uneven, cratered surface that lacquer won't smooth out. If you don't try to build thickness with it however, it provides an excellent base under lacquer.

Making a wash coat

Ready-to-spray wash coats are available from some suppliers, but you can easily make your own from a normal sealer or top coat by cutting it considerably. Sanding sealers and top coats typically have a solids content of about 21% to 23% whereas a wash coat should have about 10% solids. To produce a wash coat consistency, most lacquer needs to be thinned at least as much as 2 to 1 or more. If using shellac, thin to a 1- or 2-pound cut. We can't tell you exactly how much thinner to add because we don't know what product you'll be using. Professionals test a lacquer's viscosity using either a Zahn #2 or a Ford #4 viscosity cup, which measures how fast a given finish will drain from the cup. These cups cost upwards of $200 and more, however.

Spraying your wash coat. Most likely you'll need to spray only one wet wash coat, but thirstier woods may require two (if the wash coat seems to *completely* disappear into the wood as if nothing was applied, spray a second coat after 20 minutes). Normally, however, you needn't worry if the wet finish seems to disappear into the wood or furs it up the wood a bit. In the next step, the filler will still fill in the wood pores just fine. You can lightly sand out any roughness once the filler is dry. If it furs up badly and you feel you must sand before grain filling, try lightly scraping with a single-edged razor blade instead. A razor blade creates less dust than sanding—dust that can become trapped in the pores and keep the filler from doing a good job. Stone the sharp corners of the blade to dull them or wrap them with cellophane tape. Vacuum or blow any dust from the pores so they can accept filler. A wash coat is thin, remember, so watch out for runs.

Step 4: Filling the Grain

Paste filler, pore filler, grain filler, and grain wood filler are different names for the same stuff. These heavy, nonshrinking pastes get forced into the pores of open-grained woods, squeegeed from the surface, and left to dry. Hardened grain filler provides a smooth surface on which to apply finish coats. You can choose between oil-based or waterbase grain filler (see Chapter 2).

When you look at a piece of wood, the open pores are darkened by shadow. For that reason, wood looks more natural if the pores are filled with a grain filler that's darker than the wood itself. When they aren't already dark enough, medium-to-light shades of wood filler can be colored a small amount.

Applying grain filler

Ash, rosewood, mahogany, walnut, and others are open-grain woods that won't finish level and smooth without filler. You can fill the bare wood, or you can fill over a wash coat. Apply grain filler with a stiff bristle brush or a rag. Pack the wet filler into the pores, and quickly remove most of the excess from the surface with a squeegee so as not to drag filler from the pores. A credit card makes a good applicator-squeegee, removing excess filler from the surface as it packs filler into the pores. With any filler, but especially with waterbased, don't fill an area larger than you can wipe off quickly before the filler hardens. Hardened filler is stubborn to remove, you want the filler to remain in the pores only.

Slush filling

Some finishers apply more than one coat of grain filler, starting with a thin wet slush fill coat. This is filler cut 3 to 1 with thinner. Slush filler guarantees deep penetration, a thorough fill job, and less filler shrinkage. Slush filler should dry at least a half hour to let the solvent escape before applying normal-strength grain filler over it.

Removing residue

Squeegees will remove the bulk of excess filler but not all of it. Remove the remaining grain filler residue from the surface quickly. Use a nonabrasive, coarse material like old burlap, cheesecloth, or Scotch-Brite nylon pads. Go across the grain to keep from pulling the drying filler out of the pores. Wipe until there are no smears left on the surface. The better you remove the filler before it dries, the less sanding will be required (reducing the risk of sand-throughs).

Remove oil-base filler from the surface when a dull haze begins to form (from 5 to 15 minutes). If you filled too large an area, and it dries before you can wipe off the excess, the filler may be hard to remove with a dry rag. If this happens dampen a piece of lint-free rag, or else a Fine (grey) Scotch-Brite pad lightly with naphtha and wipe the area gently. This will dissolve the filler remaining on the surface, and usually won't pull it from the pores.

Remove waterbase filler immediately. You don't need to wait for a haze because it will happen faster than you can deal with anyhow. With waterbase filler, a haze means it's already dry, thus it's too late to easily remove the excess by wiping. Once that's happened, you'll never be able to wipe the surface perfectly clean with a rag. You may have some luck using a rag dampened with water. You're best off filling relatively small areas at a time, say 6-inch square, so that the filler won't dry faster than you can remove it. Clean a pump-spray bottle (Windex, etc.) and fill it with warm water. Lightly spritz a piece of Fine (grey) Scotch-Brite pad, and use it to rejuvenate and remove the filler if it does happen to dry too fast. Expect to sand off excess waterbase filler once it's dried.

Once filler of either type has dried thoroughly, you can lightly sand off the residue on the wash-coated surface using 220-grit Fre-Cut paper. You must not sand through your wash coat because you could open up new pores, requiring refilling. Your goal should be to remove the filler well enough with rags during the removal stage to make sanding minimal or unnecessary.

Drying and managing shrinkage

Waterbase filler shrinks so little that it normally doesn't require a second coat. It will accept a finish in as little as four hours, but it's a good idea to wait overnight. Oil-base filler, on the other hand, shrinks about 10% and some finishers apply it twice to get a level fill. It's questionable whether two or three fillings are worthwhile; if you're

TECH TIP

Some finishers leave filler to dry in screw holes. Later, the screw holes will have less tendency to absorb water during wet sanding or to over-absorb stains.

not careful you can inadvertently remove most of the filler you're applying in subsequent coats. Any last few remaining dips or sinks will fill later with sealer coats. Oil-based filler must dry three to five days, or even a week, before you can finish over it.

After filler dries completely, lightly sand the entire surface with 220- or 320-grit no-load paper to remove any residue or swirls remaining on the wash-coated surface. This smoothing will also remove any furred wood fibers raised by the wash coat.

Dealing with sand-throughs

When sanding at any stage, but especially early ones, be extremely careful not to sand through the finish to the bare wood—especially if it's stained. If you do sand through, and your wood is uncolored, touching it up by simply spraying more of the same wash-coat finish will be adequate. Not so with stained wood. Good color touchup requires much practice.

Water-soluble stains on bare wood with clear lacquer coats on top are the easiest color sand-throughs to repair. When touching up the color, the water stain bites into the wood but not the finish, which isn't water soluble, and won't add color where you don't need it. This is another reason water stains are a good choice for coloring when you're starting out. Sand-throughs to alcohol stains are a problem because restaining wood with alcohol also colors the finish around it.

Step 5: The Sealer Coat

Regardless of whether or not you sprayed a wash coat before using grain filler (many recipes call for filling the bare wood), you should follow a grain filler application with one or two coats of sealer—either vinyl sealer or other appropriate barrier finish—before spraying the topcoats. Some finishers spray the sealer coat (or coats) in a thin wash-coat fashion; others spray whatever finish they'll be using later in a normal viscosity to purposely create some build at the same time.

If you're spraying an entirely natural wood surface without stain, filler, or anything to lock in, you can skip Steps 5 through 8 and go directly to Step 9: Clear topcoats. In that case, the topcoat and sealer coat are the same thing because sealer is the first coat of finish sprayed on wood that has been prepped, stained, wash coated, or grain filled in the previous steps.

The wash coat sprayed in Step 3 was the first finish to touch the wood, so it did seal and protect somewhat. Actually, sealer coats are generally a bit heavier than wash coats and provide some build. As a wash coat finish, most of us choose barrier finishes like vinyl sealer or shellac because we also like their other properties in addition to their sealing properties.

A true sealer coat should fill the pores to some degree. Some finishers don't use grain filler at all on open-grained woods, preferring to fill the pores with sealer coats (although we'd suggest coats of clear topcoat for that).

You can use a number of different finishes as a sealer. Fifteen or more years ago, most finishers used *at least* several coats of sanding sealer, a lacquer modified with stearate to make it sand easily and with bulking agents to help it build fast. The aim was to speed up production but the tendency was for finishers to get most of their build with sanding sealer and only top it off with a couple of harder clear topcoats. However, a soft sealer substrate can cause the brittle topcoats to crack, or check in cold temperatures, and the final finish will be softer and less clear than a finish without sanding sealer.

Modern guitar finishers, especially small repair shops and individual makers, just don't need lacquer sanding sealer. One or two wash coats over the filler can serve as the sealer coat, and the finish can be built with the clear lacquer itself.

Still, sanding sealer is a viable seal coat if, after spraying it heavily enough to build a film, you then sand it back close to the surface. This leaves the pores filled with finish, but only a thin film of sealer remains on the wood surface—providing a level coat for the topcoats that follow. Used in this fashion, sanding sealer is useful.

Choose a sealer that won't interact adversely with your stain, grain filler, or the natural colors and resins in the wood. Color bleeding is the main problem. All colors will bleed to some extent, so apply them on scrap to become familiar with them! In many cases, the best sealer is the finish itself.

Sealer coats that are properly applied add little thickness to the finish, yet provide a smooth surface over which to apply succeeding finish. When you spray color, you want to avoid touching it—especially with sandpaper—until you've sprayed several clear topcoats over it to protect it. Therefore, it's especially important to do a good job of leveling the sealer coats before color is applied (so that no sanding or leveling is required for the clear topcoats to follow).

Use plenty of thinner if you want a thin sealer with less build and deep penetration to keep subsequent top coats from soaking into the wood. Mix two or three parts thinner to one part finish. If you need a little extra pore filling and want a heavier build to sand level, use less thinner. If you're not sure about your mix, test it on scrap and adjust it accordingly.

Barrier coats

If you want to lock in the stain and grain filler and create a barrier so that successive top coats won't melt into the material below, use shellac or vinyl sealer. One or two thin coats are sufficient as a barrier, and they'll also promote good adhesion. After a barrier coat dries, don't sand it unless there are dust specks in it (then quickly and lightly sand off only those). If you don't have these sealers handy, the next best choice is to use the finish itself (in our case clear lacquer).

Build coats

If your purpose in using a sealer coat is to create a level build (as opposed to just creating a barrier coat), then thin the sealer like a topcoat following the manufacturer's instructions and spray a good, wet coat or two. After it thoroughly dries, you must sand back the sealer to keep the film thin. Use 220-grit Fre-Cut sandpaper to avoid loading and sand until you're close to the wood's surface (if you're

TECH TIP

A production method for sealing bare, thirsty woods such as alder from drinking up the sealer and topcoat: use a catalyzed sealer. Alder and swamp ash will soak up finish all day, so Fender used 'Fullerplast,' which has a hardener (catalyst) added. One or two coats of Fullerplast fills the wood fast because it's thick and has far less solvent than lacquer. It doesn't penetrate as deeply and disappear into the wood. The lack of solvent also means it doesn't shrink much, so it builds quickly. Fullerplast catalyzes quickly, and once it hardens is impervious to the solvents in lacquer, so the wood is sealed, signed, and delivered!

using waterbase lacquer, be sure to use non-stearated sandpapers). Be careful not to sand through to the wood. If you do, be sure to spray more sealer, because bare wood spots will show as a different look in the final finish!

Step 6: Vintage "Primer" Under Solid Colors (optional)

The finish can only be as good as the surface it's applied over. This adage is especially true of color coats, which must lay out smoothly and flawlessly because any imperfections in color will show under clear topcoats. We want good color coverage in as few coats as possible for two reasons: first, because the pigments in colored lacquer are expensive, and second, to keep the overall finish thin and uncracked. We prepare for the color coats almost as if we were spraying a car.

Automotive finishers prepare metal surfaces for colored topcoats by spraying on several coats of (usually) gray, red oxide, or white primer (often called primer-surfacer), then sanding them smooth and level. The pigment in primer causes it to build fast, fill in imperfections, and make sanding easy. The color of a primer, highlights areas that need attention, and helps the finisher see when a color coat has covered adequately. All finishers want a thin coat to save material and avoid the cracking that can occur with a thicker finish. Automotive finishers are covering metal, not wood, so it's easy to keep the coat thin (metal doesn't soak up paint like wood does).

When we spray a solid color on wood, we like to use a white undercoat. White does the best job of blocking out the wood. White adds brightness, especially beneath the lighter colors, and makes it easy to see the coverage of the color coats. An excess of pigmented primer, however, would be at least as bad as numerous coats of the stearated sanding sealer that we have advised against. Rather than loading on coats of soft pigmented primer and watching them soak into the wood, we build up clear lacquer (because it's harder), sand it to 320-grit, and then spray a thin coat (or two if necessary) of white.

Certain colors obscure a surface faster than others. White happens to be the very best blocker and it's cheap, so it's always been the traditional primer color used by painters. If you could peel back the finish layers of most vintage Fender custom color Strats, you'd probably find a white undercoat beneath the color coat. (We've seen gray primer too, and some other colors, but white is most common). Apparently Fender used white the same way we do—as a blocker and background color.

You don't have to use a pigmented undercoat to achieve the right build under a color coat. You *can* skip the white and build up clear lacquer until it's smooth enough to spray your color onto, but in most cases a white undercoat contributes to a thinner final finish. This is because the color covers it so much better than dark primer or bare wood that a coat or two of paint is saved. Besides, it's the authentic way to reproduce the vintage Fender finishes.

If all the building, sanding, and leveling was done correctly in Step 5, the white lacquer will lay down almost as well as the color coat to follow it—like glass—and will require little or no sanding. If there are any imperfections, sand them out with 320-grit no-load paper and touch up any sand-throughs or bare spots by spot spraying with more primer.

Step 7: Solid Color Coats

That first coat of color that you've been waiting for is moments away. Enjoy your spraying, because it won't last long! One or two coats of color will usually cover.

Thin your colored lacquer so that the coat is wet and flows easily. It's just like thinning topcoat lacquer as described in Chapter 7. Two parts lacquer to one part thinner is about normal. The object is to spray as little color as possible (colored lacquer is expensive and we want the overall coat to be thin). Mix the lacquer well so the pigment distributes throughout and the color is uniform (this is important with touch ups) because you want to get good coverage with no thin spots where the primer or undercoat shows through. If you use enough thinner, you shouldn't get any of the dry, rough pebbling which is more common in color coats than clear finish coats due to the addition of the pigment to the finish.

Hopefully, because you prepared for it properly, you won't have to sand the color coat except for possibly knocking off a few dust specks. If you need to sand, be careful to avoid breaking through into the white undercoat below. If that happens, you don't have to spray an entire coat—you can touch up just a small area unless your touchup paint doesn't match, either because you're using a different lot or the sanded-through coat hadn't been mixed well enough and color had settled to the bottom. In that case, spray an entire coat.

As a rule, acrylic lacquer needs far more drying time between coats and before sanding or buffing. Nitrocellulose lacquer hardens much faster although acrylic will harden fine if you give it time. Note that some solid-color finishes are complex, requiring Steps 5, 6, 7, 8, and 9 all on the same instrument! (Check out the Candy Apple or Lake Placid Blue metallic finishes in the recipe section.)

Step 8: Shading, Sunbursting, Toning, and Touch Up (optional)

While Step 2 is for applying transparent stain to bare wood, and Step 7 is for painting solid colors, Step 8 is the third way color might be applied before the final clear topcoats go on. You can achieve both transparent and translucent colored finishes using shaders and toners made by mixing stains, pigments, or both directly into clear finish (usually lacquer). Shaders and toners are sprayed over a wash coat, a sealer coat, or a leveled lacquer surface. This step would be skipped in the case of a completely natural finish or if the color was applied at an earlier stage.

Depending upon their transparency, strength, and whether or not pigment is used to help color them, lacquer shaders and toners may hide the wood. Even at their most transparent they hide the wood to

TECH TIP

We saw an original well-used '62 Lake Placid Blue Strat that revealed the following layered colors in the worn areas (from the top down): clear, Lake Placid Blue, white, clear, 3-tone sunburst.

some extent because the color rests over the wood rather than being in it. Also, if you applied alcohol stains earlier on the bare wood, some of their colorant might be drawn out of the wood by the solvents used in the sealer or topcoat finishes, muddying the look to some degree.

Lacquer shaders can be applied now to create an entire sunburst, or to augment and complete a sunburst begun in Step 2. The terms shading and sunbursting are sometimes used interchangeably, although a sunburst is actually the result of spraying a shader and/or toner on only certain parts of an instrument. Guitarmakers spray shaders and toners to accent corners, carvings, pegheads, neck heels, and decorative areas. In fact, when furniture makers use shaders, they call the effect "highlighting," not "sunbursting." Sunbursting seems to have been coined by mandolin and guitar finishers (most likely at Gibson) to describe the light and dark shaded and toned face of a guitar or mandolin. Sunbursts are most commonly sprayed on the top or face of an instrument, but some manufacturers sunburst the sides, back, and areas of the neck as well. An example of such an overall sunburst would be the lovely tobacco sunbursts that Gibson sprayed on models like the ES-350 Switchmaster during the 1950s.

A sunburst applied *entirely* at this step is a different type of sunburst from the stain-on-bare-wood style applied in Step 2, although both are sprayed, the colors could be the same, and both versions are viable, traditional approaches to sunbursting.

Except for the 1920s hand stained sunbursts and some early 1930s coloration, most modern sunbursts are created (or completed) at this stage, including: rich and colorful Gibson sunbursts from the 1930s to the 1950s, the rather delicate transparent cherry sunburst used on late '50s Les Pauls, the more opaque sunbursts reminiscent of some of Gibson's '70s finishes, and some Gibson production finishes used today on the less expensive models. Some of these latter sunbursts, while not bad looking, lack the transparency and beauty of earlier vintage Gibson finishes or the ones created today by the Gibson Custom Shops in either Nashville or Montana. The reason for this is that when color lays on top of sealer coats, it tends to obscure the wood grain, especially when pigment is added.

Sunbursts are easier to apply now than at the bare wood stage because there's a clear base coat to spray color on top of. Bare wood fibers, no matter how much grain raising and sanding you do, always provide collecting places for stain and pigment to collect. The collected color, being more concentrated, causes tiny dark spots when it's dissolved by the solvents in the top coat. This is especially true of alcohol stain, but it can happen to a small extent with water stains if they are not protected from the top coats by a barrier sealer coat or wash coat (see Steps 3 and 5). With a clear base, you can correct mistakes more easily, either by sanding and spot spraying with an airbrush or by wiping unwanted color off with a solvent damp rag. Repairability and speed are the reasons most production sunbursts are sprayed over a clear base coat instead of bare wood.

TECH TIP

Remember that many of the sunbursts we drool over were sprayed in a production line, and often no great amount of time was spent on them. Of course, the factory finishers were pros, with daily experience most of us will never get.

Sunbursts can also be applied now to augment stain applied earlier in Step 2. There are several reasons for putting on the color in two stages:

- The edge of the burst can be darker by spraying a pigmented shader over a sealer. Shading over a sealer is preferable to staining because bare wood tends to soak up color.
- Glue spots and other marks that show up during the staining process can be covered by a lacquer shader. This is important in a production situation where sheer numbers provide more opportunities for imperfections to occur or in repair work where wood has been repaired with glue.
- You achieve a look of depth when colors are layered by putting yellow and perhaps some of the sunburst color down early. Then protect it with a couple seal coats of shellac, clear lacquer, or sanding sealer, finishing with the darker browns and blacks as shaders.

Lacquer toners used today impart an overall hue to the guitar, producing the look of PRS, Brian Moore, Patrick Eggle, and so many other modern makers. A toner can reproduce the see-through cherry-red of a Gibson SG; the neck, back, and sides of an early '60s Gibson Hummingbird; the body coloring of a see-through PRS; or add the apple to a candy apple red. An antique amber toner can give the aged vintage look to stark white bindings, tint a solid color sprayed previously, or make a reproduction gold-top finish to take you back to 1956.

Many manufacturers use Step 8 to tone the spruce tops of flat top guitars to achieve the vintage amber look. Or, at this stage you might just be doing a little repair work by touching up a sand through or lightly adjusting a color applied at any stage to better suit your taste.

Examples of colored finishes applied at Step 8

- Yellow lacquer toner base coat and red sunburst on Les Paul.
- The majority of Gibson, Epiphone, Guild, Gretsch, and other sunbursts (lacquer toner and lacquer shader colored instruments).
- PRS body coloring—the toner is sprayed now. Top stain applied to a PRS-style guitar in Step 2 would be augmented with a transparent toner at this stage to produce a sunburst.
- Some modern so-called reproductions of vintage Gretsch and Gibson transparent colored finishes. The originals were actually done with stain on the bare wood at Step 2, but many modern factory reproductions put all the color on at this stage, which doesn't get the right look.
- Any transparent stained sunburst applied at Step 2 can be color-corrected, repaired, or augmented now.
- Pre-'64 Fender two-tone or three-tone burst. Although the yellow stain would have been applied back at Step 2, the red and brown would go on now.
- All of a post-1964 Fender three-tone sunburst, including the milky yellow base coat, would be applied now.

Making lacquer shaders and toners

Make lacquer shaders and toners by putting the appropriate colorant into clear lacquer or other clear topcoat, such as shellac or waterbase finish. Use one of the following colorants (they're all detailed in Chapter 3):

NGR stain mixed in any standard dye strength can be added in up to a 1 to 1 ratio to unthinned clear lacquer. Because NGR stain uses glycol ether as one of its solvents, it can be used in place of lacquer thinner, both coloring it and thinning it simultaneously without imbalancing the mixture or changing the lacquer's drying properties. Glycol ether is a retarder, however, and since it makes up 30% of an NGR stain, it will slow down the lacquer's drying time considerably—maybe by a whole day or more.

Alcohol stain (usually made from powder; see Chapter 8) can be added to lacquer, but if the stain is straight alcohol stain (usually methanol without glycol ether), you risk imbalancing the lacquer's drying properties if you add more than 10% of the stain to the lacquer. Some powdered alcohol stains can be dissolved in NGR reducer, which is better for mixing into lacquer.

Liquid universal concentrated dye stain is the best way to color shaders and toners because the dye is so strong that you don't need much at all to get your color. Therefore, even though it has glycol ether in it, there's not much chemical altering going on. Add this within reasonable limits to your lacquer. Within the dye industry, other names for this type of liquid dye concentrate are solvent dye, metallized azo dye, nerosol, and orasol.

Traditional lacquer toners are mixed as follows: 2-1/2 pints of clear lacquer, 5 pints lacquer thinner or acetone, 1/2 pint of liquid color concentrate. This produces one gallon of a typical transparent shader as used by Gibson, Guild, and others within the industry.

Once mixed, you may want to thin the shader further with regular lacquer thinner. The color coats are only intended to achieve a color, not to create a build, so they should remain thin. Before you use a shader or toner at this step, always strain your colors well before spraying them. Also make sure your gun and cup are perfectly clean, and put a mesh strainer on the spray gun's siphon tube.

Mixing a strong shader

If your goal is a strong color but a thin finish, mix a stronger than normal lacquer shader, one with more dye and less clear lacquer. But practice first on scrap. Alcohol-soluble color in NGR dye can float up into the clear topcoats to muddy the transparency, shift color, or bleed onto white bindings. Strong thin shaders can be made several ways:

- Mix the powdered dye with half the amount of NGR solvent. You can always add more solvent later to weaken it.
- Instead of adding the NGR dye to the lacquer, reverse the process and add a small amount of lacquer to the NGR stain. Add just enough to give the mixture some body to help hold it in place and keep it from running.

- Use liquid concentrated dyes instead of NGR or alcohol stain mixed from powder. A little goes a long way.
- Instead of adding lacquer to the NGR stain, add a small amount of shellac as a binder. Shellac can be sandwiched between lacquer coats in small amounts.
- In addition, you might add small amounts of pigment (black or dark-brown liquid pigment) to the lacquer to darken it. This gives a pigmented look than straight stain, however.

Choosing the right spray guns for shading and toning

The best spray guns for shading and sunbursting are the smaller jamb guns which normally use a 1-pint capacity cup (see Chapter 4). You can also spray toners with a jamb gun, but the large quart capacity production guns are best because they can lay out a wide uniform coat. Touching up small sand-throughs is where airbrushes really excel, although some finishers also use airbrushes for sunbursting. But the small stream produced by airbrushes, and the tendency to jiggle them because of their small size and light weight, makes it difficult to lay down an even coat on a relatively large area. Also, their small reservoirs don't hold a lot of finish, and the frequent refilling can make a sunburst uneven and time consuming.

Layering the colors of a sunburst

As far as we know, there's no correct order for laying down color. Most of us start with the lighter center of the burst first, usually yellow or amber, and follow with the medium to dark edge colors. In the recipe section, we list the order in which we spray the colors, but practice by spraying reds, browns, yellows, golds, and blacks on paper, cardboard, or wood to develop your own particular tastes. Red sprayed over brown looks different than brown sprayed over red, and dark colors sprayed over a yellow base coat look subtly different than a yellow topcoat sprayed over a dark sunburst laid down first on uncolored wood.

During the finishing forum discussion at the 1997 ASIA SYMPOSIUM held in Burlington, Vermont, we were intrigued to hear that Gibson's Montana-made acoustics are sunbursted with the dark shader first, then followed with the yellow toner sprayed overall before clear coating. One expert present felt that Gibson might have shaded that way in the old days, too. Although this is exactly opposite to what most finishers do, Gibson Montana's modern flattop finishes certainly look great. To test that theory, we scraped away finish on several already damaged Gibson instruments, including a dark sunburst from the mid-1930s, a golden yellow and tobacco brown sunburst on mahogany from the 1940s, and a 1950s L5 in for partial refinishing. We still couldn't tell for sure what the color order was because everything melded together, but for what it's worth, the results of those scrapings seemed to show:

- **1935 L00:** This is one of the nearly black sunbursts with only a small golden center. The black lacquer shader was definitely put down first on bare wood (or on a sealer coat that is soaked into the wood) and the amber coat is on top of the black.

- **1940 Mahogany (steel guitar):** Clear lacquer over yellow toner over red & brown tobacco shaders on bare wood (or sealer which had soaked into the bare wood).
- **1952 L5:** Clear topcoat over red & brown tobacco shaders over yellow toner over a distinct coat of clear sealer on bare wood.

It seems most sensible to spray from the center outward to avoid spattering dark color over the center of the burst, and to produce a gradual transition to the darker edge. We see some sunbursts with dark spattering in the center, however, which suggests that the finisher could have been spraying inward, using a dirty gun that was spitting or was not atomizing the color properly.

In some cases you may want to reproduce a spattered finish—it's not hard, friend, just ask us! If not, prevent spattering by triggering the spray gun before swinging the spray stream onto the work, as well as spraying at a higher pressure with a closed down fluid setting to produce more atomization. Swing back off the work before releasing the trigger. Once you're on the instrument, don't stop spraying for any reason or the sunburst may be ruined. If you mess up, you can make the sunburst darker to hide your mistake, or use thinner to wipe it clean to the sealer coat (this is not easy). The other option is to wait until it dries to sand the color down to the clear coats, and start over. None of these solutions is desirable; you want to get it right the first time.

Since a sunburst consists of multiple layers, keep each coat as thin as possible so that the final finish doesn't get too thick. Be sure the colors are strong enough to get the effect you're after without needing excessive coats to build the color strength.

For the small shop without a separate spray gun for each color, a big advantage to starting with the light color at the center of a sunburst and progressing outward through the darker colors is that you only need to clean the gun once at the end. You can pour each color (yellow, red, brown, black, etc.) back into its respective container and add the next darker shade right into the spray gun.

Dealing with the binding

After removing any masking, and scraping off colored overspray, tone the binding now for a vintage look on refinish work, or to tone down the brightness of white binding on new instruments. There are several ways of doing this, but the simplest way is to spray a golden toner over the entire finish. More often than not this will give the look you're after without any elaborate masking.

If you don't want to tone the entire instrument, you can air brush toner directly onto the binding and let the overspray fall as it may. On darker colors, particularly sunbursts of reds, browns, and blacks, the slight overspray of yellow toner onto the dark finish is just not noticeable. However, on white, pastel, and gold-top guitars, binding toner will look almost like a secondary gold sunburst around the edges. To avoid this, mask off everything but the binding with tape and paper before you spray the toner. This is a necessity on repair work where you're simply replacing a section of binding and want it to match the surrounding finish. If you mask, you should lock in your colors with a coat or two of clear lacquer before applying masking tape. Tape can pull off finish from older guitars and the color with it. Also, the solvent in some tapes can leave strange marks, especially on soft pigmented color coats.

Avoid ridges, or steps, where the binding becomes taller from the thickness of the toner, by keeping the binding toner thin. Use mostly thinner—say nine parts thinner to one part lacquer. Whether tinting directly on the binding or on lacquered binding, the alcohol and/or thinner has a bite, easily achieving the needed strength of color. Actually, the danger here is in getting too strong a color.

Drying and sanding

After you have sprayed all your colored shaders and toners, let these coats dry for a couple of days so the solvents can escape before you lay on the coats of clear lacquer. Remember to be patient—many substandard finishes can be traced to a finisher that was in too big a hurry! Do not sand at this point. Any dust or pebble texture can be leveled after applying a couple of build coats of clear to protect the coloring.

Step 9: Clear Topcoats

If you're in doubt as to what finish to use or how to use it, refer to Chapters 1 and 7, or follow a recipe your first time out. The Recipe Chapter suggests the appropriate number of coats for a given finish.

Normally, you'll lay down between four and eight lacquer topcoats to finish the job. You'll need fewer coats if you thin normal lacquer lightly, use ready-to-spray lacquer, or work with professional equipment. Aerosol cans and propellant outfits can apply a good clear lacquer finish but they simply can't apply as much lacquer per pass as a spray gun powered by an air compressor. An aerosol finish may require a dozen coats or more. Aerosol spraying also requires attention, practice, and patience.

A few lacquers are formulated especially for guitar finishing and are ready to spray without thinning. Most need thinning, however. It's always a good idea to add a dash of retarder (a teaspoon or two per quart) to your clear lacquer to avoid blushing in humid conditions.

- Use 35 psi for spraying topcoats, unless your experience suggests otherwise.
- In case you forgot to antique the bindings in the last step, you can still do it early in this stage, before applying too many clear coats.
- Allow adequate drying time between coats, from a minimum of 30 minutes up to two hours. Three to four coats a day is a reasonable number of coats to apply in one day.
- Don't sand the topcoats until a good build up has developed (four coats or more, eight coats for waterbase lacquer). This will help you avoid sanding through into the colors.
- Don't sand if it isn't necessary! If you don't have dust or bugs in the finish and didn't get a run or sag, then don't mess with it.

TECH TIP

Scrapers play an important part in many Gibson-style finishes. Time-consuming masking can be avoided by purposely applying some stains, filler, or finish directly over the binding, then scraping the areas clean afterward. This binding scraper was made from a steel blank, ground and sharpened to any shape needed. Here, it's used to scrape just the soundhole purfling ring.

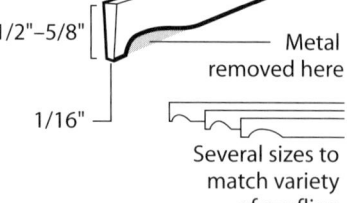

Several sizes to match variety of purfling

Knuckle of index finger against soundhole acts as a gauge

> **TECH TIP**
>
> A mix of yellow and brown transparent lacquer (sometimes a little red doesn't hurt), extended with clear lacquer and thinned a good bit, makes a good all-around toner. Practice on scrap to find your favorite mix.

Keep applying the coats, and remember that each coat of lacquer dissolves the coats under it to create one unified layer. Save your sanding until later if possible.

- If you sand at this stage, you can do so aggressively by wet-sanding with 400-grit wet-or-dry paper and water. Dry the instrument thoroughly before spraying again. You can also dry-sand if you have a nonloading paper with 400-grit or finer.
- *Four days is the minimum drying period before rubbing out!* If possible, let the clear nitrocellulose or acrylic coats dry at least a week before sanding and rubbing. The harder the finish, the more gloss the finish will have. Be patient! Once you get good at this, you'll be able to judge when you can shorten your time. A professional finisher we know often sprays 8 coats of clear lacquer, mixed 60/40 and fairly thick, every 45 minutes on good spraying days (warm and dry with low humidity) until the job is done. His finish, when dry, is .006 inches to .008 inches thick.
- Avoid runs by not spraying too heavily, not overthinning, and by holding the instrument level as soon as possible after spraying. You can clamp solidbody guitars level as soon as you set the spray gun down. If you get a run or sag in the finish, let it harden and sand it out using a block wrapped with 400 or 600-grit paper.

Spraying a flow coat

Some finishers spray a final flow coat, or flash coat, consisting of four parts thinner (or even more) to one part lacquer. This is often done with nitrocellulose but never with waterbase lacquer. This in effect melts everything together, flows out the sanding scratches, and creates a tremendous gloss. Before spraying this coat, wet sand the guitar completely with a minimum of 600-grit as if you were at Step 10, preparing to rub out or buff.

The finish coat will cure after three to four days. If there are no runs or imperfections, you can go directly to the buffing stage, without further wet-sanding. Due to the thinness of the lacquer, a finish coat is a tricky spray operation that can easily result in runs, so try it at your own risk! If you get it right however, it can look so good that you won't even want to buff it!

Step 10: Final Sanding and Rubbing Out

After at least a week of curing (two to three weeks is better) and using the techniques, tools, and materials described in Chapters 5, 6, and 8, sand the final gloss lacquer coat to a smooth, dull, satiny patina. At this stage you can easily put scratches in the finish that require additional sanding and buffing to remove. In a worst-case scenario, you'll have to go back and spray more lacquer to melt the scratches in, and to ensure that the finish is still thick enough to buff. So sand with a minimum of 600-grit if you're using traditional CAMI-grade wet-or-dry sandpaper, and P-800 grit if you're using P-graded papers. For waterbase lacquer start wet-sanding with 1200-grit Unigrit paper or finer (we go directly to 2000-grit).

The main reason scratches occur (other than using too coarse a grit) is that *the finisher doesn't clean out the clogged-up finish from the sandpaper frequently enough!* Keep the paper from clogging by wet-sanding using water, naphtha, or mineral spirits as a lubricant. Earlier in the book, we recommend water because of the obvious fire hazard and toxicity of petroleum-base solvents. Many production finishers avoid water because of its tendency to swell wood, which can cause lacquer to lift around holes, pickup cavities, and exposed end grain. But naphtha and mineral spirits are also liquid, and they can also cause problems. The best advice is to keep any wetting agent out of exposed holes or areas where it can get under the finish! Often small holes will be filled by one or more of the preceding steps; larger holes, such as tuning key holes, will get finish sprayed into them. You can take steps to help ensure that raw wood is protected from wet-sanding. Warm water mixed with a small amount of liquid detergent is the best wet-sanding fluid for waterbase lacquer.

Buffing

When the wet-sanding has been completed, buff the finish, following the advice given in Chapter 8. Buffing is the easiest and most enjoyable part of finishing, as long as the finish is thick enough to prevent a rub-through.

How Do We Get A Vintage Finish To Reveal Its Recipe?

Lacquer naturally yellows, stains fade, and wood darkens with age. The simple facts of time and chemistry force today's best finishers to be scholars, detectives, and chemists. To figure out how a vintage finish was created we must determine what materials they used and in what order. Sometimes you just have to "ask" the guitar itself by looking at a nick to see the finish layers, peeking in a soundhole to find telltale runs, or examining the crazing. The finishers, now long gone, can still have a pretty good conversation with you through their work, but you have to do some creative interpreting. Many of the finishes we admire today looked dramatically different twenty to fifty years ago when they were new.

To arrive at the finishes given in this section, we consulted with many experts in the guitar finishing field, including a few veterans. The problem is, can you remember how you did something twenty or thirty years ago? Guitar companies didn't keep detailed records of the materials they purchased or how their finishes were produced. Therefore most of us, since we didn't see a finish being sprayed, or know someone who did, have had to figure finishing out for ourselves.

We're especially voracious readers of old instruments and anything written about them. We also talk to whoever will indulge us to find out how the old finishes were created. That—and about a bazillion hours in the workshop—is how we arrived at this collection of finishing schedules, set out more or less like recipes. Most are pretty easy to follow, especially if you've gone through the first part of this book. Before we get into them, however, we'd like to divulge a few of the basic rules a guitar finishing Sherlock needs to know.

First, lacquer turns yellow. If you analyze a finish from the top down, you'll notice that the clear lacquer topcoat yellows with age. The older lacquers were supposed to remain clear, but many had an amber color to begin with. They also came in water white, or crystal clear versions beginning around the late 1940s, but many manufacturers continued to use the amber-colored varieties because they were less expensive. Regardless of how they started out, most lacquers took on an amberish cast in a few short years. (Modern lacquers have been developed that are touted to remain crystal clear, but they're still new. Whether or not they'll also yellow remains to be seen.) So you're looking through a layer of amber when you study an older finish, although it *might* or *might not* have been there to start with. Either way, you'll need to compensate accordingly when determining your finishing palette. The trick is not to overdo it because your new finish will also change. It may not yellow like the old finishes, but it will change as the wood darkens and the finish mellows.

Secondly, stains fade—especially the older NGR alcohol-soluble stains in reds and blues (today's NGR stain formulations are considerably less prone to fading). Color also migrates, so you'll be hard pressed to determine if it was applied to bare wood or sprayed over clear sealer. Stain in the wood floats up into a solvent-based finish;

stain in the finish disperses into the bare wood. This is especially true with alcohol or lacquer-soluble stains because they dissolve quite easily in lacquer, with successive lacquer coats dissolving each coat below. Nonetheless, the end result is the same: no matter when the color was applied, it ends up staining the wood. That means you don't always have to know what went on, or the order, to get approximate final results. Alcohol stains were prevalent in factory wood finishing, and still are, because they dry fast and don't swell the wood as much as water stains do.

Lastly, wood darkens as it ages from the effect of ultraviolet rays and oxidation. For example, imagine that you had shaped a mahogany neck and prep-sanded it for spraying, then were forced to drop the project for six months. You set the neck out on a shelf and forget about it. When you return to the project half a year later, the neck will have darkened dramatically—as if it had been stained. Some finishers actually use this natural darkening effect to color a neck before applying the finish. So don't forget that wood darkens on its own, and only experience and time can tell you how much.

Knowing about these forces will help you arrive at the way to duplicate the finishes you love. Even though the chemistry of finishes has undergone changes, the majority of guitar finishes today resemble the traditional ones used by larger manufacturers such as Martin, Gibson, Gretsch, Fender, and Guild. We are still amazed at how close we can come to a pre-1963 two-tone Fender sunburst or a 1920 Gibson golden sunburst.

When you're studying these finishing recipes, bear in mind that there's usually more than one way to get a particular look. Gibson and Gretsch produced the widest variety of colored finishes (and in our opinion the best looking). They've changed their finishes and finishing styles a number of times over the years, yet a certain consistency in look remained. Often one finish is so close to another, none of us will ever figure out how the process, order, or ingredients of the two differ—even though we're sure they do.

Using the main body of this book, you should be able to come up with your own methods for getting the look you want. Half the fun is in figuring out how to do it. No matter which finish you choose, it can look professional if you make sure to let the finish dry thoroughly, paying attention to craftsmanship so the finish is level, is not too thick, and adheres well. In the end, if it looks right, it is right!

Following is a variety of simple, intermediate and more complicated recipes. If you want more detail than some of the instructions offer, you'll find plenty of it in the first part of the book. Also, the materials list reflects our preferred ingredients, but you will notice that we often invite you to vary it according to taste. If you like vinyl sanding sealer better than lacquer and we've called for lacquer, feel free to make substitutions. Also, we realize that economy will sometimes dictate that you use what you have in the shop rather than buy a gallon of something else. Feel free. Again, you can always check the first part of the book to find out if one material needs any alterations in mixing, handling or applying compared to another.

Chapter 10: Finishing Recipes

Finally, trust your instincts and experience. Most of the recipes here are our versions of how we *think* finishes were applied, or how they can be applied with today's materials to get the same look. Please, alter any recipe here if you think of a better way.

Overall, finishing is not tremendously complicated. It is a craft that benefits from repetition. If you take the information on materials and technique in the book, combine it with the following recipes, add a willingness to experiment, season everything with patience, pay attention to detail—and then **practice on scrap**—you'll get the results you're after.

—*Dan Erlewine and Don MacRostie*

Weight

1 ounce = 28.35 grams
1 pound = 16 ounces

Fluid Measure

3 teaspoons = 1 tablespoon
2 tablespoons = 1 fluid ounce
1 fluid ounce = 28.35 milliliter
1 cup = 8 ounces
1 pint = 2 cups (16 ounces)
1 quart = 2 pints (32 ounces)
1 gallon = 4 quarts (128 ounces)

Stains

Powdered or liquid stains can be mixed with water, alcohol or lacquer-thinner.

Powder

Mix 28.35 grams powder to 2 quarts solvent
Mix 3.5 grams powder to 8 fluid ounces solvent
Mix 7.1 grams powder to 16 fluid ounces solvent
Mix 14.2 grams powder to 32 fluid ounces solvent

Liquid (170 drops concentrated liquid stain = 1/4 fluid ounce)
Mix 2 fluid ounces concentrated liquid stain to 2 quarts solvent

Spray Gun Capacities

Large production gun: 1 quart (32 fluid ounces)
Medium "door jamb" gun: 6-8 fluid ounces
Airbrush: 1 fluid ounce (usually)

Mixing Ratios for One Quart

50:50 lacquer/thinner = 16 fluid ounces lacquer + 16 fluid ounces thinner
5% retarder = 15.2 fluid ounces lacquer + 1.6 fluid ounces retarder
10% retarder = 14.4 fluid ounces lacquer + 3.32 fluid ounces retarder

Our first three recipes are basics that you'll use over and over. Blackening the Peghead Face is a step in many of the finishing recipes covered later in this section. And Fresh-mixed Shellac and Antique Binding Toner are also called for as parts of our recipes.

Fresh Mixed Shellac

Many finishers keep fresh-mixed shellac on hand for a variety of projects, including French polishing, sealing, wash coating, and touching up. With shellac, fresh is somewhere between two and six months, at which time we throw it out and mix a new, small, batch. A pint of shellac in a four-pound cut will go a long way (see Chapter 1 for more on shellac cuts).

Start with fresh shellac flakes. Here's how you tell. If the flakes are fresh they'll dissolve overnight. If they don't dissolve in four days, consider discarding your batch and getting new flakes, especially if the mixture doesn't dry when you test it on scrap.

Here's an easy way, measuring by eye, to mix the approximately three-to four-pound cut we use:

Shellac Cuts
One pound cut:
1 ounce dry shellac + 8 fluid ounce alcohol
Two pound cut:
2 ounce dry shellac + 8 fluid ounce alcohol
Three pound cut:
3 ounce dry shellac + 8 fluid ounce alcohol
Four pound cut:
4 ounce dry shellac + 8 fluid ounce alcohol
Five pound cut:
5 ounce dry shellac + 8 fluid ounce alcohol

FRESH MIXED SHELLAC RECIPE 1

1. Pour dry flakes into a clear glass jar with a tight-fitting lid and shake them down so they settle. We fill the dry flakes until the jar is between one-half and two-thirds full after shaking down (which is about 3 ounces, dry weight, on a digital scale).

2. Pour in denatured alcohol until the flakes are immersed and between a 1/2-inch to an inch of liquid remains on top of the flakes. On the digital scale, it took 7.325 ounces to immerse the flakes with 1/2-inch liquid remaining on top. This produces medium-thick shellac in a three- to four-pound cut that can be thinned as needed for brushing, French polishing, or spraying. Stir the mixture occasionally to keep it from forming a mound of thick, undissolved shellac at the bottom of the jar. You can also warm it gently, with indirect heat from something like a desk lamp, to speed the dissolving process.

3. Store shellac, mixed or dry, in a cool dark place.

Pint-sized clear glass jar with a good-fitting lid
Fresh shellac flakes
Fresh denatured alcohol

Antique Binding Toner

Antique toner, or antiquer, is a weak transparent amber lacquer toner used to give the aged, ambered, vintage look to a new finish or to bindings that are too white. Antique toner is made by adding transparent yellow, red, and brown dye-stain (or a ready-made vintage amber dye) to clear lacquer. It's easy to make, but you may want to practice by mixing small samples in plastic 2-ounce mixing cups. Quite frankly, most of us just dump our liquid colorant right into the clear lacquer until it looks right, and we don't worry much about it—but we still practice on scrap!

Once we started making our own transparent lacquer shaders, we soon had a good selection of "stock" colors—two favorites are yellow and gold. Gold is a combination of yellow and brown with a touch of red, but it leans toward the brown side (otherwise it would make a great antiquer alone). The yellow and gold toners together make a great antique toner, however, when mixed in a ratio of 80% thinner with 10% each of the two colorants. If you've already mixed up some nice yellow and golden brown shaders, you might try putting them together and using them as is, or extending them with clear lacquer. Otherwise, here's a good method for making a custom antique toner.

RECIPE 2	**ANTIQUE BINDING TONER**
Small amount powdered yellow, brown, and red stain (or pre-mixed concentrated liquid stain) NGR-solvent for mixing the powdered stains Appropriate amount of clear lacquer (enough for however much toner you want) Lacquer thinner as needed Several jars or small two-ounce mixing cups Pipettes	**1.** Mix each powdered stain with an appropriate amount of solvent to produce a concentrated liquid stain. **2.** Set out several cups filled with clear lacquer. Use pipettes to add several drops of yellow first, then a little brown, then only a dash of red. Mix up several more cups with slightly different proportions. Note proportions so you can duplicate them later. It's better to mix too light than too dark. Especially avoid a too-orange mix or you'll get the pumpkin look, which ruins many an otherwise good looking, vintage reproduction. **3.** Brush the colors onto a piece of clear mylar or glass laid over a piece of white paper to get a feel for whether or not the color looks right. Spray it with an airbrush if you want to really zero in on the look. If none of the batches look quite right, mix up more and test again. **4.** When you achieve the right mix, make up a larger batch using the same proportions.

Blackening The Peghead Face

The peghead faces of guitars and related instruments are often overlaid with a wood veneer as a decorative touch to match or contrast with the woods of the fingerboard and the body, to provide an even background for pearl inlay, and for a variety of other reasons. This peghead overlay hides glue joints on laminated necks and the glued-on "ears" of a peghead. Overlays also disguise the rather plain, somewhat unattractive look that results when the peghead is bandsawed at an angle through the grain of the neck wood.

Overlay veneer is usually either a dark hardwood such as rosewood or ebony (Martin's style), or a light-colored hardwood like holly that is stained a dark color or spray-lacquered black (Gibson's style). Sometimes, on economy models, the manufacturer skipped the overlay but still stained the peghead. Gibson's ES-125, for instance, had its face painted with black lacquer (although the glue lines often telescope through slightly as the lacquer shrinks).

There are several ways manufacturers have darkened the peghead faces of guitars, banjos, or mandolins over the years. Gibson used transparent dark-colored stains in the early days—you can see the wood grain of the peghead overlay in the older instruments and, unfortunately in many cases, the unsightly filler around the pearl inlays, too. By the 1930s Gibson was painting the peghead faces black. Gretsch has done it with both stain and paint and so has Guild, though Guild finally switched to using a black plastic peghead overlay with its logo stenciled in clear, which was then laid on top of a pearloid plastic to produce an inlayed look.

Whether fitted with an overlay and stained, or merely darkened with stain and/or lacquer, blackened pegheads became the norm in the industry. It may be that Gibson started using black lacquer to hide the goodly amount of filler it put around its pearl inlays. The look caught on, and now a Gibson without a black peghead face doesn't look right. For example, when Gibson hit bottom during the Norlin-owned era of the 1970s, the company left the faces of some models plain—and it looked awful.

Black stain alone works well on light or dark wood overlays, and you can finish over it with clear lacquer—if there isn't too much filler showing around the pearl. Accurate inlay work is a must if you want a stained-wood overlay because the filler will show.

Black lacquer, on the other hand, can eliminate the need for exacting inlay work, especially if the pearl rests in a bed of equally black epoxy, super glue, or other mastic. This way, even if you slip while scraping the black lacquer from the pearl, the filler around the pearl blends into the surrounding black lacquer.

As you'll see in the recipe, we recommend that you stain the wood surrounding any pearl inlay, even if you will also be spraying the whole peghead with black lacquer. Then, when you're scraping the lacquer from the pearl, especially if the pearl isn't perfectly inlaid, you'll hit a black background when you scrape. It won't hurt anything if you stain the whole overlay for that matter; the black lacquer will cover faster and thinner. You may even decide that you like the stained look, and skip black lacquer entirely, especially if the inlay work is accurate. Don't worry about getting black stain on your pearl, by the way. Pearl is hard, smooth, and nonabsorbent, so stain comes off easily with an eraser.

You can decide which stain you prefer. Water stain is nice for overlays because it's less apt to bleed into the lacquer and onto pearl or binding. On the other hand, NGR or alcohol stain dries faster and is less invasive to a wood veneer. This recipe calls for waterbase stain but gives you a variation for alcohol soluble ones.

Some finishers mask pearl before putting on lacquer, and others leave the inlay bare, then scrape off the lacquer afterwards. Either gives fine results. The choice really depends on whether you can mask easily and have the right masking tapes or papers (Gibson actually masks off its delicate logo with a spare logo secured with a spritz

Chapter 10: Finishing Recipes

of lacquer. The spare pops right off after finishing). If you decide to mask, skip the scraping step.

You can blacken the peghead as your first guitar-finishing step or anytime up until the clear coats go on. In most of the recipes, we suggest that you paint directly after you've sealed or wash coated any bare wood staining or grain filling. Here's how to blacken a peghead with pearl inlay.

RECIPE 3	BLACKENING THE PEGHEAD FACE

400-grit "no load" sandpaper (such as Fre-Cut)
 Masking tape
 1 ounce black water-soluble stain (you may use an alcohol stain if you prefer, and most likely you'll have to mix either stain yourself)
 Artist's gum or pink pencil eraser
 4-6 ounce black lacquer thinned to a ready-to-spray topcoat consistency (use ColorTone Aerosol Guitar Lacquer in Black Gloss right from the can)
 Optional: Frisket paper
 2-4 ounce clear lacquer or a wash coat
 Optional: Antique Binding Toner (see Recipe 2)
 Utility knife blades, micro-chisels or small chisels for scraping
	1. Be sure that the peghead face is smooth and has been damp-sanded with 400-grit Fre-Cut sandpaper (pearl inlays must be scratch free, otherwise black stain will show every mark).
	 2. Mask off the sides and back of peghead, the nut, and the fret board.
	 3. Using a small brush or cotton swab, apply black stain to filler around pearl, and entire peghead. Let dry several hours if waterbased. Alcohol or lacquer stain can be worked on almost immediately.
	 4. Clean stain from the pearl with an eraser.
	 5. Mask off anything you don't want black lacquer on (some finishers choose to leave their pearl bare, then scrape off the lacquer afterwards). Large areas, such as Gibson's crown inlay, are easy to mask with fine line or masking tape. For trickier delicate inlays, such as the block-script Gibson logo, use frisket paper like this:
	     Lay frisket over the pearl inlay and trace the outline onto it.
	     Remove frisket to a cutting mat, cut the pearl shape out of it.
	     Carefully lay cutout over pearl.
	 You can also mask thin lines with masking tape cut with a razor knife, or block mask the entire inlay with one piece of tape. In the latter case, simply doctor up any missing black afterward with an airbrush and/or small brush. Experiment on scrap first!
	 6. Spray one wet coat of black lacquer. One coat will usually cover an overlay—and coverage is all you're after. Let dry to touch, and remove masking tape before finish becomes hard, but not more than an hour. It's easier to scrape the pearl before the lacquer's gotten too hard and starts to chip when worked. In about 10 or 15 minutes, the lacquer will have shrunken back differently on the wood than on the pearl, making it possible to see the outline of the inlay.
	 7. If you did not mask your pearl inlay, scrape off lacquer using the widest tool that will fit within the perimeter of the inlay since small tools are more likely to leave scratch marks.
	 8. Let dry several hours, and seal with clear lacquer or wash coat the black lacquer.
	 9. Optional: spray a thin coat of Antique Binding Toner to give the pearl a vintage look.

Mixing Solid-colored Lacquers

Finding solid-colored opaque nitrocellulose lacquer in good guitar colors isn't easy. Off the shelf, you *may* find a usable black, white, blue, or red, but that's about it. You'll have to mix other colors that are usually tints or shades of two or more existing colors.

As we explained in Chapter 3, black darkens a color's value to create a color **shade**; white lightens a color's value to create a color **tint**. Fender's Daphne Blue and Fiesta Red are tints because white lightens the base. Dakota Red is a shade because black darkens the base. The dark burgundy or cordovan Cherry Red used on Gibson SGs, although transparent, is a shade of red.

White can be turned into a pastel guitar color like Fender's Sonic Blue or Seafoam Green pretty easily just by adding a little of the appropriate color liquid pigment, or other type of lacquer-compatible colorant you may already have around the shop. Traditionally, the correct way to tint the white is with pigment, but you can use transparent dye colors and get almost the same look. White lacquer, with a little concentrated liquid stain or a strong concentration of an alcohol-soluble stain powder mixed into NGR solvent, can yield beautiful color variations. You have the best assurance that the pastel won't fade if you use pigment, but these days transparent dyes are very light fast too.

By the same token, when you want a dark custom color, you can start with a dark base, such as red or blue, and mix into it one or more darker or lighter colored liquid pigments to alter it. You can use dye stain too, but it won't be as effective on dark colors as it is with light colors.

Here are some custom solid colors and instructions for making them in your shop. Watch that you don't load too much color into your lacquer—it's very easy to do. Add pigment in small increments, and test the mixture on a piece of acrylic sheet or plate glass; carefully add more if it's too light, test again, and so forth until your mix is just right. These mixtures can be stored for at least 18 months and sometimes longer.

SHOP-MADE WHITE LACQUER (AND OTHER OPAQUE LACQUERS) **RECIPE 4**

If you have white lacquer to start with, you can make all the pastels quite simply. But if you don't, here's how to make white lacquer (or any solid color) using liquid pigment.

1. Place the liquid pigment in a jar suitable for mixing. Add small amounts of thinner to the liquid pigment until you get a slurry, and then keep adding thinner until you get a mixture like heavy cream that seems as if it will mix into the clear lacquer well.

2. Add clear lacquer to the slurry, a little at a time, and continue until you get a strong colored lacquer. Mix well, and you should have a usable lacquer that

10 ounces of ready-to-spray lacquer, or clear lacquer thinned 1 to 1 (5 ounces lacquer to 5 ounces thinner)

1 to 2 tablespoons lacquer liquid pigment

Lacquer thinner

Chapter 10: Finishing Recipes

is still ready to spray. The liquid pigment won't thicken it much; if it does, add thinner to suit yourself.

RECIPE 5	**SONIC BLUE PASTEL**

10 ounces ready-to-spray white lacquer

Small amounts (drops, not ounces) of blue liquid pigment, blue concentrated liquid dye, or blue transparent lacquer toner

Lacquer thinner as needed

This recipe adds the blue color in stages so that you have a good chance of achieving the color on the first try. If you happen to overdo the blue, you can add more white. Avoid this if possible, though, because it's way too easy to mix more than you want or need.

1. Pour an ounce or two of the white lacquer into a suitably sized mixing jar. Add blue colorant in small amounts

2. When it starts looking like the blue you're after, you'll now have a feel for how much blue it takes to make the white into a pastel shade. Remember, paint lightens when it dries, so you won't know for sure how the color looks until you let it dry on scrap. Also, the shade of blue can be shifted by adding red or purple to lean it toward violet, or green or yellow to lean it toward turquoise (see Chapter 3 for more information on shifting colors).

3. Pour the new blue mixture back into the remaining white and mix well. Now it'll be too light again. Pour off an ounce or two of that into a jar and add blue as before. Mix and pour back into the main mixture. Any time you feel confident with the proportions, dump it all together and keep adding small amounts of blue until you reach the desired shade.

RECIPE 6	**FIESTA RED**

10 ounces ready-to-spray clear lacquer, or clear lacquer thinned 1 to 1 (5 ounces lacquer to 5 ounces thinner)

1 to 2 tablespoons red liquid pigment

1/4 teaspoon white liquid pigment

Several drops of yellow liquid pigment (or dye colorant)

If you have a dark red lacquer, you can lighten it in a jiffy with white lacquer or liquid pigment, then add tiny amounts of yellow to make a Fiesta Red. Or you can make the entire color from scratch just as you did with the white lacquer. The only difference is that you're starting with a dark liquid pigment instead of with white.

1. Place the red liquid pigment in a suitable jar for mixing, and add small amounts of thinner until you get a slurry.

2. Add clear lacquer to the slurry, a little at a time, until you get a red lacquer. Mix it well.

3. Add white until you are close to the lightness of the pastel color you envision, and mix well again.

4. Add just enough yellow (in *small* amounts) to give it the slight orange quality of Fiesta Red.

Solid Color Spraying with Aerosols

Here's how to go about spray painting a guitar body a solid color without using an air compressor and other expensive equipment. This is the easiest recipe for a colored finish in the book, and there are no fancy paints or vintage tricks.

Don't be intimidated by the list of materials and number of steps. It takes a lot of stuff to paint guitars, especially with a solid color, but these techniques are simple enough for a beginner.

It is virtually impossible to brush on a professional looking paint job using nitrocellulose lacquer, so a spray setup is required. To keep things simple your first time out, spray the color coats using Preval fill-it-yourself spray units, available at most automotive stores for a few bucks. A Preval unit contains a jar for the paint and a compressed gas can that turns it into an aerosol unit. You may need several units for this project.

We recommend nitrocellulose products here because they are simple to use, low-tech, high gloss, and give professional results. Nitro is the original guitar lacquer. You may be able to find equivalent colors and materials at your local automotive store, but remember that all materials used on a single guitar must be compatible with each other. The materials list below tells you how many aerosol cans you might need for the average job. To be safe you may want to get an extra of each just in case you get caught short or to practice on scrap with.

SOLID COLOR SPRAYING WITH AEROSOLS   RECIPE 7

1. Prepare the instrument with at least one damp-sanding to raise the grain (explained in Chapter 8) Choose a method of holding the body from Chapter 4.

2. Shake up two cans sanding sealer or lacquer so both are mixed and ready to spray when you need them.

3. In a jar, mix 5 parts thinner to 1 part clear lacquer—enough to make about 6 ounces of wash coat. Then spray a little of the aerosol blush retarder into the mixture to help slow down drying time. Pour this mix into the Preval spray bottle and spray a wash coat on the instrument. Let it dry at least several hours.

4. Fill open-grained wood with grain filler. Remove surface residue carefully and let the filler dry the recommended time.

5. Spray on another wash coat just as you did in Step 3, using the remainder of the already mixed wash coat. Dry two hours.

6. Spray three coats of sanding sealer one hour apart. Let dry for four hours.

7. Scuff sand with 220-grit Fre-Cut paper. Don't sand too hard yet, and stay off any sharp edges.

8. Spray two more coats of sanding sealer one hour apart. Let body dry overnight.

3 to 4 cans clear nitrocellulose lacquer (aerosol)

2 cans sanding sealer (aerosol)

1 can blush retarder (aerosol)

Optional (for open-pore woods only): 4 to 6 ounces of waterbase grain filler

1 quart or less clear lacquer

2 quarts or less lacquer thinner (some is for cleanup)

Optional: 1 quart or less lacquer sanding sealer

1 ounce or less lacquer liquid pigment

3 Preval or other pressurized touchup spray propellant units (You'll need two for the project and one for any emergencies)

220-, 320- "no load" sandpaper; 800- (or finer) wet-sanding finishing paper

9. Using 220-Fre-Cut again, level-sand the finish. You want to remove the majority of the sealer at this step, leaving only what it takes to eliminate any sinks or shiny spots. Avoid sanding through on corners and narrow spots such as the edges of a peghead. If you do sand to bare wood, coat again with sanding sealer, let it dry several hours, and then sand again if needed to get the level surface required for the next steps.

10. Mix up your colored lacquer (or use store bought) and fill two Preval jars with it. Spray enough colored lacquer to cover, probably two coats sprayed one right after the other lightly. Don't get runs! Start with one can and when it cools, switch to the other to keep the coat flowing. Let dry overnight.

11. Use 500- or 800-grit Fre-Cut paper to wipe-sand extremely lightly, and only to remove bumps or pebbly texture.

12. Apply six coats of clear lacquer. Always try to get your first coat on as early in the day as possible, even if you're only spraying three coats with an hour's wait between each. This allows the surface to dry enough that you can scuff sand lightly at day's end, then leave it overnight. With the surface opened by sanding, solvents gas off quicker and the film cures faster. Apply coats as follows:

Spray three coats, allowing one hour drying time between each. Dry overnight. If the finish seems hard near day's end, scuff-sand lightly with 220-grit open-coat dry paper to let the solvents escape overnight. Avoid sand throughs!

Spray three coats with an hour or so between each. At day's end scuff-sand lightly with 320-grit no-load paper and let dry overnight.

Inspect the instrument and level-sand lightly with 320-grit no-load. You should be able to sand out the entire finish (careful on edges). Spray two more coats, with one or two hours between coats. Let the finish cure a week or two.

13. Wet-sand with 800-grit or finer wet-sanding paper and buff as usual (according to the instructions in Chapter 8).

Mixing and Using Metallics

A metallic finish is produced by mixing colored bronzing powder into clear finish before spraying it. It's the finish on Fender's Lake Placid Blue, Shoreline Gold, Inca Silver, Sherwood Green, and Burgundy Mist, as well as Gibson's Les Paul Gold Top, and ES-295.

Of the commonly used bronzing powders, the gold powders and probably the copper are the only ones that actually contain bronze metal. The others are aluminum anodized to the respective color. Because gold powders really are bronze, they have a brief shelf life once mixed into lacquer. In two or three weeks they'll start to turn green from oxidation. The aluminum colors appear to remain usable indefinitely. We have the remains of a quart of Gibson Sonic silver metallic from 1986 that still seems fine.

Keep sandpaper away from metallic coats. If you must sand a metallic finish, cover the metallic with clear lacquer before touching it. This is especially true if you're using an anodized aluminum powder because if you sand into the metal it will turn from the color it appears to be (red, blue, etc.) to shiny silver aluminum! This won't happen with golds but you still shouldn't sand gold either; it creates a uniformly flat surface on the flakes and takes away from their depth and shimmer.

You can use the bronze finishes with clear topcoats or turn them into candy finishes by applying a transparent colored toner over a silver or gold metallic base. In other words, if you took a Les Paul Gold Top and sprayed a cherry toner over it, you'd have a Candy Apple Red Les Paul.

Bronzing powders are available from art supply stores and paint stores. The powders most finishers use are made by Crescent Bronze Powder Company in Chicago, Illinois. The colors you're most likely to use are blue, silver, green, copper, purple, and any of several golds. With these you could reproduce all the colors we mentioned above as well as a host of candy colors.

Crescent Bronze has a color chart and a big selection of colors. Some of the colors we like and the guitars they emulate almost perfectly are:

Gold #256 (Les Paul Gold Top, ES-295; base for candy colors)
Silver #242 (candy color base coat; metallic silver)
Gold #255: (Les Paul Gold Top variation—Dan's favorite)
Blue #1 (Lake Placid Blue)
Green #5 (Sherwood Green)

Bronzing powders are incredibly messy, so here are two caveats. We advise you to mix them outside if you're able. Secondly, it's a good idea to dedicate one inexpensive spray gun to being used just for metallic paints. It is almost impossible to clean every single flake from your gun. Just when you least expect or want it, a flake will break lose and show up in a finish sometime later.

| RECIPE 8 | **BASIC GOLD BRONZING LACQUER** |

This recipe is for gold lacquer, but the method for making it holds true for any bronzing powder. Gold lacquer is what makes a Les Paul Gold Top a Gold Top. (In the Gold Top recipe, you'll find that the materials list calls for a half recipe from recipe shown below). Gibson sprayed some of its earliest Les Pauls gold from head to toe. On others it sprayed the face only. The amount of bronzed lacquer mixed below would spray an entire Les Paul—cut this amount in half (use a pint doorjamb gun) if you're spraying only a guitar's face.

Small disposable 2-ounce mixing jar
1 ounce Crescent Bronze Gold #256 powder
1 ounce lacquer thinner
2/3 quart ready-to-spray clear lacquer

1. In the mixing jar, mix one ounce of powder into 1/4 ounce lacquer thinner, or enough thinner to turn it into a thin slurry. You want it runnier than a paste.
2. Pour small amounts of the remaining clear lacquer into the small jar until you have a thinner, syrupy texture.
3. Transfer the contents to a larger jar and continue adding clear lacquer. Stir it until you have 3 or 4 ounces and the powder is suspended evenly throughout the lacquer. Transfer mixture into remaining clear lacquer.
4. Pour entire mixture into a quart spray gun cup. Use immediately. Once mixed, gold bronzing lacquer doesn't keep well, so mix only as much as you need for the job. It also settles out of the solution quickly, so stir it often during the spray schedule.

| RECIPE 9 | **METALLIC BLUE—AS BLUE AS LAKE PLACID** |

To be authentic, this finish would use the same undercoat of yellow stain and white primer as the Candy Apple Red finish (see Recipe 11), and it would be used only on an alder body (not ash, which has an open grain that requires grain filler). If you don't care about reproducing a vintage look, however, and just want a nice looking Lake Placid Blue, you can follow the simpler parts of this finishing schedule and skip the optional steps (except for grain filling ash if you use an ash body).

Optional: 4 ounces yellow stain
Optional: 2 to 4 ounces or neutral grain filler
6 to 8 ounces sealer or your choice (vinyl sealer, lacquer sanding sealer or clear lacquer)
Optional: 6 ounces white lacquer
220-grit and 320-grit open coat sandpaper for level-sanding
Optional: 2-4 ounces of neutral grain filler for open grain wood
6 to 8 ounces of blue metallic lacquer (see Recipe 8: Basic Gold Bronzing Lacquer, substitute Crescent Bronze Powder Blue #1 for the gold powder)
1-1/2 quarts clear lacquer

1. Optional: Wipe body of guitar with yellow stain and let dry appropriately.
2. Optional: Fill open grain wood with grain filler. Let dry appropriately two days for oil-based filler, two hours for waterbase.
3. Spray two to four coats of sanding sealer (enough to allow you to sand level without sanding through).
4. Optional: Spray one or two coats of white lacquer to give a nice thin cover that provides enough build for level-sanding. Let dry at least several days, until it shrinks back from the evaporation of the solvents. (All lacquer shrinks back, but the shrinking is more noticeable in a metallic finish that in a plain clear finish).
5. Level-sand with 320-grit open-coat paper.
6. Apply metallic blue lacquer with 30 to 35 pounds of air pressure and a full pattern, spraying medium dry to get a feel for it. Once you get the feel, and you

start to get coverage, open up the nozzle and spray up to two medium-wet coats. It's especially important to avoid runs with metallics because you cannot sand them out, so control the wetness of the coat by balancing the adjustment of the spray gun's fluid regulator knob with the air regulator knob (see Chapter 7 for details). To keep the metallic blue powder in solution, shake the can to mix the paint before every coat.

7. Let dry several hours. Do not sand. Seal with two coats of clear lacquer, allowing an hour or two between coats, to protect the blue metallic.

8. Spray four to six coats of clear lacquer, allowing two hours in between. Let dry a week or more, and sand and buff as usual.

Gold Top Finish

Gibson's Les Paul Gold Top finish, sprayed on the earliest Les Pauls, is one of the most special of all electric guitar finishes. On some Les Pauls, it wasn't just the top that was finished in gold, the whole guitar was gold (the ES-295 model, which Scotty Moore made famous in Elvis Presley's band, sported this all-gold finish, too). "I've always favored the Gold Top version used in 1957," says Dan Erlewine. "On the ones I've seen, only the top is gold, and mated with a second tone of either a dark-walnut or light natural stain on the mahogany neck, back, and sides.

"I never wanted a Les Paul until I saw Mike Bloomfield playing his beat-up Gold Top in the Paul Butterfield Blues Band at the Chessmate Lounge in Detroit, Michigan in early 1965. (I ended up owning that guitar several years later, after Bloomfield traded me out of the cherry sunburst '59 Les Paul, which I had traded my '63 Jazzmaster for the day after seeing him play). Soon I started noticing Les Pauls on record jackets—Hubert Sumlin in Howlin' Wolf's band, Freddy King on his first album *Freddy King Sings*—and of course it wasn't long until blues players over the pond helped make them famous. However no Les Paul will ever be as beautiful to me as that beat-up Gold Top of Bloomfield's."

As stated above, the mahogany of the neck, back, and sides of a true Gold Top are not sprayed gold; the mahogany shows in either a dark-walnut version or a light golden natural one. The dark version has the same dark walnut stain and filler found on most Gibson instruments with mahogany necks, backs, and sides, and it stood out in stark contrast to the Gold Top. The lighter one, which gets its color from the light honey-colored grain filler, is the most common Gold Top finish and the version used in the recipe here. If you wish, you can use most of the same recipe for a dark version (see variation); you'll borrow the stain and filler steps from the ES-125 Generic Tobacco Sunburst recipe.

Spraying a Gold Top finish isn't that hard, it's just messy because the bronze powder gets everywhere. It's the same gold base coat used for a candy apple finish as described in "Mixing and Using Metallics", but the topcoats are clear instead of colored. The key to any good metallic finish is the coat on which you spray the metallic. It must be smooth and flat because any imperfections will telegraph through the gold and become accented by it. Dan says, "For that reason I prefer ample coats of clear lacquer or sanding sealer—the Gibson method—instead of Fender's white base coat."

> **TECH TIP**
>
> At Gibson, they hang a Les Paul (and many other models) with an eye-hook screwed into the butt-end (later to become the strap-button hole). The guitar is free to swing up and out so the operator can grab the neck and spray the peghead, cutaways and shoulders, and then return it to the vertical hang for the majority of spraying.

RECIPE 10 — **GOLD TOP FINISH**

1. Prep guitar, mask off all areas not to receive grain filler (peghead face, fretboard, top, and binding). If you're careful with filler you don't have to mask.

2. Fill the mahogany neck, back, and sides with the light pore filler. Wipe off any excess carefully and let it dry several days.

3. Spray a double wash coat, 15 minutes apart, on the filled mahogany so it can be handled. When dry to the touch, about 45 minutes, remove the masks from the peghead, binding, and top, and let the wash coats dry for another hour, or until the guitar can be handled.

4. Blacken the peghead face, and scrape the pearl soon after blackening the face. Scrape the binding while you're at it.

5. Spray two wash coats on the top, 15 minutes apart, mostly to prime the wood but also to catch the top up to the rest of the guitar. It's okay to let the wash coat overlap onto the sides because it will seal the binding a little bit. Let it dry two hours, or overnight if it's getting late in the day.

6. Scuff-sand the top lightly and spray two wet coats of full-bodied clear lacquer or sanding sealer 1 hour apart. Dry several hours.

7. Level-sand the lacquer with 320-grit Fre-Cut paper, and to be safe, spray one more coat. Let dry several hours and scuff-sand lightly to release solvent. Let the guitar hang overnight.

8. Level-sand the top smooth with 320-grit, then mask the sides including the binding, the back, the fretboard, and the neck at least halfway up to protect it from gold over spray. The thin top edge of the binding on the face can be left untaped and scraped after the gold is laid down. A good way of taping the body is to use a cut-out paper mask for the back first, and then pre-mask tape on the sides folded over the back mask. A bag of any size that fits makes a quick neck mask.

9. This step should be done outdoors, weather permitting:

   Spray one or two coats of gold metallic lacquer 15 minutes apart.

   Spray more gold if you see any weak areas.

   Do not touch the gold coats, and let them dry an hour or so.

10. Remove all masks, scrape the top edge of the binding, gently blow everything clean, seal in the gold with two coats of clear. Let lacquer dry overnight.

11. Spray two or three coats of clear lacquer, an hour apart, on the back, neck, and sides to catch them up to the top. Let dry several hours or overnight.

12. Spray four to six coats clear lacquer on entire instrument.

Variation: Dark Walnut

For the darker version mentioned in the intro to this recipe, use the following three ingredients instead of the stain and filler in the main recipe:

1. After Step 1 and before Step 2, stain the bare mahogany with the dark walnut.

2. In Step 2, substitute the dark walnut grain filler for golden, honey brown filler.

3. Optional: If you want the antique effect, use Antique Binding Toner right after sealing the gold in Step 10.

Masking supplies

2 ounces light honey brown grain filler

4 ounce Black Peghead Face Lacquer (see Recipe 3)

1 pint Basic Gold Bronzing Lacquer (see Recipe 8), substitute Crescent Bronze Gold #255 (Dan's favorite) for Gold #256

1-1/2 quarts of ready-to-spray clear lacquer

1 quart lacquer sanding sealer (or use clear lacquer)

320-grit Fre-Cut sandpaper

Using pre-mask tape to mask a solidbody.

Tobacco waterbase stain, which is dark walnut

Dark walnut grain filler

Optional: Antique Binding Toner (see Recipe 2)

Candy Apple Red Circa 1964

This finish came about after we saw a 1964 Candy Apple Red Fender Stratocaster, with chipped and worn areas that distinctly showed the following layers of colored finish from the bottom up: yellow stain, clear, white, gold, transparent red, and clear lacquer. The Strat we saw must have been one of the last of the Pre-'63 or '64 stain-on-bare-wood bodies. Around 1964 or '65 it's believed that Fender begun using Fullerplast, a clear catalyzed sealer coat, on bare *unstained* wood.

If you don't care about reproducing a vintage look, skip the yellow stain and white lacquer steps, because nobody will see it anyhow. Our recipe, however, includes the necessary steps to replicate the original Fender we saw (which had an alder body, by the way)—but you can use this recipe to finish other woods, too.

RECIPE 11	CANDY APPLE RED
Optional: grain filler	1. From Chapter 4, select a method of holding the body.
Pre-'63 yellow water stain	2. Optional: Grain fill open grained wood (alder does not require filler).
1 quart of lacquer sanding sealer or clear lacquer	3. Wipe a waterbase pigmented yellow stain onto the bare wood. The grain will not be hidden; it will stand out.
320-grit Fre-Cut sandpaper	4. Spray 3 to 4 sealer coats, waiting 2 hours between coats. You must lay down enough sealer to create the build needed to level-sand. Because alder soaks up sealer, you may need more than usual. This is why Fender switched to Fullerplast; once the first coat cures (catalyzed), subsequent coats don't sink in. Dry overnight.
500- grit Dry-lube paper	
6 to 8 ounces white lacquer (you need that much to fill a spray can, but you won't use that much—the same thing goes for the gold metallic)	
6 to 8 ounces Basic Gold Bronzing Lacquer (see Recipe 8)	5. Level-sand with 320-grit Fre-Cut paper. Next spray only enough white lacquer to cover and to withstand a little sanding to smooth out dust. Keep it thin—but white; two coats will probably do. Let the white coats, and the sealer coats below, dry at least several days so the finish can shrink back as the solvents evaporate. It's better for this shrinking to occur before the metallic goes on, because metallic tends to highlight fills and imperfections caused by shrinkage. Level-sand lightly with 500- grit Dry-lube paper.
1 to 1-1/2 quarts ready-to-spray clear lacquer	
800-grit Fre-Cut for wipe-sanding	
800-grit and finer wet-sanding papers for wet-sanding	
8 ounces transparent red lacquer toner (dye-based) for the candy apple color	6. Prepare the metallic gold lacquer and be sure that it is well stirred every time you spray a coat. Two coats should be plenty, and spray them fairly light and dry. Wet coats tend to run, and you don't want that because you cannot sand on gold. Let dry several hours (overnight is better) and do not sand.
	7. Seal with two coats of clear lacquer to protect the gold lacquer. Wipe-sand only using 800-grit or above. Let dry two hours before going to the red.
	8. Spray one or two coats of transparent red lacquer toner to cover, waiting 20 minutes between coats. Dry overnight (or several days is better).
	9. Spray four to six coats of clear lacquer, waiting two hours between coats.
	10. Continue as normal with wet-sanding (800-grit and finer) and buffing.

Basic Martin-style Finishes

This finish, with a natural top and stained back and sides, is our version of the recipe that many of the modern flattop and archtop acoustic builders who use nitrocellulose are following. This is an amalgamation of the approaches used by several prominent makers, and the result of many hours spent talking with some of the world's best makers. With it, you can produce a professional finish on acoustic instruments made from rosewood, mahogany, maple, spruce, and other tone woods. This is not the look of the older Martins and Gibsons, many of which were stained and grain-filled on bare wood (see variation at end of recipe). This is the modern, clean look of a wash-coat-before-filler, as used in the '90s by the majority of hand-makers and manufacturers.

Most of us use a dark walnut stain on mahogany and light amber, if any, on maple. Rosewood often doesn't need a stain. (See Chapter 3 for details on mixing your own stain from either a water-soluble powdered stain or a concentrated liquid dye stain.) Mix up a quart or two; it lasts for years. On mahogany, you can replicate the color of many Martin guitars made since the late 1930s by mixing 1 part red mahogany stain to 1 part dark walnut (both water-stains).

BASIC MARTIN-STYLE FINISH USING NITROCELLULOSE LACQUER — RECIPE 12

1. Prep sand entire instrument down to 180- or 220-grit (mahogany stains best when it's been sanded to 220-grit).
2. Mask white or ivoroid binding.
3. If the instrument is mahogany or other wood that requires stain, wipe water stain on the neck, back, and sides. Dry overnight.
4. Spray instrument with one thin wash coat of vinyl sealer. Let dry several hours or better yet, overnight if time is not a problem.
5. Fill pores with grain filler following the instructions in Chapter 9: Step 4. Wipe off any excess cleanly. Let dry several days for oil filler, several hours for waterbased.
6. With a clean cloth, wipe the dry surface clean of any filler residue, or lightly scuff with a gray Scotch-Brite pad if necessary. Be careful not to sand through to the bare wood and hit the stain!
7. Spray another wash coat to lock in the filler and let it dry an hour or two.
8. Unmask binding and scrape any color that may have bled under the tape.
9. Spray nine coats lacquer following this schedule:

    Day 1: Spray three coats, two hours apart.

    Day 2: Sand with a sanding block and 220-grit Fre-Cut paper in the morning to help solvent escape.

    Day 3: Spray three coats, two hours apart.

    Day 4: Sand again with the 320-grit, in the morning, to help solvent escape.

    Day 5: Spray three coats, two hours apart.

Materials:
- 180- and 220-grit no-load sandpaper for wood prep
- Masking supplies
- 4 ounces water stain in the color of your choice
- 1/2 quart or less of vinyl sealer or thin clear lacquer for the washcoat
- 2 ounces of dark walnut grain filler
- 1-1/2 quarts of clear, ready-to-spray lacquer
- 800- and 1000-grit (or finer) wet-sanding paper
- Buffing compound

Chapter 10: Finishing Recipes

10. Let hang for a minimum of one week; wet-sand with a minimum of 800-grit wet-or-dry paper, graduate to 1000- or 1200-grit if you choose, and buff.

Variation: Grain filler on bare wood

For the older Martin and Gibson look, stain and fill the bare wood by substituting the following steps for Steps 4 through 7 above:

4. Fill pores with grain filler following the instructions in Chapter 9: Step 4. Wipe off any excess cleanly. Let dry several days for oil filler, several hours for waterbased.

5. With a clean cloth, wipe the dry surface clean of any filler residue, or lightly scuff with a gray Scotch-Brite pad if necessary. Be careful not to remove any stain!

6. Spray instrument with one thin wash coat of vinyl sealer and let dry several hours.

7. Spray another wash coat, slightly heavier, to lock in the filler and let it dry several hours.

8. Continue basic finishing at Step 8.

RECIPE 13 — **BASIC MARTIN-STYLE FINISH USING WATERBASE LACQUER**

This version of the traditional acoustic look (natural top and stained back and sides) is what modern flattop and archtop acoustic builders who use waterbase lacquer are following.

Waterbase finish doesn't look wet and glossy as you're spraying, unlike nitrocellulose lacquer. Be careful not to lay it on thick, looking for that glossy wetness. Good lighting is very important. Spray light coats, carefully overlap your spray pattern by 1/3-1/2 for coverage with uniform thickness.

1-1/2 quarts of ColorTone Waterbase Sanding Sealer

1 quart of ColorTone Waterbase Clear Topcoat

Fine-grit (grey) Scotch-Brite Pad

Optional: Waterbase grain filler, retarder and stain

220-, 320-, 400-grit Fre-Cut gold sandpaper

1200-grit Unigrit wet-sanding paper

Rubber sanding pads

Buffing compound for hand buffing or pedestal buffing

1. Prep sand the entire instrument down to 180- or 220-grit (mahogany stains best when it's been sanded to 220-grit).

2. Mask any binding.

3. If the instrument is mahogany or other wood that is commonly stained, wipe or spray water stain on the neck, back, and sides. Spray stain on neck at 60 psi with the fluid needle almost closed, producing a fine mist that is not too wet. Be careful not to get stain on the spruce top! Some finishers go to the effort of sealing the top to protect it—even masking off the body to protect the bare mahogany from the sealer. Or, they may carefully mask the top before staining. Let the stain dry 4 hours.

4. Spray 2 dry wash coats of sanding sealer on the neck and body, waiting 2 to 3 hours between coats. A wash coat is a thin coat of sanding sealer mixed 50/50 with water.

5. Fill the open pores with grain filler, following the instructions in Chapter 9: Step 4. Remember to work small areas at a time since waterbase filler dries so

quickly. Let the filler dry four hours, then reapply a lighter second coat of filler just as above, and let the filler dry overnight.

6. With a clean cloth, wipe the dry surface clean of any filler residue, or lightly scuff with a gray Scotch-Brite pad if necessary. Be careful not to sand through to the bare wood and hit the stain!

7. Unmask the binding and scrape any color that may have bled under the tape.

8. Sanding sealer: 12-16 coats • 3-4 coats per day • 2-3 hours apart.

Nearly three-quarters of your final finish thickness will be sanding sealer (this is an important point that will seem odd to finishers experienced with nitrocellulose). Scuff-sand with 320- or 400-grit dry Fre-Cut sandpaper after about 8 coats. Only knock off high spots and dust specks; don't try to level "sinks" and low spots below the surface. Then spray four more coats of sanding sealer if you feel it is needed. The goal is to build the finish to the point that you'll be able to sand it smooth without sanding to the wood.

9. Clear gloss topcoats: 9-12 coats • 3-4 coats per day • 2-3 hours apart.

Level-sand sealer with 320- or 400-grit dry sandpaper until all shiny spots are gone, then spray your first topcoats (four coats two hours apart). Drop-fill any sinks or low spots with gloss topcoat applied with a small artist brush. You may need to do this twice, with two hours drying in between. Spray another round of topcoats. Lightly sand the drop-filled areas with 400-grit Fre-Cut dry sandpaper, and then spray more topcoats.

10. Let the finish cure for at least a week (longer is better). Wet-sand it level with 1200-grit Unigrit sandpaper or finer. This will work if the sandpaper has been soaking overnight—that is how wet-sanding papers are supposed to be used. Buff the finish.

TECH TIP

Waterbase sanding sealer has a 48-hour "burn-in" window; successive coats will bond best when applied within 48 hours of each other. When this time is exceeded, sanding with 320-grit paper is required to roughen the surface for good adhesion of the coats to follow.

A Brief History of Gibson Guitar Finishing

Many of our favorite finishes are the work of the Gibson Guitar Company, and we're guessing many readers feel the same, especially fans of sunbursts. We've included our renditions of several of Gibson's best in the recipes. We've devoted more time than you might imagine to figuring out how Gibson achieved its finishes over the years. Sometimes arduous, always interesting, the research has turned up the art, craft, and foibles that went into Gibson's repertoire of vintage instruments. The findings were too good not to share. So we offer you a brief history of Gibson. Even if you don't intend to finish a guitar, you will learn how your favorites got their look.

The Early Years

At the turn of the century, Grand Rapids, Michigan, was the heart of America's furniture industry. The Gibson Mandolin-Guitar Company was located just sixty miles south of Grand Rapids in nearby Kalamazoo. With musical instruments being essentially small pieces of furniture, it's logical to assume that Gibson finishers were influenced by the same materials, techniques, and colors utilized on the era's best furniture. After all, musical instruments are used—and prominently displayed—in people's homes, just like furniture. Grand Rapids was also an easy source for the stains, fillers, shellac, and enhanced-shellac spirit varnishes of the time.

For these reasons, we believe that from the early 1900s, until they began using lacquer and spray equipment in the 1920s, Gibson probably finished a majority of instruments with a reasonably fast-drying spirit-varnish furniture finish.

That wasn't always the case, however. In Gibson's golden mandolin period, between 1910 and 1925, there are distinctive finish periods that overlap as varnishing evolved into spray-lacquering. For instance, from about 1914, in Catalog J under the heading Varnish, Gibson claims: "A finish must be tender and in a manner soft; that is, yielding to the movement of the wood; most assuredly not to encase the instrument as with French polish like a film of glass....[The finish] must not impede, obstruct, or hinder in any way, which is the case if the varnish be too hard, or flint-like as French polish, which is the hardest finish known....The yielding qualities of oil varnish give it a vast superiority over spirit varnish or French polish. The oil varnish is more difficult to apply and takes longer to properly dry; therefore, most manufacturers do not use it."

These statements, however, were lifted verbatim from a popular violin-making book of the time, *Violin Making As It Was And Is*, by Ed Heron-Allen, and they may have no bearing at all on what Gibson actually used for a finish! (The catalog was written a long time before truth-in-advertising laws. For example the catalogs often advertised the use of maple when in reality the advertised models were birch.) From a production perspective, you'd have to wonder how Gibson could possibly have finished so many instruments with a slow-drying oil varnish. They built huge numbers of instruments, especially mandolins, because of the popularity of mandolin orchestras. It's possible they used oil varnish on custom instruments; it's hardly probable they used it on the majority of production instruments.

Experts believe that Gibson's Master Model instruments, which debuted during the early '20s, differed from the production instruments of the time in that they *were* finished in a type of oil-varnish and then French polished to the final shine. These Master Model instruments were designed and built under the guidance of Lloyd Loar, one of Gibson's greatest and most-revered design engineers, who was with the company from 1921 until 1925. Perhaps Loar decided to turn Gibson's catalog claims about violin varnishing into reality. He was certainly under the influence of the violin world (he introduced F-holes to the mandolin and replaced the top's cross brace with longitudinal tone bars). Oil varnish finishes do have a certain look, color, and quality that set them apart from other finishes, and Loar's instruments were certainly perceived to be a cut above Gibson's other instruments.

"In their golden mandolin period, from 1910 to 1925, it's true that there are distinctive finish periods that overlapped or evolved into others. ...What Gibson published in their catalogs and what they actually produced weren't always the same thing," says renowned mandolin builder Steve Gilchrist. He has spent the last 20 years studying Gibson's early finishes, seeking to duplicate them.

"I saw a photograph in an old Gibson catalog of what looked like a finishing room. The caption read 'Varnish & Shellac Division.' The same photo is in *The Gibson Story*, by Julius Bellson. Certainly instruments up until the early '20s had a good quality spirit varnish consisting of gum resins such as sandarac, copal, benzoin, or shellac dissolved in ethanol. This would produce a relatively fast-drying, durable, thin, light-colored finish."

From his research, Gilchrist has been able to reconstruct Gibson's techniques, at least to his own satisfaction. For instance, he has found that less expensive models appear to be finished by and large in orange shellac (or straight shellac)—even over rosettes. On the other hand, all models with logos, including orange top models, have only a light amber colored varnish over the head stock.

Gilchrist believes that Gibson used oil or oil-composite varnish as a sealer, with a thin glossy spirit-varnish topcoat until late 1925. "This produced a more flexible finish that in time has checked only slightly compared to the all spirit-varnish finishes of the earlier period," he says. "This matches my experience with repairing Loar varnish as well as studying varnish remnants of destroyed instruments. The thin topcoat is a spirit varnish that wipes off very easily with alcohol. Underneath is a finish that at best only becomes rubbery with strong solvents such as lacquer thinners and acetone, and sure acts like an oxidized oil varnish."

Gilchrist even had some of Gibson's finishes analyzed. It showed that the finish was shellac and "who knows what" in the topcoat, and that the foundation coat contained Truly Natural (TN) shellac, a very dark brown shellac that could have been one of the components of an oil-composite varnish. It also showed dichromate, which violin makers use for preoxidizing the bare spruce to give it an aged look prior to staining.

"I've looked at numerous Loar instruments through the end pin hole," Gilchrist says. "All instruments to some degree have a mess around the inside area of the soundboard with dribbles and patches emanating from the sound holes," he says, particularly referring to Master Model F-hole instruments and most oval hole models through the eras. "This usually includes yellow water stain and very dark TN-colored varnish dribbling or flowing in a uniform direction that would be consistent to the angle if held while brushing."

Gilchrist believes the advent of spray finishing ushered in a drop in the quality of workmanship, visual aesthetics, and overall attitude to the product Gibson was producing. "I can imagine the disillusionment of the old varnishers in the finishing department when they were told to throw away their brushes and rags." Gilchrist can relate. "Stains enhance every grain and figure in the wood, and varnish with its amber shade, maximizes the subtle and beautiful refraction of light on wood," he says. "For example, a light curl of maple will turn to dark when rotated in the light like no other technique will effect—particularly with hard maple, the only maple they used."

Color Arrives

You can get just as good a feel for the history of Gibson finishes by studying the vintage Gibson Mandolins (or guitars of course). Gibson mandolins are more plentiful than their guitars, and instruments from the teens abound. This is probably because the mandolin orchestras required *lots* of instruments, and the orchestral musicians were, as a rule, more educated, sophisticated, and affluent than your average blues players or cowpokes. Therefore, they were more likely to take better care of their instruments.

The top colors of the earliest instruments (made by Gibson founder Orville Gibson, himself) were transparent amber, walnut brown, or opaque (pigmented) black, on the more expensive models. The same colors were used on the earliest factory-made models and received names like Golden Orange for amber, Sheraton Brown for walnut brown, and Ebony for black. A few models were Ivory, an opaque white.

Golden Orange-shaded tops were unstained, and received their color from the amber color of the orange shellac finish. Golden Orange tops were mated with Rich Dark Mahogany (red brown) backs and sides on the A, A-1, most A-3 mandolin models, and many L-1 guitars. Earlier models can be quite orange, though you'd see lighter shades of orange shellac as well. These variations were described in the catalog as Amber Brown, Light Amber, Beautiful Orange, and Golden Orange. Amber *was* the dominant top color until about 1914 when it was joined by the same red-mahogany being used on backs and sides.

Sheraton Brown was a popular top color too, even used as an all-over color on some mandolin and guitar models such as the A-2 and L-1. Sheraton Brown was the predecessor for many of the walnut brown shades, later used for sunbursting and coloring the necks, backs, and sides.

Ebony, a coat of black varnish finished with clear varnish, coupled with Rich Dark Mahogany back and sides, was the predominant finish used on higher-end models between 1910 and 1914 (models such as the A-4, F-2, and F-4 model mandolins and the L-3 and L-4 guitars). In 1914, Ebony was replaced almost entirely by the Red Mahogany Sunburst; you will find exceptions but this was Gibson's standard at the time. Ebony was still being used right into the 1930s, however, although it was lacquer instead of varnish and it was no longer used only on high-end models. On the low end, the top of the 1932 L-00 and the entire finish of 1935's little L-30 archtop were Ebony. On the high end, the 1934 catalog describes the L-10 with an Ebony finish, although we've never seen one, but we have seen a 1936 Nick Lucas Special in Ebony. Some late-'30s L-0s sport white pickguards against an all-Ebony finish—and we can't figure out why Gibson would discontinue such a simply *stunning* look!

Ivory finishes are rare but the color was an option on the A-3 mandolin, H-2 mandola, K-2 mandocello, and the L-3 guitar between 1918 and 1922. Ivory, by the way, was one of two "new" finishes described in Gibson's 'M' catalog of 1921.

Gibson's finishers used a clear satin lacquer over Sheraton Brown on styles A, A-2, H-1, K-1, L-1, J, A-Jr. & L-Jr. We assume that the lacquer would have been sprayed on. According to a reputable source, Gibson may have changed all finishing to lacquer about late 1925. We have confirmed that F-5 #81250 was finished in varnish, and that F-5 #82630 was finished in original lacquer. Regardless, we know that they definitely used the "new" lacquer finish in 1921.

In 1914, Gibson introduced Dark Mahogany, a red brown used as a back and side color. It was the maker's first move into a bolder, brighter top coloration. It used a hand-blended staining effect that furniture finishers up the road called shading or highlighting. We like to think that Gibson finishers coined their own term for the look—sunbursting. If that's true, then the sunburst was born in 1914!

The new red sunburst graced the A-4, F-2, and F-4 model mandolins and the L-3 and L-4 guitars. The mahogany stain on earlier models was quite light with a subtle transition to the golden burst, getting darker as the period evolved. By 1918, the application of the stain was heavier, on top of a distinctly yellow base coat. As the sunburst evolved, the red edge shading grew darker, and the golden center grew yellower, intensifying the effect of the finish. By 1921, Cremona Brown became a stain option.

In the old Gibson catalogs, under the heading "Finish and Decorations," Golden Sunburst is used to describe the golden brown, amber, yellow, or golden yellow area of the top around the bridge. A typical catalog description in the late 1920s of the F-4 mandolin and the L-4 guitar reads: "...British Honduras Mahogany neck, shaded to match the sounding-board and back-board which are finished in rich dark mahogany shaded to golden 'sunburst'."

By 1922, the Red Mahogany Sunburst had a three-shade look with a very dark brown at the rim, blending to a bright red, blending to the golden burst. The catalog described the finish as "rich dark mahogany shaded to a golden 'sunburst'…reflected lights and shadows in the dark red mahogany finish…exquisite blending from the dark shades to the glowing sunburst in the center."

Basically, shades of walnut brown and red mahogany (or a blend of the two) have colored the tops, necks, backs, and sides of Gibson instruments made from spruce, maple, birch, and mahogany, from the earliest days until the present. Sometimes these browns—especially in the 1940s and early '50s—appear to have a subtle hint of green in it, probably from the yellow and black pairing. If you added green however, you'd be wrong, and every model doesn't have this look. Red became less prevalent during the 1940s and early '50s, but it was always used, returning in force as Cherry Red in 1958.

Gibson generally stained the birch backs and sides of the instruments we've seen—the majority of which have been mandolins—with this deep transparent red mahogany brown, also described as Rich Dark Mahogany in Gibson's 1912 catalog. We've also seen models with backs and sides (or backs, sides, and *tops* as well) stained in the Sheraton Brown.

When Gibson introduced the original Lloyd Loar-signed Master Model instrument family in June 1922, the majority were shaded a dark Cremona Brown over a golden, almost olive-oil colored center, and red was absent. (Loar's family of Gibson instruments included the L-5 guitar, F-5 mandolin, H-5 mandola, and K-5 mandocello.) Toward the end of the Loar era, which ended in December 1924, the sunbursts on these 5-style instruments became even darker and "greener." Throughout the period, however, a significant number of Loar instruments received a lighter shading, resembling more what many call tobacco today.

Mandolins and guitars underwent change as the Roaring 20s approached. Gibson mandolin necks were made from cherry up to about 1912 and mahogany thereafter, although most of the guitar necks from the same period were mahogany. Later, Gibson introduced maple as a neck wood on higher-end models of the Master 5-style instruments. The necks were finished in natural until the sunburst evolved, at which time some areas of the neck and peghead received sunbursting to match the body. Prior to 1914 or 1915, most necks were unstained, and the body staining stopped cleanly at the neck joint. After 1915, the body staining continued onto the neck, fading out down the neck just past the heel area.

By the early 1930s mahogany necks received the same overall dark walnut or dark mahogany stain or "toner" that the backs and sides received. Maple-neck Master Models usually received a sunburst. However, maple necks on some guitar models received an all-over dark walnut stain to match the body color.

According to some sources, Gibson began spray-finishing with lacquer around 1925. Spray-finishing brought a new, one might say cleaner, look to sunbursting, since most of the colors were applied by spraying as well. Although, to many, nothing quite equals the deep, dark, moody, golden-olive quality and chatoyance of the hand-rubbed Loar Cremona Brown sunbursts, we believe that the early-30s sprayed finishes are stunningly beautiful in their own right with such subtle combinations of yellow, gold, red, amber, brown, and black. The 1934 L-5 is an example of spray-lacquer sunbursting at its best—the type that became the new inspiration for the sunbursts we know today.

Gibson seems to have had a variety of names for what in reality were only a couple of shades of the dark walnut brown, and deep, wine red mahogany used as stains and shaders over a golden yellow base when sunbursting the top or back, or as an overall toner for the backs and sides of non-sunbursted models. These included: Cremona Brown, Rich Chocolate Brown, Deep Red Mahogany, Transparent Chocolate Brown, Brown Mahogany, and Sheraton Brown.

A Changing Order—Gibson at Mid-century and Beyond

Gibson's approach to coloring changed in the 1930s. The stains went from being in the wood to lying on top of the wood over clear sealer coats. Spray lacquer finishing lent itself to applying colored lacquer quickly and easily to the instrument. The tell-tale sign of this change is that the figure and grain character of the wood becomes somewhat or completely obscured at the dark edges. By the mid-1930s few instruments got on-bare-wood staining or many other hand-applied treatments.

Color changed too, especially red, which waned during the 1930s. With the advent of lacquer finishing and lacquer-compatible products, perhaps red became a bother to use with its tendency towards fading and bleeding. Perhaps red just wasn't as popular a color as it had been. It simply may have been an expensive color, and we certainly know it can be difficult to use in terms of bleeding onto bindings and into surrounding finish. Red didn't disappear entirely, and of course we see red in many sunbursts throughout Gibson's history, but it seems Gibson reserved it for the more expensive models during the '30s. The lower-priced models, which Gibson cranked out, got an orange amber centered sunburst with very dark brown or black shaded edges.

By the early 1940s, the name Golden Sunburst truly was an appropriate name for the ambered brown look of Gibson guitar models (mandolins had long since taken a back seat). The finish often lacked any visible red, though surely red was a component of the ambers, golds, and browns. These plainer Gibson sunbursts were still beautiful enough to become the benchmark of the industry, however, and they changed very little until well into the 1950s.

In the mid-to late-50s, Gibson began using red more prominently again. At the same time, Fender seemed to have followed Gibson's lead because they added red to change from a "Two-Tone," to a "Three-Tone" burst.

In mid-1958 Gibson replaced the Les Paul Gold Top and brown shading with a cherry-over-yellow sunburst top accompanied by a cherry-shaded neck, back, and sides. At the same time, it seems that

TECH TIP

"Chatoyance" is a jeweler's term to describe the movement, depth, and brilliance of a rare stone. In woodworking it describes the depth and flash of beautifully figured wood grain.

stronger reds again became prevalent on Gibson's finishing palettes, even extending to lower-priced guitars. Certainly the color and the term Cherry Red had joined Gibson's finishing history forever.

The term Tobacco Sunburst, which is used by so many today to describe almost any vintage sunburst, seems to have first appeared in a 1976 Gibson price list, describing the somewhat lackluster two-tone sunbursts used on lower-end instruments at that time. Tobacco may well describe Gibson sunbursts of the 70s, even on many from their top-of-the-line instruments at the time, which left much to be desired when compared to earlier finishes. But tobacco does not describe the gorgeous sunbursts inspired by Lloyd Loar and developed by his successors during Gibson's fifty year reign as the "king of color" lasting from the teens into the 1960s.

Gibson-style Tobacco Sunbursts

This is the most common Gibson sunburst. Found on models from the ES-125 on up, it features a golden brown sunburst top with a dark walnut stain on the neck, back, and sides (on higher-end models the back, neck, and sides are also sunbursted). Typical of the Gibson sunbursts from the 1940s until the present, this finish inspired the modern term tobacco sunburst in the mid '70s. You'll find it on models with either mahogany or maple backs and sides, necks of either mahogany or maple, and tops of either maple, or spruce. This finish was used not just on the ES-125, but on lots of models, including: flattops like the J-45 and SJ; archtops and archtop electrics like the L-4C, L-7C, ES-150 and ES-175; and on semi-hollowbody models such as the ES-225, ES-335, ES-345; and the list goes on.

As we stated before, this is our guess at how a vintage 1950s Gibson sunburst was probably done. Note that it has less taping and fewer steps than the recipe which follows it. Gibson may have bolder than we can emulate since they sprayed hundreds of any given model. They were able to cover up mistakes by simply spraying a darker color, and even had the luxury of being able to destroy a guitar from time to time if things went too far wrong. Also, the dark grain filler is applied directly to the bare wood, a time-saving short cut.

Since most of you are not in a factory situation with hundreds of guitars to practice on, you might want to consider more masking at various stages of this recipe. For example, you'll probably want to mask off the spruce or maple top while grain filling and spraying dark stain on the back and sides. Also, some extra masking keeps color off the binding at almost every stage. This means that you will not end up with a deep "trench" from scraping color off the binding (the trench is typical of vintage Gibson finishes, however the choice is yours). Masking around the peghead area while coloring the face black keeps overspray off the rest of the peghead. These extra measures are cheap insurance against mistakes that could happen to your precious, once-in-a-lifetime refinishing job and hand-built instruments.

ES-125 TOBACCO SUNBURST — RECIPE 14

1. Mask off the fingerboard, nut, and fingerboard edges (bound or unbound). On flattop acoustics, use a soundhole plug as described in "Masking-off the instrument" (see Chapter 9).
2. Wipe or spray walnut brown water stain on neck, back, and sides. Let it dry.
3. Fill mahogany surfaces with dark walnut grain filler (quick-mask a maple body adjoining a mahogany neck). Let dry several days.
4. Spray two wash coats, 30 minutes apart, on the entire instrument; make an extra pass on the top to get more build there. (Note: It appears that Gibson recently removed the fingerboard edge mask, most likely to avoid a built-up ledge of clear along the edge of the fingerboard. We say this because the top shader about to be sprayed often covers the fingerboard edge on the extension as well as part of the heel).

- 4 ounces walnut brown water stain or NGR stain
- 3 ounces dark walnut grain filler
- 6 to 8 ounces wash coat of choice
- Small amount black peghead lacquer
- 6 to 8 ounces yellow lacquer toner
- 2/3 quart or less ready-to-spray lacquer sanding sealer
- 4 to 6 ounces walnut brown (and/or red brown mahogany) lacquer shader
- 1-1/2 to 2-1/2 quarts clear lacquer ready-to-spray (you'll use more lacquer if you don't use the sanding sealer)

5. Scuff-sand the peghead face to clean off any brown overspray, and shoot a coat of black lacquer on the face. Shoot the lacquer from the center out and always off an edge, not onto one, so that the color doesn't get on the sides. (Option: You may want to run a quick-mask around the edges of the peghead before spraying the black lacquer, but it's doubtful that Gibson did.) Scrape pearl inlays clean while the lacquer's still soft.

6. Shoot yellow lacquer toner on the top. If there are dust specks, you may color-sand them off with 500-grit or finer, but don't actually scuff-sand. (Color-sanding is simply wiping a smooth sandpaper across dust specks in a color coat—preferably while blowing the area with compressed air to prevent scratches.)

7. Optional: Spray a coat of clear lacquer or sanding sealer over the yellow toner to protect it. Make it smooth, and do no sanding other than wipe-sanding.

8. Spray a sunburst with your choice of a brown lacquer shader. Do not sand! Let dry several hours then spray a coat of clear lacquer to lock in the colors and protect them when you scrape the binding. Let the clear dry 30 minutes to an hour so the lacquer is still soft.

9. Scrape the binding and scrape any color from the fingerboard side dots.

10. Spray 6 to 8 coats of clear lacquer, hang to cure for a week or more, then final-sand and buff as normal.

RECIPE 15	**MODERN FACTORY COLOR JOB**

Here's a modern factory approach to getting the same basic look as the above recipe. If you compare the two, this one will not be as handsome, but *you avoid numerous problems* by not staining or filling the bare wood. Most factories would skip the maskings.

Optional: 2/3 quart ready-to-spray vinyl sealer or lacquer sanding sealer

6 to 8 ounce wash coat (vinyl sealer, lacquer sanding sealer, or clear lacquer)

3 ounces dark walnut grain filler

320-grit no-load paper

4 to 6 ounces yellow lacquer toner

6 to 8 ounces walnut brown lacquer toner

Black Peghead Face Lacquer (see Recipe 3)

Optional: 4 to 6 ounces a red brown lacquer shader in addition to the walnut brown mentioned above

1-1/2 to 2-1/2 quarts ready-to-spray clear lacquer (you'll use the higher amount if you don't use the sanding sealer)

1. Mask off the fingerboard, the nut, and the peghead face (masking body binding is optional). On flattop acoustics, use a soundhole mask.

2. Optional: On a spruce top, spray two coats of a heavier-bodied sealer or vinyl sealer. If you're using clear lacquer instead of a sealer, spray three or four coats.

3. Wash coat the entire instrument with a thin wash coat of your choice.

4. Protect top with mask, or else be careful. Fill open-pore necks, backs and sides using a dark walnut grain filler, wipe off any residue carefully (a rag damp with an appropriate solvent may help), and let it dry at least several days.

5. Wash coat filled surfaces to lock in filler.

6. Optional: Scuff-sand a lacquered spruce top.

7. Spray one coat of sanding sealer or vinyl sealer (or two coats of clear lacquer) on entire instrument. Let dry. Scuff-sand lightly if necessary to remove dust specks.

8. Optional: Quick-mask sides from yellow toner.

9. Spray yellow toner on top and let dry to touch.

10. Optional: Quick-mask top from brown body toner.

11. Tape off fingerboard edges.

12. Spray walnut brown toner on neck, back, and sides.

13. Sunburst top with a walnut brown shader. You may choose to use the same toner just used on the neck, back, and sides, or simply add some darker pigment to it.

14. Remove peghead face mask, quick-mask (optional) exposed areas around peghead, and blacken the peghead face.

15. Scrape color from binding, pearl, and other areas as needed.

16. Spray four to eight coats clear lacquer, allowing two hours between coats and drying overnight halfway through. Proceed with finish-sanding and buffing.

TOP O' THE LINE SHADED FINISH — RECIPE 16

Here's how you can reproduce the beautiful all-over shaded finishes used from the 1920s until the present on Gibson's higher models. These guitars, such as the Nick Lucas, the J-200 flat tops, and a host of fancy archtops, were made of maple or maple and spruce. For us, this type of finish brings to mind in particular Gibson's 1950s finishes on the L-5, ES-5 Switchmaster, Super-400, ES-350, and others of similar stature.

In this recipe, all the color is on top of clear sealer coats. This finish is more than just a sunburst. The top and back are sunbursted in normal fashion, but areas of the sides, waist, butt, shoulders, neck heel, rear of the peghead, and even the tips of the peghead are also highlighted with the sunburst colors.

1. Sand the maple well, to about a 220-grit, and consider combining grain raising with grain enhancement as described in the "Vintage-style Sunburst on Figured Maple and Spruce" recipe.

2. Quick-mask around the peghead and the fretboard, leaving the face exposed, then spray the peghead face with Black Peghead Face Lacquer. Scrape the black from the pearl inlay within an hour or less of spraying so it removes easily. Let dry an hour or two.

3. Unmask the peghead and scrape away any black lacquer that might have gotten on the binding.

4. Spray a thin wash coat on entire instrument to prime the wood.

5. For spruce tops only: Spray a coat or two of ready-to-spray sealer or clear lacquer on the top only because spruce soaks up finish more than maple does. Allow 30 minutes between coats.

6. Seal the entire instrument with a coat of sealer, or clear lacquer if you don't use sanding sealer. This will be the top's second or third coat. Dry several hours or overnight.

7. Scuff-sand the instrument lightly with 220-grit no-load paper. Tape off the binding now if you want to avoid heavy scraping later (optional).

8. Spray a coat of transparent yellow lacquer over the entire instrument. Only include the peghead face if you want the aged look over the pearl or black; otherwise just avoid the face, which you really shouldn't need to tape off.

Black Peghead Face Lacquer (see Recipe 3)

6 to 8 ounces wash coat material

1 quart clear lacquer sanding sealer (or sealer of your choice)

220-grit no-load sandpaper

8 ounces each lacquer shader or toner (or enough to fill your sunbursting spray gun) in the following colors (or any mix of the colors—use your eye)

Transparent yellow

Transparent red

Transparent brown

Pigmented brown/black (pigment add to a transparent brown base)

1-1/2 quarts clear lacquer

800-grit wet-or-dry paper (or finer)

Optional: 8 ounces of a 1-pound or 2-pound cut of shellac

9. Spray two coats of clear lacquer to lock in the yellow toner. On this round, spray the peghead face too.

10. Spray the remaining transparent colors, beginning with red, then brown, then darker brown black. Work from the center out to the edge for the sunburst. Spray other portions of the guitar as you please to highlight them (sides, waist, butt, shoulders, neck heel, and so forth). Overall, you want to use as little color as possible to keep the finish thin.

11. After the color coats have dried several hours, lock them in with a coat of clear lacquer. Let dry until the surface can be touched.

12. Remove masking (if any) and scrape all color from binding.

13. Spray two light coats of lacquer, 30 minutes apart, to lock in the color and the scraped binding. Let dry an hour.

14. Spray four coats lacquer two hours apart. Dry overnight.

15. Scuff-sand with 220-grit Fre-Cut paper and let instrument hang a day to release solvents.

16. Spray four more coats lacquer two hours apart. Dry two weeks.

17. Wet-sand with 800-grit wet-or-dry paper (or finer) and polish or buff as normal.

Variation

If you've learned to handle shellac, a wash coat of fresh shellac used at Step 4 will make the wood look gorgeous. It will also stop up the wood enough that less sealer will be needed in Steps 5 and 6. If you use shellac, let it dry four hours before sanding with 220-grit no-load paper. If you sand through, touch up the area with more shellac, or spray a second coat.

Some of Gibson's most beautiful sunbursts weren't sprayed with lacquer shaders at all. The stain was wiped or sprayed on the bare wood (see Chapter 9, Step 2: Transparent Stain on Bare Wood). You look through the coats of clear lacquer at wood which has been beautifully colored, not obscured by shading. You can see some of these older sunbursts at vintage guitar shows or by visiting stores that handle vintage instruments. Once you've seen the best (and photos aren't enough), you'll do a better job of sunbursting with lacquer shaders because you'll have that beautiful goal in your mind's eye. If you're trying to duplicate the beauty of stained wood, you'll layer your colors more thoughtfully, perhaps a bit more lightly, and certainly you'll be less likely to obscure the wood needlessly with shaders that are too strong.

Here's our version of an old-style sunburst that combines the best of both worlds: 1920s-style staining applied directly on the wood and a sunburst applied with a spray gun in 1930's fashion for uniformity and a modern look. This is a great looking sunburst finish on any instrument with maple back and sides and a spruce top. Don MacRostie developed this finishing schedule over a period of twenty years and uses it on his acclaimed Red Diamond mandolins. What makes this method most unique is the use of a water stain, instead of plain water, for raising the grain during the wood prep stage.

Grain enhancement is not widely used in production, and is a technique more likely to be used on hand-crafted instruments made in small batches by craftsmen who are not under production schedule pressures. It's done during the damp-sanding stage of wood preparation. If you have to damp sand anyway, using color isn't really adding much extra work.

We're using water stain for our color and applying it in two steps: Step 1 enhances the grain, or figure of the wood, prior to final sanding; Step 2 creates the sunburst. The initial coloring is a sprayed sunburst that gets sanded back almost to bare wood, but some of the color remains down in the figure of the wood grain. When it is followed with the final sprayed sunburst, the enhanced grain really stands out, making even mediocre wood look great! The wood grain is not obscured because the color is directly in the wood, and the water stain is not dissolved by the topcoats. Water stains are very light fast, so the color stays true. Other advantages of this approach to a sunburst are that water stain sand-throughs are easily touched up and the entire finish can be thinner without the build up of color coats.

To reproduce the lovely yellow tones of a vintage sunburst we have made another adjustment to modern materials, specifically the yellow stain. In the late 1960s the mainstay yellow dye became no longer available (it was rumored that the colorants were carcinogenic). The new yellow was more fluorescent looking than the older yellow, which had been nice and warm. In this recipe, we add a bare hint of red to the yellow to get that golden yellow look.

VINTAGE-STYLE SUNBURST ON FIGURED MAPLE AND SPRUCE — RECIPE 17

One caveat: Because the finish is water based, you must take care to go lightly and not warp the wood by over wetting it. Finally, be sure to save some of each stain color for touchup later if necessary. That will be easy because we call for 3 to 4 ounces of stain to fill your spray gun cup properly. That will leave plenty left over for touchups.

1. Mix the sunburst stains with distilled water in at least three colors, namely yellow (amber), red brown (mahogany), and dark brown (walnut). Distilled water makes stains last longer because it resists microbial growth.

2. Spray or wipe (wiping is quicker) the yellow stain on the center of the top and back, center of the neck, and spots on the sides and peghead that require the light shade of the sunburst. You may also color areas that will later be covered with darker stain, but it is not necessary.

3. Spray or wipe at least two coats of red brown stain around the edges of the yellow center, overlapping and reducing the yellow areas. Let stain dry 30 minutes between coats under good conditions. If spraying, use a higher air pressure, around 60 psi, and keep the fluid valve fairly closed. This will provide a finely atomized spray and a droplet-free look. Keep away from the center! Be

- 3 to 4 ounces yellow stain to which a small amount of red is added in a ratio of about 200 to 1
- 3 to 4 ounces red brown stain
- 3 to 4 ounces dark walnut brown stain (mix this with 10 to 20% black stain if a darker sunburst is desired)
- 150- to 180-grit no-load sandpaper
- Masking and pinstriping guide tape
- 4 to 6 ounces shellac in a 2-pound cut
- 1-1/2 pints clear ready-to-spray lacquer

Chapter 10: Finishing Recipes

careful not to spray so much stain that it runs. It may take two sprayings of any one color to obtain the shade of darkness you desire.

4. Spray or wipe the dark brown water stain around just the edge. You could add some black to the dark brown stain mix to darken it even more. Let dry thoroughly, overnight at least.

5. Next day, sand back to the wood using 150- to 180-grit paper. Sand until the instrument is almost to the white wood stage. Spots in the figure will be impossible to sand back white because they've absorbed stain and become highlighted. Look for areas that need extra work, such as glue residue around bindings, sanding scratches left by previous coarse grits, or dings and sinks in the wood.

6. For enhancement repeat steps 1-5. This serves as the final sanding of the wood. Now proceed to the final sunburst.

7. With pinstriping guide tape, mask off the binding where you're able, especially the sides. You needn't tape off the top edge of the binding because it scrapes easily. Mask the nut and fingerboard, and block off sound holes.

8. Repeat the sunbursting procedure in steps 1 through 4. On this final burst, carefully shade one color into the next. This can be done by maintaining good atomization and by keeping a good distance between the gun and the instrument. Keep the color even and symmetrical from one side to the other—this is the artistic part! Be careful to fade the yellow out so as not to leave a hard edge of color. Let it cover a little further toward the edges than the first application. Also, keep the red brown away from the outer edge so it will be a good neutral brown unaffected by the red tones. Spray two to three dark walnut coats to reach the level of darkness desired. Don't spray so much that the color runs, though, or you will have to redo that portion of the instrument. Let dry a day or two.

9. Spray a wash coat or two of shellac. This will protect the sunburst from any handling while you remove the masking and scrape the bindings. It's especially important to seal in the water soluble stains when you are using a topcoat of lacquer, which will redissolve stain. Let shellac dry 6 to 8 hours.

10. Remove the tape and scrape your bindings. The top edge of the binding will need the most scraping if it wasn't taped. A trick used by Gibson is to leave a little (.005 inch) of the innermost layer of white binding unscraped and thus covered with the darkest sunburst color. This reveals enough binding and creates a clean edge between binding and color without the risk of scraping into bare wood which always shows, and looks bad.

Another solution is to use an inner layer of black binding which gets overpsrayed with color along with the innermost white layer. Then, when you scrape the white, you're actually scraping to black. If you screw up, you have a margin of safety with the black.

11. Spray five to eight coats of clear lacquer, allowing 45 minutes between coats, and sanding between every two or three coats to level the surface. After spraying the last two coats, let the finish cure three or four days or longer.

12. Wet-sand and buff as normal.

TECH TIP

A close look at vintage Gibson pegheads might make one think they just wiped a bare fingertip (maybe wrapped in a rag)—alongside the peghead to remove any slight overspray of black—like wiping a runny nose (this author will admit to having performed both acts). Also, we've known finishers who use a rag dampened with a mixture of 1 part lacquer thinner to 5 parts naphtha as an overspray wipe in this situation—just enough thinner to cut, and the naphtha washes things clean.

Very Cherry Reds

Transparent cherry red is a great looking color on mahogany, and in our books Gibson does it best. The look first appeared on its 1958 Les Paul Standard, and soon the color appeared on many models including the SG, ES-335 (and others in the semi-hollowbody series), and acoustic flattops such as the J-45 and Hummingbird. We've even seen a high-end maple-and-spruce archtop, a George Gobel L-5, entirely finished in cherry red. Cherry red is a very popular finish, and there are many subtle differences between the reds of different eras. That's why we devote a good bit of space to it here.

Between 1958 and about 1970, Gibson used a cherry red grain filler on many models with mahogany necks and bodies. The filler was colored with red, or a reddish brown pigment combined with a transparent cherry red dye, and it served as both a stain and filler. The pigment colored the filler; the dye not only stained the wood but, being soluble in lacquer, it bled instantly into clear lacquer sprayed over it. This bleeding turned the clear lacquer, to some degree, into a transparent red lacquer toner. So the red filler really accomplished three jobs: pore-filling, staining, and toning.

Former Gibson Kalamazoo shop supervisor Marv Lamb got Gibson to eliminate the cherry filler. "You'd see those blurry spots floating around in the clear finish when the red migrated into the lacquer," says Lamb, now a part owner and veteran guitar builder at Heritage Guitars. "And another problem with the old red filler was that it would bleed onto the binding and turn it red. Red is the one color that always wants to bleed."

Worse yet, the process contaminated the shop. "We wiped the filler on with what we called hemp—it was coarse cloth, like burlap, with hairy fibers. Dry, red hemp fibers would float in the air throughout the finishing area, and any natural instrument—even a hundred feet away—would get red spots in the clear finish from those fibers."

Lamb says Gibson dropped the red filler around 1970 and switched to using a walnut filler on the bare wood with a red toner sprayed over it (see Recipe 24, "Modern Factory Cherry Red"). The walnut filler didn't bleed onto the binding as the red did. When Gibson switched to red toner from filler, it used two processes: red toning of the back and sides with a weaker red shading of the sunburst top to make it brighter and more transparent.

Despite what Lamb and others at Gibson thought of the shortcomings of cherry filler, vintage guitar lovers don't mind the floating red spots or the reddish tinge of the binding. In fact, they'll pay for a finisher who can achieve the look. However, Gibson used several shades of red filler over a dozen years, changing the color. The earlier red filler produced a brighter, more cherry color than the filler of the late '60s, which was a darker, more burgundy color.

It's also common knowledge that some of the red dyes Gibson used in the late 1950s and early 1960s faded quite dramatically when exposed to ultraviolet light. Finishes colored with these reds had become significantly lighter as early as 1966, and of course, they have faded even more in the thirty years since. (Like most aspects of vintage guitar appreciation, the look is popular—a vintage Les Paul with a faded cherry sunburst, neck, back, and sides is known as an "Ice Tea" sunburst and is highly desirable).

If you study a number of cherry red finishes from 1958 to 1964 you'll find that all the reds did not fade equally. The red stains used on maple portions of given models, such as ES-335 and other models from that series, or a cherry red 1959 'George Gobel' maple and spruce model that we've seen, have held their red nicely.

As a rule, it's the mahogany parts colored with cherry grain filler that have faded most. This leads us to believe that the red grain filler was colored with a different (cheaper, perhaps) red dye than Gibson's NGR-stains, water stains, lacquer toners and shaders. It's now known that lacquer/oil-soluble dyes in general tend to fade more than water- or alcohol-soluble dyes do (especially reds), and we generally avoid using them for that reason.

When duplicating the old cherry filler, however, the old style lacquer-soluble dyes are just what the doctor ordered because the finish will fade in direct sunlight. However, the old-style fading dyes are being replaced by modern dyes that are better because they don't fade. So do some experimenting on scrap, using weaker mixes of modern pigments and dyes to come up with a cherry stain or filler that gives you the look you want today, without waiting thirty years.

RECIPE 18	**CHERRY RED GRAIN FILLER**

In researching a Gibson cherry filler that gives an old vintage look, we tried adding a number of colorants to both dark-brown walnut grain filler and natural filler. We found that by adding the red colorant to an already dark grain filler, we got a good facsimile of the later '60s dark burgundy filler. But to color a filler for the old faded look, we used the neutral grain filler as our base and experimented with different colorants until we got what we wanted. Our mixing method of milling the powders into a solvent-based paste before adding it to the filler prevents any undissolved chunks of powder that could cause dark streaks of color in the finish. Here's our secret revealed.

1 ounce Mohawk 242 red Blendal™ powdered fresco pigment stain

Small amount naphtha

1 quart natura colored grain filler (any brand)

2 ounces Mohawk #363 02424 red lacquer/oil-soluble powdered red dye

1. In a small dish, using the back of a spoon, mill the fresco powder into a small amount of naphtha until it becomes a smooth paste. Then add a little more naphtha, working it in until it becomes a thick liquid. Then add it to the filler and mill it in.

2. Using the same milling method, add the powdered lacquer/oil-soluble dye into a small amount of naphtha, then add it to the filler which already contains the milled fresco powder. You could cut the dye into a small amount of lacquer thinner instead of naphtha if you prefer.

3. In a tightly capped jar, this filler will be good for several years.

'58 VINTAGE CHERRY SUNBURST

RECIPE 19

How did a '58 Gibson Cherry Sunburst Les Paul get its subtle red tones? We give you the original recipe below, but it's followed by a variation for the post-'70s approach, just in case your vintage leanings are to a slightly later era. The post-'70s schedule can produce a good-looking cherry red finish too, and it can be done with the same dark walnut grain filler you may already have in your shop.

1. Mask or quick-mask the fretboard, fretboard binding, top, body binding, and peghead face.

2. Apply cherry red filler to the neck, back, and rims. After removing the residue let it dry at least two days.

3. Unmask the top and the bindings. Clean any red filler from the bindings with solvent, sanding, and scraping.

4. Seal the entire instrument, except the peghead face, with two coats of clear lacquer or lacquer sanding sealer: wait 30 minutes between coats. The lacquer-soluble red dye in the filler will pop to life when the lacquer hits it, and the guitar will be much redder than you might have thought. Let dry overnight.

5. Quick-mask around the peghead and the fretboard, leaving the face exposed, then spray the peghead face with Black Peghead Face Lacquer. Scrape the black from the pearl inlay within an hour or less of spraying so it removes easily. Let dry an hour or two.

6. Scuff-sand the top with 320-grit Fre-Cut paper to smooth it. Quick-mask the sides, the neck heel, the fretboard binding, and the side of the body binding with paper and a light adhesive masking tape like draftsman's tape. Spray a coat of transparent yellow lacquer on the top. This "toner" should be well-thinned but strong, without turning watery or runny, so it colors quickly without producing a thick coat. Remove the masks and let the yellow dry two hours, or overnight if possible.

7. Wipe-sand the toner lightly to remove dust specks, and seal in the yellow with two coats of clear lacquer, waiting an hour or so in between. Spray these over the entire instrument so the number of coats is consistent on the guitar overall. Dry overnight.

8. Wipe-sand the top lightly, and mask off the fretboard binding and the side of the body binding. Don't worry about getting red on the thin top edge of the body binding—it scrapes easily. Spray the 'burst with transparent red lacquer. Dry 30 minutes.

9. Remove the binding mask and scrape the red from the top edge of the body binding.

10. Spray from 6 to 8 coats of clear lacquer, applying three coats a day, with two hours between coats.

11. Hang two weeks then wet-sand and buff as usual.

Masking tape

2 ounces Cherry Red Grain Filler (see Recipe 18)

1-1/2 quarts clear ready-to-spray lacquer (or more, if you are also using it as your sealer)

320-grit Fre-Cut sandpaper

Quick-mask, masking paper, and draftsman's tape (or similar masking materials)

6 to 8 ounces transparent yellow lacquer

6 to 8 ounces transparent cherry red lacquer

Black Peghead Face Lacquer (see Recipe 3)

Variations

Cherry red using walnut grain filler. Substitute the following steps into the above schedule where indicated:

At Step 2, instead of cherry filler, use the dark walnut grain filler on the bare wood.

After Step 7, quick-mask the top, fretboard binding, and body binding (use light adhesive), then spray transparent cherry lacquer over the sides, back, and neck to imitate the cherry-filler-under-lacquer look. You may need to mix a second, darker version of transparent cherry lacquer for the mahogany to get the effect you're after, so practice on scrap!

Unmask the top (leave a mask on the bindings) and go on to Step 8—sunbursting the top. Again, you may use the exact same transparent red for everything or you may choose a darker red for the mahogany portions.

Proceed with remainder of recipe.

Pigmented shader

For a year or two, around 1960, Gibson used a red pigmented shader because their transparent red dye was fading so badly. Color your cherry shader with red liquid pigment instead of red transparent dye if you want the different look of this era.

Skip masking step before the filler, if you want to emulate the big guys. Gibson didn't mask before putting on filler because, as Lamb points out, for a large guitar company that is an expensive, time-consuming step if you can get by without it. Instead Gibson finishers applied the filler with a brush. "We were careful, and we were good at it. Whatever little bit of red got onto the top we sanded off once it dried," Lamb said. Nor did Gibson finishers tape off the fretboard or bindings. Binding was scraped clean after the sunbursting, toning, shading, and sealing steps.

RECIPE 20	**CHERRY RED 335**

Unless you get a job at Gibson, most of you will never have a chance to put this finish on a new ES-335 (one of Gibson's ES-series semi-hollowbody guitar models which have laminated plywood maple bodies and solid mahogany necks), because laminated guitars are just too tough to build. Other models in the series include the ES-330, ES-345, and ES-355. Originally these models were finished in sunburst, with natural as on option, until cherry red became popular at the end of the 1950s. You may have cause to refinish an ES-series semi-hollowbody in your careers, though, and this recipe will help you get professional results.

Here is our recommendation of how to put a cherry red finish on a guitar with a maple body and mahogany neck so it looks like a late '50s or early '60s ES-335. This finish replicates the beauty of a new ES-355 before succumbing to the inevitable fading that many red-stained Gibsons from this era suffered.

1. Mask the fingerboard, fingerboard binding, and flat, wide side of body binding. Taping body binding is optional; you may prefer to scrape it just like Gibson would have done.

2. Quick-mask around the peghead and the fretboard, leaving the face exposed. Then spray the peghead face with Black Peghead Face Lacquer. Scrape the black from the pearl inlay within an hour or less of spraying so it removes easily. Let dry an hour or two.

3. Mask several inches of the neck heel at the body joint, and wipe or spray a red stain on the body. Mask the neck close to the body joint, but not right to the line. Then lay down a second, more temporary, mask on top of the first tape to bring you up to the line. You can peel off this secondary mask to inspect after the coloring operation, and before shooting a seal coat, without undoing the entire masking job.

4. Exchange the secondary mask for a fresh one, and with the mask still protecting the bare neck, spray two wash coats on the body, allowing 15 minutes between coats. Remove any neck masking and let the wash coat dry several hours. Now the body can be handled and taped when necessary.

5. Quick-mask the body in the area around the neck joint using low-tack draftsman's tape, and fill the neck with a cherry red grain filler. This will also stain the wood. Remove the excess filler; remove the quick-mask, and let the filler dry several days if possible. (Note: You can use dark walnut grain filler instead of the cherry filler and get the red look entirely from cherry toner in Step 7. Other cherry red on mahogany options are given in the next recipe, "SG Red".)

6. Wipe the neck clean of residue and spray two wash coats on the neck, fifteen minutes apart. Let dry two hours.

7. Check the neck for color. If you're not happy, use a cherry red toner to highlight it or to even out weak areas, but try to avoid toning too heavily. This is where you might add some yellow, orange, or brown to shift the hue of the cherry red.

9. Remove binding mask and scrape any color on the binding (there shouldn't be much).

10. Optional: If you toned the neck, spray one light coat of clear lacquer to lock in the toner, and let it dry 30 minutes.

11. Spray clear lacquer on the entire guitar. Make sure the first two coats aren't too wet to avoid moving color around. Spray four coats the first day, waiting two hours between coats, and dry overnight.

12. Level-sand (but carefully, you must not sand into color) with 220-grit no-load paper. Spray four more coats of lacquer two hours apart, then let the guitar hang for two weeks.

13. Wet-sand and buff as usual.

Masking tape, draftsman's tape, and clean paper

Black Peghead Face Lacquer (see Recipe 3)

4 to 6 ounces red stain (see Chapter 3 for advantages and disadvantages of water and alcohol stain). You may need to add yellow, orange, or brown to an existing red stain to get the shade you're after (which could be a burgundy, orange, or cherry depending upon the era and look you're after).

4 to 6 ounces wash coat of choice

1 ounce Cherry Red Grain Filler (see Recipe 18)

Optional: 4 to 6 ounces cherry red toner, with a hint of yellow, orange, or brown to shift color to your taste

1-1/2 to 2 quarts clear lacquer

Optional: 6 to 8 ounces vinyl sanding sealer or lacquer sanding sealer

1-1/2 quarts clear lacquer (more if you use the clear lacquer for your sealer)

SG Reds

There are numerous ways to go about most finishes, and SG Reds are no exception. Here's several approaches to replicating the cherry red finish used on a Gibson SG or Les Paul Junior; the neck of a cherry red ES-335; the neck, back, and sides of a '59 Les Paul; Hamer's Eclipse, Parker's Fly; and other transparent cherry-on-mahogany-colored guitars that we love so much.

The old way is to use a cherry red grain filler, which you have to make yourself. While we used cherry filler in the last few recipes, these use an of-the-shelf dark walnut brown grain filler. Using the materials listed below, you can concoct recipes 'til the devil won't have it. Finishing materials are like pieces in a Scrabble game; all you need is a good vocabulary. Hopefully, by giving you several recipes, as we do below, we'll inspire you to be creative.

RECIPE 21 — CLOSE-TO-THE-WOOD CHERRY RED

This is as close as you'll get to using a red grain filler without using one. The dark-filled pores won't have the '58 to early '60s look but will replicate the later burgundy look quite nicely. An advantage of this recipe over the Modern Factory Cherry that follows is the thinner finish due to teh lack of toner coats.

Masking tape

3 to 4 ounces dark-walnut, oil-based grain filler

4 to 8 ounces red NGR stain

6 ounces vinyl wash coat (vinyl sealer thinned to wash coat consistency). Vinyl sealer provides a barrier coat between the NGR stain and the clear lacquer.

Black Peghead Face Lacquer (see Recipe 3)

6 to 8 ounces sealer coat: vinyl sealer, lacquer sanding sealer, or clear lacquer

320-grit no-load sandpaper

1-1/2 quarts clear ready-to-spray lacquer

Lacquer thinner as needed

Optional (for touching up a sand through): 4 ounces of red lacquer toner made from the NGR stain above added to clear lacquer

1. Tape off peghead face and fingerboard.
2. Fill neck and body with a dark walnut oil-base grain filler. Remove residue carefully so you'll barely have to sand it after it's dry. This way, the brown colorant of the filler stains and darkens the mahogany as it fills the pores. Let the filler dry three days.
3. Wipe or spray a red NGR stain on all mahogany surfaces. Wait several minutes, then burnish the surface dry by rubbing lightly and briskly with a clean, dry rag.
4. Spray two vinyl wash coats, one hour apart. Let dry two hours.
5. Remove peghead face mask, quick-mask (optional) exposed areas around peghead, and blacken the peghead face. Dry two hours.
6. Spray two coats vinyl sealer or sanding sealer on entire instrument.
7. Scuff-sand lightly with 320-grit no-load paper. This is where a sand through is likely to happen!
8. Spray 6 to 8 coats of lacquer two hours apart. Let dry overnight half way through schedule. Sand with 220-grit and finish applying coats as above. Let dry one to two weeks. Wet-sand and buff as normal.

Variation

Aerosol option. The finish can be done entirely with aerosol products. Replace sealer and lacquer with two aerosol cans lacquer sanding sealer and 4 cans aerosol clear lacquer. Two Preval or other brands of spray propellant outfits will allow you to load and spray vinyl sealer. You can use red lacquer toner for touching up sand throughs.

MODERN FACTORY CHERRY RED — RECIPE 22

This is how Marv Lamb, founder and key member of the Heritage Guitar Company, described spraying a cherry red finish at Gibson around 1970, after they'd dropped the cherry grain filler. This is still the approach most guitar factories use today.

1. Mask fretboard and peghead face.
2. Fill instrument with dark walnut grain filler. Let dry three days.
3. Clean filler residue from fretboard edges by scraping or sanding.
4. Spray one vinyl wash coat. Let dry one hour.
5. Quick-mask around the peghead and the fretboard, leaving the face exposed, then spray the peghead face with Black Peghead Face Lacquer. Scrape the black from the pearl inlay within an hour or less of spraying so it removes easily. Let dry an hour or two.
6. Spray entire instrument with two coats of vinyl sealer, allowing 30 minutes between coats. Dry several hours.
7. Scuff-sand lightly and very carefully with 320-grit no-load paper, tape off the fretboard edges, and spray a coat of cherry lacquer toner over entire instrument. Dry 30 minutes.
8. Spray a second coat of cherry toner if needed. Let dry another 30 minutes.
9. Spray one coat clear lacquer to protect the toner. Dry one hour.
10. Unmask fretboard edges and clean by sanding or scraping. Scrape bindings and remove all residue. Let dry overnight.
11. Spray 6 to 8 coats clear lacquer, waiting two hours between coats, and sand once with 220-grit in the mid-schedule.
12. Dry a week or more, wet-sand, and buff.

3 to 4 ounces dark walnut oil-based grain filler
4 to 6 ounces vinyl wash coat
Black Peghead Face Lacquer (see Recipe 3)
6 to 8 ounces vinyl sealer
320-grit no-load sandpaper
6 to 8 ounces cherry red lacquer toner
1-1/2 quarts ready-to-spray clear lacquer

EASIER CHERRY RED — RECIPE 23

Here's a cherry red which is a little more user friendly because it substitutes water base products for some of the components.

1. Stain the instrument with a dark walnut water stain. This will help give the necessary dark brown which is not easy to get with waterbase filler. Let dry overnight.
2. Spray a vinyl wash coat. Let dry one hour.
3. Fill the grain with dark brown filler. Within 5 minutes, while the filler dries, sponge off any remaining residue with a damp sponge. With a clean, dry rag, clean up sponge marks and wetness while you work. Dry several hours.
4. Wipe the surface with a red NGR stain. The stain will etch, or color, both the vinyl wash coat and filler at once.
5. Spray a vinyl wash coat to lock in the stain and filler.
6. Quick-mask around the peghead and the fretboard, leaving the face exposed, then spray the peghead face with Black Peghead Face Lacquer. Scrape

2 to 3 ounces dark walnut waterbase stain
6 to 8 ounces vinyl wash coat
2 ounces darkest brown waterbase grain filler available
4 ounces red NGR stain
Black Peghead Face Lacquer (see Recipe 3)
1-1/2 to 2 quarts clear lacquer ready-to-spray

the black from the pearl inlay within an hour or less of spraying so it removes easily. Let dry an hour or two.

7. Proceed with a 6 to 8 coat clear lacquer finishing schedule as described in the previous recipe.

RECIPE 24	**MOSTLY WATERBASE CHERRY RED**

Here's an even friendlier version. It only uses one solvent-based component (a red NGR stain). It still gives a good finish without the usual shop toxicity.

3 to 4 ounces dark walnut waterbase stain
1-1/2 quarts clear waterbase lacquer
2 ounces dark brown waterbase grain filler
2 to 3 ounces cherry red NGR stain
Black Peghead Face Lacquer (see Recipe 3)
220-grit no-load gold sandpaper

1. Wipe-stain the instrument with the dark walnut water stain. Let dry four hours or overnight.

2. Wipe on a coat of waterbase lacquer. Since it's wiped with a rag and straight from the can, the lacquer will go on thin like a normal wash coat. Some, but not much, of the brown stain will come off on your rag, but don't be concerned. Dry two hours.

3. Fill the grain with grain filler. Within 5 minutes, while the filler dries, sponge off any remaining residue with a damp sponge. With a clean, dry rag, clean up sponge marks and wetness while you work. Dry several hours.

4. Once dry, wipe the surface with a red NGR stain. The stain will etch, or color, both the waterbase wash coat and filler at once. Let dry one hour.

5. Spray a light waterbase wash coat to lock in the stain and filler. Let dry one hour.

6. Blacken the peghead as done in the previous recipes.

7. Spray 6 to 8 coats clear waterbase lacquer, sanding halfway through the schedule with 220-grit no-load paper (or sand more often if you feel the need). Gold paper is a better choice than a stearated paper if you're sanding on waterbase lacquer.

8. Cure two weeks or longer; then wet-sand and buff as usual.

RECIPE 25	**FADED CHERRY RED ON MAHOGANY**

Study original examples of a faded cherry red finish on mahogany. Except for the telltale red filler remaining in the pores, it's as if they had never seen cherry at all, and some of those old ES-335 necks look golden brown! The red pigment in the filler remained stable, but the red dye faded because it wasn't a very lightfast. The red also disappeared because certain unstable materials in a coating migrated to the surface. Once it reached the surface, some of the red dye was worn away by the player's hand, on polishing rags, and on the guitar case lining. The faded look, with its warm golden browns, occasional hint of cherry, and distinct splashes of red in the pores, is sought after by guitar lovers (does anyone here remember the popularity of "Madras" shirts in the late '50s and early '60s—and how the reds faded to nothing—but we loved the look?).

1. Stain the neck with a golden yellow brown stain—possibly with a hint of red if you think it's needed. Let dry one hour for alcohol stain and several hours or overnight for waterbase stain.

2. Seal in the stain with a wash coat. Let dry 30 minutes for lacquer and several hours or overnight for shellac wash coat.

3. Fill the grain with the cherry grain filler. Let dry several days for oil-based, or several hours for waterbase.

4. Seal in the filler with a wash coat (again, shellac would be good). Let dry same as Step 2.

5. Optional: Spray Antique Binding Toner if you think you'd like an even more amber look. Let dry two hours.

6. Spray 6 to 8 coats of clear lacquer, allowing two hours between coats, 4 coats a day. Sand after the first four coats with 280-grit paper. Hang two weeks after the last coat and wet-sand and buff as usual.

- 2 to 4 ounces golden yellow brown stain, either waterbase or alcohol-based
- Optional: small amount of red stain of same solubility
- 4 to 6 ounces wash coat of choice (shellac in a 2-pound cut is our favorite because it gives a nice amber tone to the wood)
- 2 to 3 ounces cherry pigmented grain filler that contains no red dye or, at most, very little.
- Optional: Antique Binding Toner (see Recipe 2)
- 1 to 1 1/2 quarts clear, ready-to-spray lacquer

TV Yellow

Gibson's answer to Fender's blond finish was Limed Mahogany, a tan or beige finish first used on the single-cutaway Les Paul TV and Les Paul Special models between 1955 and 1957. Fender and Gibson simply copied the popular blond furniture finishes being used in the 1950s on console television, pianos, and all types of furniture made from mahogany, maple, birch, and ash.

Blond finishes are similar in look to pickled finishes, and they are always light colored (normally a milky, translucent white). The blond finish was formulated to be used on light furniture woods. Ash is a favorite because, although light, it has a strong grain pattern that shows through the milky topcoat with a pleasing effect. Then furniture makers who favored the properties of mahogany decided they could duplicate the blond look so popular on the lighter woods. They whited out the natural brown of mahogany with a thin layer of white or off-white lacquer to make it look light and then toned it with a translucent tan lacquer to give the white a natural wood tone. Then, by filling the pores with a medium toned, raw sienna colored contrasting filler over the white lacquer (this filler is very similar to the golden amber filler that Gibson uses on its natural-filled mahogany instruments like the Les Paul Gold Tops), the mahogany took on the look of a lighter wood—"grain" and all.

Gibson appreciated mahogany and used several variations of limed mahogany between 1955 and 1959, then reissued it 40 years later as both a production and a custom-shop finish at its Gibson USA facility in Nashville, Tennessee. Although an entirely different look than blond on ash, limed mahogany is a great looking finish that today's guitar builders and refinishers imitate often; a look today's players demand.

Though the terms TV-Yellow, TV-Style, and TV-Finish are often used to describe the colors of the finishes we're discussing here, vintage Gibson catalogs never used any of those terms to describe a version of their limed mahogany finish. The TV color names were nicknames that came from the players, not Gibson.

Dan Erlewine remembers, "I always thought TV finish meant the guitar looked like the blond TV sets my parents and most of our neighbors had in the 1950s. Then I heard the name referred to where the guitars would be seen, not how they looked." Gibson formulated the finish to show up better on the new color televisions, which were then hitting the market. And of course TV in the name couldn't hurt marketing; Gibson guitars were prominently featured in Les Paul & Mary Ford's TV show in the '50s.

The blond and limed finishes went through several transformations. When the Les Paul TV and the Les Paul Special became double-cutaway guitars in 1958, their finishes changed too. The TV and Special traded the first rendition of limed mahogany for a "brand-new shade of limed mahogany, much finer than the former one," Gibson's 1958 catalog boasted. This brighter, almost banana colored version of beige was described in 1958 and 1959 catalogs as both a "new shade of limed mahogany," and a "cream finish." Whether you call them Limed Mahogany, Cream, TV Yellow, or something else, these finishes are very similar, and if you can do one you can do them all.

When viewed today, some good original examples of the finish will still be tannish-white or beige in areas not exposed to ultra-violet rays. (For the original color, look in the control cavity, the pickup cavities, or under the pick guard.) Time plays tricks with color, too. Exposed areas may have yellowed until what was a beige limed mahogany finish in 1957 now resembles how the yellower Cream version must have looked when new in 1959 (but of course the cream versions yellow over time, too).

If you're fortunate enough to get one of these vintage beauties in your hands, inspect the chips, scratches, and wear areas. You'll see that white was laid down first with a distinct secondary tan, beige, or light "chocolate milkshake" color applied extremely thin on top. Occasionally some of us have seen original examples that rarely ever saw daylight, and they are still tan. The yellowed tan we see today on early models was not an intentional color until the new improved Cream finish was introduced in 1959.

The recipe below will give you a nice limed mahogany look. See the variations if you want more of a TV finish.

TV YELLOW — RECIPE 26

To get the right limed mahogany color, mix up some white wash coat and spray on scrap mahogany until you can get quick coverage with a thin white wash coat that doesn't block the pores. You are going to be following this with a tan wash coat that also must not block the pores, so it may take practice to get the technique right.

1. Sand the wood until you are down to a 220- or even a 280-grit paper. Carefully vacuum and blow free any dust. The pores of the wood must be open.
2. Mask the fretboard, fretboard edges, fretboard binding and peghead face.
3. On the bare mahogany, spray an extremely thin white wash coat that's substantial enough to cover but not so thick that you flood and fill the grain. The mahogany's pores must remain open; the few that get covered will usually reopen as the trapped air and the wash coat solvents escape. Let dry at least several hours or overnight.
4. Spray a thin layer of tan wash coat. The pores must still be open. Let dry overnight.
5. If the surface feels too rough to fill cleanly without catching lint off the rag, make a couple of passes with a single-edge razor blade to scrape off the fuzz.
6. Fill the open pores with the grain filler. A slush filler will slip past the white paint that has built up on the edges of the pores. Wipe off the filled surface well, changing rags often, and leaving filler only in the pores. Let dry at least several days.

Masking tape and sign painter's tape

White wash coat made from 1 part white lacquer (or white liquid pigment) to 4 to 5 parts well-thinned lacquer. Mix enough material to not only fill your spray cup but have some left over for making the tan wash coat for the next step.

Tan wash coat made by mixing small amounts of brown colorant into the white wash coat left over from above

2 to 4 ounces neutral oil- or waterbase grain filler tinted to raw sienna (with a hint of red) thinned as a slush filler (see the slush filler mixing ratio, Step 4 of Chapter 9).

6 ounces clear lacquer wash coat

1 to 1-1/2 quarts ready-to-spray clear lacquer

Lacquer thinner for mixing and cleanup

Black Peghead Face Lacquer (see Recipe 3)

Optional: Antique Binding Toner (see Recipe 2)

220-grit no-load dry sandpaper

P800 dry sandpaper

P1000 wet sandpaper

7. Mix clear lacquer 3 to 1 with lacquer thinner. Spray one wash coat of it, and let it dry 45 minutes.

8. Spray three or four coats of clear ready-to-spray lacquer to protect all the color coats, waiting two hours between each coat. Let dry overnight (or several days if possible), then sand level with 220-grit.

9. Quick-mask around the peghead and the fretboard, leaving the face exposed, then spray the peghead face with Black Peghead Face Lacquer. Scrape the black from the pearl inlay within an hour or less of spraying so it removes easily. Let dry an hour or two.

10. Spray 6 to 8 coats of clear lacquer (or fewer if using the Toning option described below).

Spray three to four coats every two hours. Dry overnight.

Scuff-sand with 220-grit and let hang a day to cure.

Spray three to four coats every two hours. Dry overnight.

Scuff-sand lightly with the 800-grit and let hang a week or more to cure.

11. Level-sand with 1000-grit wet, and buff.

Variations

Cream option:

To get more of the banana-colored Cream effect, add a small amount of yellow colorant to the tan wash coat.

Toning option:

If you decide to antique over the tan, do it right after the wash coat that locks in the grain filler. If you overdo the antique toner, you can get a fake mustardy look—and of course who knows how it may look in twenty years—so practice on scrap. The following antique toner steps would replace Step 8:

- Spray three coats of clear lacquer two hours apart. Allow to dry overnight.
- Level-sand lightly with 320- or 400-grit to smooth the surface for the toner, and spray the toner. Dry two hours.
- Continue to Step 8.

Bleachtone option:

For a TV finish try using 'Bleachtone' in place of the white and tan wash coat. Bleachtone is a thin, white-pigmented, lacquer-based blond stain formulated to produce a perfect-looking blond finish on mahogany and other dark woods (the formula, as near as we can tell, is similar to our white wash coat formula above). Furniture finishers have used it since the 1950s, and some guitar builders of the 1990s rave about it. It does make a very good white wash coat, and it can be tinted tan or yellow easily.

Fender: Chasing After Blonds

When Richard Smith was writing his definitive and complete history of the Fender guitar company, *Fender, The Sound Heard Round The World*, he described some papers he'd come across while going through Leo Fender's personal notes. In the "Telecaster" folder, on pencil-written note paper from October 1951, Leo had jotted down the following finishing schedule and time study for a Telecaster Blond finish (Blond is Leo's spelling). Richard provided the info to us, and we're passing it along to you. Draw your own conclusions, as we have drawn ours.

Standard body

Primer Coat: 60% primer coat #1362 Duco; 40% #3661 Duco thinner mixed. (3/4 pint will do ten bodies. Twenty minutes to put on primer coat).

Filler: Natural #563 6825 Dupont mixed with 1/2 pint #200 thinner to 1 pint filler. (Time: 10 filled per hour).

Stain: Harpers # L-804 Blond stain mixed with 40% primer #1362. (Time: three minutes to stain each. 1/2 pint will stain four).

Sealer: Duco # 1991. 1-1/2 quarts used on 4-1/2 bodies. Time: 6 minutes to do each body, this includes the spraying of each coat. Sealer sanding: Averaged 25 minutes each.

Gloss: #1665 Duco mixed with 10% thinner #3661 Duco (2 pints on five bodies. Four bodies sprayed in 5 minutes).

What interested us most about Leo's notes was that the "stain" (it was actually a lacquer shader) was listed right after the filler and before the sanding sealer. Most finishers today lay down smooth coats of sealer first, and then put the color on top, as a shader or toner. Right away we had several questions: Was the primer clear? How did the primer differ from the sealer that followed later? What was the solvent-base, color, and viscosity of the Harper blonde stain? Were the sealer and gloss topcoats clear or ambered?

Leo's notes described the order in which Fender must have applied a blond finish, or at least the order in which we apply the finish in our shops to end up with a finish that looks and feels like the old ones. In recent years, some of us—the Fender Custom Shop's Alan Hamel, Fred Stuart, and me—have had the opportunity to scrape, chip, dissolve, sand, and strip to the bare wood areas of original Fender blond finishes. This is what we found:

The white color does seem to be on the wood, so to speak, and under all the clear coats, lacquer or sanding sealer. If the "penetrating" primer had soaked in and had no build (see Dupont notes below), the white stain would look as if it was on bare wood.

The white, at least on some guitars we've seen, seems to have been brushed or wiped on. There are telltale runs and drips running down the walls of routed cavities that probably would not have come from spraying even heavy spraying. This does not mean that Fender wiped or brushed on the white stain in later production, but they may have at least started out that way.

Fender seems to have applied a second color over the white, call it tan, butterscotch, amber, or what you like (and surely the finishers would have used more than one color). The TV Finish recipe describes why and how two tones are used to create a blond finish. This second color must have been almost all thinner, like the white stain but more so. Our experience also confirms this. We've used solvent to dissolve the layers of an original Tele one at a time; when we get through the clear and hit the amber layer, we're through it in a second to the white. Bare wood comes next and last.

Before we had a chance to feel too smug about our great "discovery," we happened to speak with George Fullerton, who strongly disagreed with our findings. He stated adamantly that the sealer coats went on before the white. George started working at Fender in 1948 and was there from the inception of Fender's blond finish. He convinced us that Leo may not have been concerned about the order of the finishing steps in his note taking, and simply switched the stain and sealer steps by accident.

"We put the primer coat on the raw body. It was clear, and seemed like it was mostly thinner because it disappeared—soaking down into the wood and tying it together. Then we rubbed in the filler, let it dry, and lightly sanded it," Fullerton said.

Speaking with George Fullerton was like going back in time! "We always used a couple coats of clear sealer, after the filler had dried, of course, then sanded it smooth as glass, before the color went on. And 'stain' isn't the right nomenclature for the white, either—it wasn't a stain, it was a lacquer shader," Fullerton said, adding that if they'd put white under the sealer and then sanded through it by mistake, it could ruin the finish. "You cannot touch that spot up because you'll be suspending white between layers of clear, and it'll show. So, if you want to put the finish on a Telecaster the way we did it in the early '50s, then you have to put the white on top of the sealer coats—at least if you want it to look right."

Nor, according to Fullerton, did Fender finishers brush on white primer, or any other finish. "We used a small spray gun that was bigger than an airbrush but smaller than a production gun. The same guns were used for sunbursting later on." (Note: George is describing a 'jamb' gun—used for spraying the door jambs of automobiles on the finish assembly line—editor).

By Fullerton's account, our guess about a second color over the white was off track also. "The shader was a milky white color, and pretty thin once it was mixed with the primer. There was not a secondary tan, amber, or yellowed color sprayed over the white as you describe—any yellowing must have come from the slight amber color of the lacquer." Instead, on top of the white Fender applied three coats of clear lacquer, sanded, then put on a couple more clear coats. "Once that dried sufficiently, at least twenty-four hours, we wet-sanded and polished out by hand with a white automotive polishing compound. This was in the '50s—later on they went to the pedestal buffers and such, but originally we did it all by hand."

The necks, said Fullerton, had sealer alone or maybe primer that was almost all thinner. "We'd spray a neck with three coats of lacquer, water-sand it, and then give it another couple of shots just like the bodies. Then we'd water-sand again and polish by hand."

After speaking with George, we were a little disheartened because we wanted to think that Leo's notes held the answer. Instead we now speculate that if the color went on after the sealer, then the white pigment must have settled toward the bottom of the sealer coats when the solvent in the clear lacquer topcoat dissolved the finish coats below. The majority of such settling would occur as soon as the lacquer coats were sprayed, but you wouldn't be able to see or feel it happening. Then over a long time (in the case of the guitars we see, almost 50 years) the solvents continue to evaporate, the lacquer film oxidizes, and the overall finish becomes thinner and thinner. This process leaves behind a dry, white pigment resting close to, if not actually on top of, the wood with a thin clear layer on top of it.

By the same token, if the white settled downward, perhaps a yellowish colorant within the white (the "blond" part of the white) remained behind in the sealer coat. Or, maybe it was just the amber color of the lacquer as George recalls. Anyone who has sprayed a white finish knows how certain colors, red and yellow especially, will sometimes bleed and float to the surface when you least expect them to. The only way we can duplicate this look today is with a slight secondary tint, even though it doesn't seem to have been part of the original finishing schedule.

No matter what, we can assume that when new, an original Tele blond finish didn't look as it does today. If you don't have 30 to 50 years to wait for the right look and want to reproduce the look of an old blond Tele finish today, you must start out by putting the white on the wood, or extremely close to it, and then keep all the coats over it very thin.

Well, thanks to Richard Smith, George Fullerton, Fred, Alan, and a few others, we knew a lot more than ever about how old Teles were finished—but we wanted more. Probably hoping to add a spray cap to his Fender memorabilia collection, Richard Smith had searched long and hard for "Harper's Stain & Lacquer," once a local finish supplier to Fender, but to no avail. If Richard couldn't uncover anything, we knew we couldn't. Instead we called the Dupont company in Lionville, Pennsylvania, and spoke with Calvin L. Rowland, a senior technical specialist in the automotive products division.

Mr. Rowland found a 1976 price sheet and some product information sheets from 1953. All Leo's product numbers, except for the grain filler, were listed on one sheet or another, but with minimal product descriptions. We got an overview of some of Dupont's (no longer available) furniture lacquers, however. Of the seven lacquers listed, here's what we found:

- All were supplied at spraying consistency.
- Five were listed as being slightly amber.
- Two were listed as "water white".
- Six of the seven were high-solids (around 26%).

- One of the two water-white lacquers was recommended for "finishing Blond Wood surfaces."

This information tells us several things. "Water White," crystal clear lacquer was available in the very early 1950s. This doesn't mean it didn't yellow, however, and we don't know if Fender used it. It backs up our long-held feeling that the majority of wood lacquers of that era were amber colored. Blonde finishes, or blond wood surfaces (they could be referring to blond woods such as maple and ash, and not a blond finish), were given special consideration with regard to the color of the topcoat. It's been our understanding that from about 1956 on, clear lacquer became available in non-yellowing formulations. This must be the reason that blond finishes from '56 on haven't ambered like the early butterscotch-looking versions have.

Following is any information we could find from Dupont on Leo's particular product numbers, along with our views on Leo's notes:

Primer Coat #1362: This is described as a "Clear Penetrating Furniture Primer." Its purpose, as George Fullerton said, was to get into the wood and "tie it together," creating a bridge between the smooth bare wood and a relatively thick finish since lacquer sticks well to itself and some other finishes, but not to smooth, bare wood. A close, modern facsimile of a penetrating primer would be shellac or vinyl sealer, extremely well thinned, to create a penetrating wash coat (see list of materials in Tele Blond recipe). For three-quarters of a pint to be enough to do ten bodies, it must have been laid down quite thin. This sounds like an ultra-thin wash coat, just something to get into the wood and create a bridge for everything to cling to.

Thinner #3661: This is described simply as "Mid-temp" lacquer thinner.

Filler, Natural #563 6825: No information available.

Stain: Dupont couldn't help us here, but this must have been a good strong shader sprayed short of the point that would completely opaque the wood grain—thus, Leo Fender called it a stain. It was probably on the thin side, and perhaps it was more of a stain consistency than most lacquer shaders or toners.

Sealer, Duco # 1991: Listed simply as a "Clear High Solids Sealer" with no color listed. We don't know if it came in spraying consistency, but it probably did. Leo's notes imply that more than one coat was sprayed, as if six minutes was an accumulated time for all the coats on each body: "...this includes the spraying of each coat...". If sanding really "averaged 25 minutes each," as Leo wrote, perhaps that included scuff-sanding between coats, and a very careful level-sanding at the end—that would add up to 25 minutes' worth of sanding in most shops.

Gloss #1655: We found the most information on the gloss. It was number 1655, not 1665 (as Leo had written), supplied at spraying consistency, was slightly amber, and had 26.2% solids. A ready-to-spray, high-solids, clear lacquer mixed with 10% thinner would spray nicely. "Two pints on five bodies..." must be the amount of lacquer necessary to build three to four coats on each body, and the time must be the time for spraying only, without drying time included.

Conclusion: Only a blond's hairdresser knows for sure!

There are any number of possible stain, lacquer, and technique combinations that may have been present in the old days; you can draw any number of conclusions from all this combination of hearsay and fact. For example:

- If the primer was amber colored (and the Dupont records don't say), it could have tinted the blond stain a little, and therefore the blonde stain could have been slightly ambered as it went on.
- Even if the blond stain was bright white, after three to five ambered lacquer or sealer topcoats, the earliest Fender Blonds had to be a little yellowed when new.
- Perhaps Fender finishers tinted some batches of the blond stain with brown or yellow so the stain would take on the tan cast of certain blond furniture at the time (and much like Gibson did in 1956 with its tan "Limed Mahogany" finish).
- In addition, the wood showing through the blond stain would age and darken.
- If you're replicating an old butterscotch blond, you'll need to add some color to the white coat or spray a second shade before the clear coats go on.

Even with all this new information, you still need to interpret Leo's notes, and what George and the rest of us say for yourself. Then adapt them to available finishing products and your own preferences. We do have proof here of how simple the original Tele finish was, however, and we're able to replicate any look.

Blond on Ash

Most of the reproductions we've seen of Fender blond finishes from the 1950s look good but not great. And they all look different, because there are dozens of shades of white. They're applied simply by adding white pigment to clear lacquer and spraying that as a transluscent milky-white film over clear sealer coats. A thin coat of amber can turn this finish into the yellowed early-50s butterscotch version; un-ambered, the blond remains whiter and is more reminiscent of the blond finishes of 1956 and later. EZ-Make Blond, the first recipe below, is our version of this simple blond finish.

Good Looking Old Blond, the second recipe below, is much more complex. It's our approach to nailing down the look of a vintage blond as it would look today—if you found a 10-grade Telecaster under grandma's bed without any dents, dings, scratches, and weather checking. You must read our history lesson, "Chasing After Blonds", before trying to capture the nuances of this more complicated version. It amply demonstrates the extent to which we went to research this recipe, although it might be more than you ever wanted to know about a blond Tele finish! If that's the case, skip the history lesson and stick with the first recipe. It's not too complicated, and you can spray it without the history lesson.

Chapter 10: Finishing Recipes

RECIPE 27	E-Z-MAKE BLOND

Here's the simplest way to apply a blond finish on an ash body to replicate the transluscent, white look of Fender Telecasters and Mary Kay Stratocasters made after the mid-to late '50s. This is how most modern day finishers have been approaching this finish for years, including the factories.

- 2 to 4 ounces natural, or neutral grain filler (Fender used a neutral with a golden butterscotch tone)
- Naphtha
- 1/2 teaspoon white liquid pigment
- Lacquer thinner as needed
- Optional: small amount yellow and/or brown pigment
- 1-1/2 quarts ready-to-spray clear lacquer
- 2/3 quart lacquer sanding sealer, vinyl sealer, or clear lacquer
- Optional: 6 ounces of weak Antique Binding Toner (see Recipe 2) to imitate the butterscotch look
- 220- and 320-grit no-load sandpaper

1. Fill the bare ash body with a neutral grain filler. Prepare the filler by cutting it 2 to 1, filler to naphtha. Let it dry several days for oil based filler, several hours for water based. (NOTE: Some finishers would spray a wash coat of lacquer before the filler—either way works.)

2. Lightly block-sand the dried filler with 220-grit no-load paper to remove residue.

3. Seal with three coats of clear lacquer or sanding sealer, allowing about two hours between coats. You need enough build to withstand some level-sanding without getting down to the wood and filler. Let dry overnight.

4. Level-sand adequately with 220-grit paper. This is not a full level-sanding, but it's not just a scuff-sanding either. If you sand through to bare wood apply another coat or two of sealer, wait overnight again, and lightly level-sand again.

5. In a small mixing jar, mix a small amount of white liquid pigment with a little lacquer thinner to reach a consistency that will mix into the clear lacquer easily. Add it to the clear lacquer in small amounts, testing on scrap, until you get the hiding power you want.

6. Spray the translucent white on the entire body. Start with the sides, and if you dial the spray fan pattern down small and round, you'll be able to get the color on the sides without getting much on the top or back. Approach the sides from two angles, shooting off the edge, and let the two patterns meet in the center. When the sides are covered, including the cutaway, dial the spray pattern into a wider, wetter fan and color the back and top. Fender usually sprayed the sides whiter and more opaque than the top and back, so you may need to touch them up with a tad more white once the top and back look right. Try to keep this white coat as thin as possible. Let the white dry for several hours.

7. Spray two coats of clear lacquer, one hour apart, to lock in the white and let the body dry overnight.

8. Wipe-sand for dust only and spray 4 to 6 coats of lacquer, two hours apart. Hang to cure as long as possible (a week or two).

9. Wet-sand and buff as usual.

GOOD LOOKING OLD BLOND RECIPE 28

Some Tele lovers drool over a battle-scarred guitar that's played every bar in Bakersfield. Others dream of finding one mint, untouched in grandma's yard sale down the street. This is our attempt at reproducing the latter—Fender's early 1950s blond finish as it could look today if it had never seen a gig. (It's now stylish to apply a relic finish by distressing brand new work with the wear marks just mentioned—an art that some finishers are getting quite good at.)

At first glance, this recipe doesn't look much different than the one above; but it is. The color is on the wood, not suspended in between many coats of clear lacquer. Whether or not this is how Fender did it in 1953 is your guess—one you can only make after reading "Chasing After Blonds".

To get just the right look, you'll have to mix some of the components yourself, and we use more steps than Fender probably did forty or fifty years ago. For instance, to make the white pigmented toner, we have you combine a hand made blond stain with a primer wash coat that you also have to mix yourself. While the stain acts as a colorant, it also thins the already-thin primer. This means you won't have a very heavy mixture, which helps keep the overall finish thin.

1. Mix primer coat and experiment on scrap, if necessary, until you obtain a quick wash that primes the wood, but doesn't close the pores. Spray or wipe the primer coat (a very thin wash coat) on the wood and let it dry several hours.

2. Fill the pores with the natural filler and let it dry several days for oil based, several hours for waterbase. Lightly sand with 220-grit paper when dry to remove residue. We specify a neutral, or "natural" grain filler, because we think that's what Fender used. The natural filler often looks like blue-grey specks showing through the translucent white color coat.

3. Prepare the first stain coat by combining the blond stain with the thin wash coat primer so primer amounts to 40% of the mixture. If brushing, add a dash of Butyl Cellosolve to slow down the stain's dry time, and to let it bite in to the primer. After practicing on scrap for viscosity and coverage, spray a coat of stain until it covers the way you want it. Fender usually sprayed heavier on the sides to hide end grain and glue joints (sort of like sunbursting). Let dry several hours, then wipe-sand if you need to knock off dust specks, but do it lightly to avoid sanding through.

4. Prepare a second stain by adding yellow and/or brown pigment to lacquer thinner and/or acetone, to make a butterscotch-colored thinner. As before, add primer to this stain (so it equals about 40% of the mixture) to give it some body, but this coat will be much lighter and thinner than the first stain. Spray one coat onto entire instrument and let dry an hour.

5. Seal with three coats of clear lacquer (or sanding sealer), allowing about two hours between coats. You need enough build to withstand some level-sanding without getting down to the color. Let dry overnight.

---

4 to 6 ounces of primer (a thin wash coat). Use clear lacquer or vinyl sealer thinned at least 1 part finish to 2 parts thinner (a one- to two-pound cut of shellac would also work nicely).

2 to 4 ounces natural (neutral) grain filler cut 2 to 1, filler to naphtha

220-grit no-load sandpaper

Blond stain: 4 to 6 ounces of lacquer with a 1/2 teaspoon white liquid pigment

Small amount (drops) of yellow and/or brown pigment—transparent dye-stain will also work

Lacquer thinner and/or acetone

Optional: small dash of Butyl Cellosolve

1-1/2 quarts ready-to-spray clear lacquer

6. Level-sand adequately with 220-grit paper. This is not a full level-sanding, but it's not just a scuff-sanding either.

7. Spray three or four more coats of clear lacquer, again allowing two hours between coats. Dry a week or more.

8. Wet-sand and buff as normal.

Variation

For the 1956 look or later, (one that is less butterscotchy), skip Step 4 above or make the tint very weak. And remember, any heavy sanding on amber lacquer coats will remove color, and show as a subtle color difference. Also, the finish you apply today will yellow over the years (we won't know how much today's "nonyellowing" lacquers have fared until well into the next millennium, however).

Fender sunbursts, according to "Yas"

Yasuhiko Iwanade is a well-known vintage guitar expert, builder, repairman, and prolific photojournalist, who spent his youth playing, building, repairing, and studying vintage American guitars in his native Tokyo, Japan. "Yas" took a particular interest in the Fender company, and we consider him an authority on the subject. He worked in the Fender Custom Shop from early 1990 until mid-'93, when he returned to Tokyo. Two of Iwanade's years at Fender overlapped with his good friend Michael Stevens, who cofounded the Custom Shop along with John Page. Here, Iwanade shares his opinions on how Fender sprayed their three-tone sunburst on alder, and their shop methods for holding the work. He also has a few tips to share.

"Because alder varies so much in color from piece to piece, Fender bleached its alder bodies, starting when they switched from ash to alder in '56 so that glued-up bodies would have a uniform color to receive the yellow stain, which was applied to the bare wood as a background for the sunburst. I discovered the bleaching technique only after doing a number of restorations which required the finish to be completely stripped.

"I removed finishes very carefully, layer by layer, and paid close attention to my work. After stripping, and while sanding on a body, I noticed that the wood got darker as I sanded into bare wood—this told me that the surface might have been bleached. And the only way I could get back to the right color when I re-finished was to bleach the wood.

"I was finally convinced when I realized that what I'd thought was rubbing compound slopped into many of the body routs during buffing, was actually bleached sawdust! The bleach ran into the cavities and bleached the lumps of sawdust clinging to the cavity walls. The bleach turned the sawdust into a grain that clung even better as it dried, and they finished right over it. I should have known all along because the sawdust was under the finish. Rubbing compound wouldn't have been under the finish. This was the final strong evidence for the bleaching that I'd been looking for.

"In very late '63 or very early '64, because production was up, they dropped the time-consuming bleaching step in favor of a semi-transparent whitish-yellow "shader" sprayed over a clear sealer coat to simulate the effect of bleaching the wood a uniform color. Like the earlier yellow, the '64 shader was a pigmented color—but solvent-based, of course, so it would be compatible with clear lacquer.

"The '64 sunburst looks different because the yellow-pigmented coat has white in it too, producing a slightly milky-yellow look. White pigment was mixed in because of its hiding power. Yellow alone can't always take care of the strong color contrast between two different pieces of unbleached alder. With the pre-'64 finish, the yellow stain was applied to the bare wood, and the brightness comes from the bleached wood; since the stain had no white, it doesn't hide the grain underneath as the later '64 yellow shader coat does. The '64 shader coat is translucent, and hides the grain somewhat because of the hiding quality of the pigments—especially the white. Both the white and yellow pigment suspend in the clear lacquer, they don't dissolve in it as a dye would. This suspension clouds the mixture. The yellow pigment alone doesn't have tremendous hiding power, but white is the greatest blockout pigment, and even a small amount of white pigment will turn any clear film transluscent quickly. So depending on the year, the yellow was either under, or over, the sealer coat,and possibly both during the period when the two methods overlapped."

The sealer underwent changes, according to Iwanade, when Fender introduced Fullerplast into its finishing schedule. None of us, including Iwanade, have hard facts on when Fender began using Fullerplast, and even experts don't agree. One expert swears he saw a worn '57 Tele sunburst with a Fullerplast base coat; another describes a classically worn '59 Jazzmaster with weather-checking and chips that could only be lacquer. Most of us feel that Fullerplast didn't come in until around 1964 or after, and that lacquer, or lacquer sanding sealer, was the main build coat until that time.

To keep his Fender-style bursts authentic, Iwanade uses the Fullerplast that the guitar maker adopted. He has refined the technique of using this somewhat peevish sealer.

"By the time the yellow was on top of the sealer, sometime after 1964, we believe Fender had begun using Fullerplast as a sealer. This is a catalyzed finish that hardens chemically. It has very little thinner— 5% to 10% versus lacquer's 50%. I'm guessing Fender began using Fullerplast as a sealer to prevent the finish from going too deeply into the wood. Alder really sucks up lacquer. You can spray lacquer sealer on it all day and it keeps disappearing. That's no problem if you have plenty of time for the solvents to escape from the wood; then lacquer sealer will do a great job. But since lacquer dries faster on the surface than at the bottom of the film, it's easy to trap solvents under the finisn—creating poor adhesion, discoloration, poor drying, and other problems—especially in a production situation.

"The disadvantage of Fullerplast, and other finishes like it, are that it will dry in the gun, it's more expensive, it requires constant cleanup, and, I suspect, the Synol thinner and other solvents may be more hazardous than lacquer. But used with care in a proper spray environment, it definitely does the job! Certainly Fender had fewer worries with Fullerplast than they would have with conventional lacquer—not to mention that lacquer has been hard to procure, and use, in California for many years.

"Fullerplast soaks in on the first coat only. I keep the first coat fairly thin for it to go into the wood to get good adhesion. I usually lay on a few more full-strength coats to ensure a relatively flat surface for the Sunburst to land safely on. If you shoot within two hour intervals, you don't need to scuff-sand between coats because you will get enough chemical bond between coats. If you wait longer, scuff the finish so that succeeding coats cling well. I always level-sand the final sealer coat, catching the highs and missing some lows, then spray a wash coat of lacquer just before the color—an added insurance.

"The color," says Iwanade, "was most likely a pigment, not a dye stain." He doesn't use any dye stains, which are fully transparent, on either a two-tone or a three-tone Fender sunburst. He believed that even the yellow Fender used was a pigment because if you use bleach you can't use dye—especially in production. Any unneutralized bleach residue could easily affect a yellow dye, causing it to fade or discolor, even months down the road after the guitar had left the factory."

Iwanade uses a wiped-on water-soluble pigmented stain because he hand applies it and has control over using it. Fender used a lacquer-soluble one because they were dipping the bodies in color and they would never have submersed a wood body in water. We think Fender may also have used a yellow water stain at times, because reputable sources have described bodies stripped to the bare wood that were stained with a water-soluble yellow, though the source couldn't confirm a date. On the contrary, the January 1958 body we stripped had a yellow that was only soluble in lacquer thinner.

Iwanade has other reasons for using pigment:

1. It won't fade or discolor over the years, as many dyes will.
2. Pigments also cause the light to come back up through the finish so the sunburst glows. But the pigments used are finely ground, and the effect is subtle. The more common, course, pigment grind should not be used because it will block out the wood color and make it look somewhat artificial.

"Both the red and brown of the sunburst are also pigment colors. The brown I use is made from concentrated pigment paste, which is cut with lots of lacquer thinner. You can use a ready-made brown if you have one that you like. There's a little clear lacquer added in also, but just enough to thicken the spray viscosity, and to help the color stick to the surface it's sprayed on. The consistency is like a wash coat of lacquer or sealer; because the pigment is strong, there's very little color buildup during the sunbursting, and the finish remains thin.

"Fender used two shades of one brown, which they referred to as Salem maple and dark Salem maple, for the sunburst. The dark brown color went on the edge, or rim, because it covered quickly with little buildup. It was too strong to create a nice, delicate sunburst, however, so Fender thinned the dark Salem to a lighter shade for the top and back burst.

"As for the red, when I study most original three-tone sunburst finishes, I see two layers of red. The first is almost like a 1-inch to 1-1/2-inch band of red inside the brown transition area. You can only achieve this banding effect by shooting outwards. The second layer of red is a weaker, more oversprayed, wider pattern that subtly graduates the red area into the center. The red thins out towards the center in such a subtle manner that it covers almost the entire yellow center area including the area under the pick guard. This latter effect can only be achieved by spraying inwards and also from farther away. In other words, you shoot the red twice: once to smooth out and sweeten the brown transition area, and the second time to smooth out the red's transition area.

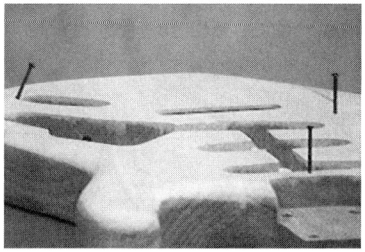

"My red is made the same way as the brown. I use pigment paste, mix it with clear lacquer, and shoot it very well thinned. I can't tell you what color of red it is because it has no name—it's just a red pigment paste. There are many reds of course, so you'll have to use what you can find. It's important to shoot the red after the dark brown. The red sweetens and beautifies the transition area from brown to yellow, and gives the brown that beautiful chocolate look! I was never able to find the exact finely ground pigments in the U.S. that we have in Japan, but that doesn't mean none are available."

Iwanade not only studied Fender's finishing materials and techniques, he studied (and as usual, refined) the way Fender handled instruments in the finishing room.

"Up until sometime in '64, and I've never seen a '65 body with this, Fender drove nails into the face of the guitar as a 'stand' to support the wet body after it was turned over onto its face for spraying the back side. For years I'd heard that these nail marks were clamping marks for tooling, but that never really made any sense to me. If production methods had required indexing, the marks would've been in the exact same spot each time—but they weren't. Finally, I saw an old factory picture in which the guitar seemed to be floating off the surface of the table. The photo was quite small and a casual observer wouldn't have noticed anything out of the ordinary. Then I knew! It was very exciting, and soon I talked with a couple of old timers who verified my suspicions.

"I do not know when Fender started using a turntable, but I'd guess it would have been in the '50s. They drove a nail at a 60-degree angle in the jack cup hole. Otherwise, there's no room to get close enough to the edge without splitting the wood, yet still have the hole be hidden by the jack cup. Actually the only safe, solid nail hole is the one under the pick guard near the bass side, front edge of the bridge. Even the hole between the neck pocket and front pickup hole is often split from lack of wood. If you look at a Tele, you'll see a similar thing. The hole is either right by the screw hole, which often causes splitting there, or else on the wall of the control cavity, which is probably a better place for it.

"The bodies were sprayed while resting on a board. The finishers hit the face first, and then flipped the guitar over onto the nails, to spray the back. I don't know, but I would guess they were using a turntable. They probably set the board on the turntable for spraying, and then lifted the board—body and all—to set it somewhere to dry. The big reason to spray horizontal is so that the finish won't sag or run. You want it to flow out flat and even, without moving the pigment around.

"Somewhere in the early '60s, Fender switched from using the spray table to using a right-angle stand for spraying bodies. We don't know exactly when Fender began using the stand for spraying, but we do know that in '62 Fender began bolting a handle into the neck pocket, because that's when a shadow of it started showing up in the paint. Initially, the handle was used just to store the bodies for drying—otherwise they wouldn't have continued to use the nails. The handles allowed the bodies to be hung, stored almost horizontally, actually, on the branches of what Fender calls a tree for drying bodies. The tree holds forty-four bodies on one stand, and can be rolled about on wheels. Both the handle shadow and the nail-hole marks overlapped for the three years, from '62 to '64, so it must have been very early in '65 that someone looked at the hollow-tube handles and thought of using them on a stand, over the turntable, for holding bodies while spraying.

"To accommodate my spray technique I use a special spray table, which has a circular plywood turntable resting on it. The turntable has three wheels and is center pinned to the table so it can be revolved without running off onto the floor. This is my version of the spray turntable used at Fender. The circular shape lets the operator turn the table easily with a free hand without needing to look away from the work while spraying.

"The stand I use is made from two pieces of three-quarter-inch plumbing pipe, an elbow, and a flange to mount the whole contraption to the edge of the carousel table. The body holder is a one-inch electrical conduit pipe flattened on one end, with holes drilled through the flat area for screwing it to the body cavity. The handle fastens into the two neck-mounting holes on the bass side of the neck pocket with two sheet metal screws. Only enough of the sharp sheet metal screw thread cuts into the wood to hold it, and no sign is left when it's removed. The tube slides onto the stand and becomes a no-fatigue rotating handle for spraying. Combined with the revolving turntable, it allows the finisher complete mastery over the work.

"You can take the handle trick one step further by using it for necks, too. Take a piece of the one-inch tubing, weld or tape a piece of three-eighth-inch steel rod to the outside, and tap one end to fit the 10-32, or whatever size you need, truss rod thread. Bend the other end into a hook. Now you can slide the neck handle onto the hanger and use the spray carousel for careful neck spraying. It offers especially good control for tinting necks a vintage color or for spraying, and the hook lets you hang the neck out of the way for drying. If I'm spraying clear I'll leave the neck on the hanger so it remains level while the finish sets up. The lacquer flows out level and without sagging, and turning it once or twice avoids any sags."

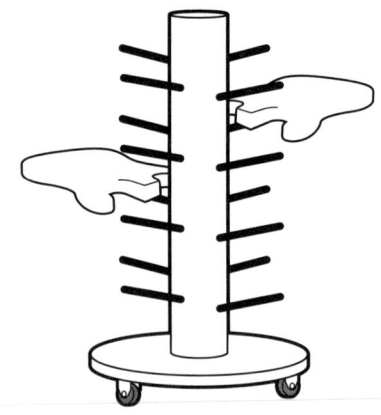

Body up on nails sits on "spraying board"

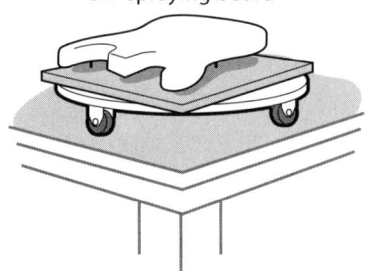

1" electrical conduit flattened on end (sheet metal screws fasten to neck mount holes).

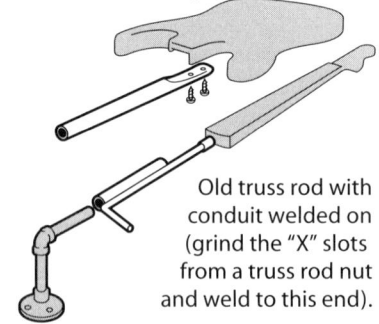

Old truss rod with conduit welded on (grind the "X" slots from a truss rod nut and weld to this end).

The plumbing pipe and the elecrical conduit are two slightly different sizes, allowing one to slide over the other.

Fender-style Stains and Shaders: Components of the Fender Sunburst

If you want to reproduce authentic vintage finishes on old work or new, follow one of the base coat recipes given below for all Fender-style sunbursts, and for some of their metallic and opaque colored finishes. These two are close to the techniques Fender used.

Here's a little history on how Fender applied the yellow undertone to its sunbursts from 1956 up until approximately 1963 or 1964. Whether they were to be sunbursted or painted a solid color, Fender bleached alder Strat bodies, stained them with a pigmented-yellow stain, and sealed them with clear lacquer sanding sealer. It was probably easier to put all their Strats through this process rather than finish ready-to-sunburst guitars separately from those that would get solid-colored finishes. Then the nicest-looking bodies were selected for sunbursting, while the others were primed (usually with white) to accept a solid color.

George Fullerton, who was with the Fender company from 1948 to 1970, confirms this. After bleaching the alder, Fender dipped the bodies in a solution that resembled colored lacquer thinner. "We dipped the alder bodies so the wood soaked up a lot of color and then they wouldn't sand it off."

After '64, Fender dropped the time-consuming steps of bleaching and yellow-staining the bare wood in favor of spraying Strats with a translucent pigmented yellow lacquer toner with a touch of white pigment. In these post-'64 sunbursts, because of the order of finish layering, the yellow toner was in such close proximity to the red toner that when the red faded, the remaining weak red, with the strong yellow showing through it, looks somewhat orange. This is now a look that vintage guitar enthusiasts have come to love. It's part of Fender's sunburst history, and you may need to reproduce it—or repair it—upon occasion. You may even want to imitate it on a new finish.

After the '64 transition, bodies must have been sorted to receive either a sunburst or else an opaque color before the yellow toner was sprayed. We know this because worn areas on opaque custom-color guitars from this era show a white primer undercoat sprayed directly over the clear Fullerplast, without the layer of translucent yellow-white lacquer toner used under a sunburst. However, repairmen who specialize in finishing report a good number of variations in this finishing schedule.

If you're a vintage nut, and want to do things the way Fender did it, here's how to reproduce the yellow base coats from the two different eras. The first is for a pre-'64 look, with the stain on bare wood. The second is for a post-'64 look, with the toner resting on clear sealer. These colorants are easy to make but you'll probably have to do some shopping to find the materials. Actually, a great deal of finishing is leg work. If you're patient, you'll find what you need, and don't be afraid to experiment on scrap with colorants you find on your travels or have around the house. Why won't a child's finger paints or poster paints work? Only practice on scrap will tell!

Fender used the following four versions of either a two-color or three-color sunburst:

Pre-'56 two-tone sunbursts in yellow and brown were on ash from '54 until '56 when ash was replaced by alder as the body wood for a Stratocaster. On ash-bodied Strats, the yellow undercoat is a golden-yellow lacquer toner sprayed over clear sealer.

Post-'56 two-tone sunbursts were still yellow and brown, but the wood is bleached alder so that it would be as bright as the earlier ash sunbursts. The golden undercoat is a pigmented yellow stain on the bare wood instead of lacquer toner.

Pre-'64 three-tone sunburst on alder. This is identical to the post-'56 just mentioned, but Fender introduced the third tone, red, in 1958 to brighten up the look.

Post-'64 three-tone sunburst on alder. Though similar to the pre-'64 variety, the look is different because Fender dropped the bleach-and-yellow-staining operations in favor of a whitish-yellow toner sprayed *over* clear sealer coats.

PRE-'64: YELLOW STAIN — RECIPE 29

When they stained the bare wood, as George Fullerton described, Fender used a lacquer-thinner-soluble yellow stain—at least during the era when they were dipping bodies in color. That's because they would never have submersed a wood body in water. We can verify that we stripped one alder body, dated January 10, 1958, with a yellow stain deep in the wood that was only soluble in lacquer thinner. To the contrary however, we've heard of other stripped alder bodies where the yellow was only soluble in water (we don't have a confirmed date, though). Fender may have used both lacquer-soluble and water-soluble stains at different times.

Before you begin, take time to read Yasuhiko Iwanade's description of two-tone and three-tone sunburst colors in the previous section, as well as the information on pigmented stains, toners, and shaders for creating them. Yas uses a wiped-on, water-soluble pigmented stain because it's nontoxic, easy to apply, and very lightfast. Since it's not soluble in lacquer, it won't move around under clear lacquer or sanding sealer.

Water-soluble stain

1. Put the liquid pigment into a small mixing cup, bowl, or jar and work in small amounts of water at a time. Mix in the water gradually until you have a yellow stain with no lumps, testing on scrap.

2. Work the white pigment into a small amount of water, and then add it to the yellow mixture.

3. Optional: Add the yellow dye and test on scrap. Add waterbase lacquer to give slight body to the mixture, and help it cling to the wood.

1/4 to 1/3 ounce yellow waterbase liquid pigment

4 to 6 ounces water (enough liquid to dampen a rag or sponge as many times as needed to apply the stain)

1 drop (the size of a pea) white waterbase liquid pigment

Optional: 1/8 to 1/4 ounce waterbase lacquer

Optional: 10 drops, more or less, yellow liquid concentrated dye stain to add brilliance and strength to the mixture

Chapter 10: Finishing Recipes

1/2 to 1 ounce yellow lacquer liquid pigment

4 to 6 ounces lacquer thinner (mix enough to suit your application method—either wiping or spraying)

Optional: 1/4 to 1/2 ounce—just a splash—of Butyl Cellosolve to slow down the drying time and make the stain easier to wipe on

Lacquer-soluble stain

1. Put the lacquer liquid pigment into an appropriate mixing cup, bowl, or jar and work in small amounts of lacquer thinner until it becomes liquid. Keep adding thinner until you know the pigment is dispersed.

2. Add the remaining lacquer thinner (from 4 to 6 ounces) to the mixture and test on scrap until the color is strong and pleases you. Too much liquid pigment can cause drying problems so follow the specific mixing instructions on the brand you use.

RECIPE 30	POST-'64: YELLOW TONER

This is like making a transparent lacquer toner in that it doesn't take much colorant to color the clear lacquer, but the colorant is a pigment instead of a dye. Unlike a stain, a toner is actually a thin coat of finish. Don't overdo the color; you want this toner to be translucent, not opaque!

1/8 ounce (or less) yellow lacquer liquid pigment (or a bright yellow lacquer)

4 to 6 ounces clear gloss ready-to-spray lacquer (mix enough to spray)

1 or 2 drops white liquid pigment (or white lacquer)

1. In a mixing cup, gradually cut the yellow liquid pigment with lacquer until the paste becomes a yellow lacquer. Then gradually add small amounts of this to the clear lacquer, testing often. Test on a clear piece of glass or acrylic laid over a piece of alder or other wood, until the effect you want is achieved.

2. Add a small amount of white lacquer to give it brightness and to imitate the look that bleached alder would have. The white will instantly decrease the translusence—too much will ruin the mix!

Variations: Quick Vintage Yellow

You can make a reasonable facsimile of the above Post-'64 toner without yellow liquid pigment by adding small amounts of white opaque lacquer to a transparent yellow lacquer toner. The effect will be slightly more transparent.

RECIPE 31	DARK SALEM MAPLE SHADER

This recipe is for our version of Dark Salem Maple, the dark brown-black pigmented shader that Fender uses for the outside color on a Strat-style sunburst (in either the two-tone or three-tone variety). It starts with a Van Dyke brown liquid pigment (brown darkened with black).

10 ounces ready-to-spray lacquer, or clear lacquer thinned 1 to1 (5 ounces lacquer to 5 ounces thinner)

1 tablespoon Van Dyke brown liquid pigment

2 ounces black ready-to-spray lacquer, or black lacquer thinned 1 to 1

Lacquer thinner

1. Place the liquid pigment in a suitable jar for mixing. Add small amounts of thinner to the liquid pigment until you get a slurry.

2. Add clear lacquer to the slurry a little at a time, until you get a brown lacquer. Mix well.

3. Add black lacquer until you achieve the final color you're after, and mix well again.

PRE-'56 TWO-TONE SUNBURST ON ASH

RECIPE 32

1. Spray wash coat and let it dry two hours. (Fender probably used the same ultrathin penetrating furniture primer described in the Blond recipe, and they may have wiped or brushed it on.)

2. Wipe on filler, let dry several days. To remove any surface residue, sand lightly with 180- or 220-grit Fre-Cut paper.

3. Spray two to four coats sealer, with 2 hours drying time between each application. As always, you want the sealer coat as thin as possible, but thick enough to sand nearly flat. Let dry overnight in a warm place.

4. Using 220-grit Fre-Cut sandpaper on a sanding block, level-sand to eliminate the majority of shiny spots.

5. Spray one or two coats yellow lacquer toner to cover, allowing 30 minutes between coats. Let dry two hours.

6. Seal with two coats of ready-to-spray clear lacquer, allowing 30 minutes between coats, and dry overnight.

7. Wipe-sand with 320-grit paper just to knock off dust. Avoid sanding through into the color and stay off sharp edges.

8. Spray dark brown tone, beginning with the sides and shooting outward to avoid overspray. When the sides are dark enough, begin shooting the edges of the top and back where they meet the side. Again, shoot outward to avoid overspray on main body.

9. Let dry for 15 to 30 minutes, then brush off any dry overspray using a soft, clean brush. Work from the center toward the edge.

10. At this point, switch to the lighter brown by adding clear lacquer to the brown just used. Finish the sunburst from the center out to where the lighter brown meets the darker brown as it wraps over the corner. Let dry one hour.

11. Spray one wash coat of thin clear lacquer to stabilize the color. Let dry four hours or even overnight.

12. Apply a single coat of clear lacquer; wait twenty minutes. Then follow with 3 to 4 double coats, allowing two hours between applications. (A double coat means that you spray around the body once, then immediately go around again without letting the first coat dry.) After the second double coat has dried for two hours, sand with 320-grit no-load paper.

13. Hang to dry for a week or more. Wet-sand and polish as usual.

---

6 ounce wash coat your choice

4 to 6 ounces natural (golden) oil-based grain filler

180- to 220-grit Fre-Cut paper

1/2 quart or less sanding sealer: Choose from sanding sealer, vinyl sealer, or clear lacquer

8 ounce transparent yellow lacquer toner (see "Making lacquer shaders and toners" in Chapter 9: Step 8)

1 to 1-1/2 quarts clear lacquer

320-grit no-load paper

1 to 1-1/2 quarts lacquer thinner

8 ounces pigmented brown toner. You will use a dark and light version of the same toner—the lighter version is simply the dark version extended with clear lacquer to weaken it (see Recipe 31: Dark Salem Maple Shader)

RECIPE 33 — POST-'56 TWO-TONE OR PRE-'64 THREE-TONE SUNBURST ON ALDER

These two sunbursts differ only the use of red in the three-tone sunburst, so we list them as one recipe.

- 6 ounces wash coat your choice
- 4 to 6 ounces of Klean-Strip Wood Bleach
- 1/2 quart or less sanding sealer (or sealer of choice)
- 220-grit Fre-Cut sandpaper
- 1 to 1-1/2 quarts clear lacquer for topcoats
- 320- to 400-grit dry-lube paper
- 1 to 1-1/2 quarts lacquer thinner
- 8 ounces pigmented yellow stain in the solvency of your choice (see Recipe 29 Pre '64 Yellow Stain)
- 8 ounces pigmented brown toner. You will use a dark and light version of the same toner—the lighter version is simply the dark version extended with clear lacquer to weaken it (see Recipe 31: Dark Salem Maple Shader)
- 8 ounces red toner for three-tone only

1. With a sponge, apply bleach in half to full strength to top and back of guitar.
2. To stop the bleaching action, neutralize it with a 3% solution of acetic acid, following the instructions that came with the bleach kit. You can also use white vinegar. If you skip this step, the bleach will attract moisture to the instrument. When wood is dry, sand off any fir, or raised fibers.
3. Spray or wipe on the yellow pigment stain (this will not obscure the wood). Let dry at least six hours.
4. Spray two wash coats of well-thinned sanding sealer, or plain lacquer. Let dry two hours and scuff-sand.
5. Spray two to four coats of ready-to-spray sanding sealer or lacquer, allowing two hours between each coat. You want the sealer coat as thin as possible but thick enough to sand somewhat flat. Let dry overnight in warm place.
6. Sand to 70%–80% flat, being careful not to sand through to wood. Sand just enough to dull the surface and eliminate the shiny spots.
7. Spray the sunburst. Begin with the dark brown and spray the sides. Avoid overspray by shooting outward. When the sides are dark enough, begin shooting the edges of the top and back where they meet the side. Again, shoot outward to avoid overspray on main body.
8. Switch to the lighter brown and finish the sunburst, spraying from the center out to where the lighter brown meets the darker brown as it wraps over the corner. Let dry for 15 to 30 minutes, then brush off any dry overspray using a soft, clean brush. Work from the center toward the edge.
9. If you are doing the three-tone version, spray the red coat, keeping slightly farther away from the surface so that the coverage is not too heavy. You may need to raise the pressure and/or thin down the paint (wetting it) to keep the red from drying before it hits the surface. Shoot outward first to establish a distinct 'band' of red (see Yasuhiko Iwanade's description in "Fender Sunbursts, According to 'Yas'"), then shoot inward with the gun held even farther away. The paint must be well thinned, because the farther spraying distance means the finish has more time to dry and create overspray buildup. The red is too delicate to brush off overspray. You will ruin the look if you mess with it.
10. Let dry, then wash coat with thin lacquer to stabilize the color.
11. Apply a single coat of lacquer, then follow with 3 to 4 double coats, allowing two hours between applications. (A double coat means that you spray around the body once, then immediately go around again without letting the first coat dry.) After the second double coat has dried for two hours, sand with 320-grit no-load paper.
12. Hang to dry for a week or more. Wet-sand and polish as usual.

POST-'64 THREE-TONE SUNBURST ON ALDER RECIPE 34

Whether the dark color at the edge of a Fender sunburst is very dark brown or black is anybody's guess. Maybe it's both. To us, the sunbursts from the '50s seem browner and ones from the early '60s on seem blacker. For this recipe, add plenty of black to your brown and keep this mystery alive. If you choose to use it, this is the era that introduced Fullerplast as a sealer.

1. Spray one coat of wash coat of your choice. If you use Fullerplast, dilute it 1 part thinner to 2 parts Fullerplast. Let dry 2 hours.

2. Shoot two to four double coats of full-strength sealer (Fullerplast needs fewer coats for build), allowing two hours between coats. You want the sealer coat as thin as possible but thick enough to sand somewhat flat. Let dry overnight in a warm place.

3. Sand to 70% to 80% flat, being careful not to sand through to wood. Sand just enough to dull the surface and eliminate the shiny spots.

4. Do this step only if you used Fullerplast in previous steps: Apply one mist coat of thinned lacquer to give the succeeding coats of lacquer something to cling to. When dry, lightly sand with 500-grit no-load paper get to get rid of any grime or dust that may have been trapped, which will eliminate unwanted shadows on the finished instrument.

5. Spray one or two coats yellow pigmented toner to cover. If a second coat is needed, allow 30 minutes between coats.

6. Seal with one or two coats of clear lacquer, allowing two hours between coats.

7. Shoot Sunburst: From here on, the recipe is exactly the same as the previous Recipe 33. Follow steps 7 through 12.

---

6 to 8 ounces washcoat (vinyl sealer, clear lacquer or Fullerplast)

1 quart sealer of choice (vinyl sealer, clear lacquer or Fullerplast, but not thinned as a washcoat)

220-grit no-load sandpaper (and 500-grit if using Fullerplast)

6 to 8 ounces Post-'64 Yellow Toner (see Recipe 30)

8 ounces pigmented brown toner. You will use a dark and light version of the same toner—the lighter version is simply the dark version extended with clear lacquer to weaken it (see Recipe 31: Dark Salem Maple Shader)

8 ounces pigmented red lacquer toner for three-tone only

1 to 1-1/2 quarts clear lacquer for topcoats

Finishing A Bolt-on Maple Neck

If you wind up doing a lot of guitar finishing or repair work, you're bound to find yourself putting a clear lacquer finish on a bolt-on replacement neck made of maple. The neck may have a rosewood fingerboard, in which case only the maple is finished; or the neck may be made entirely of maple—in which case the entire piece is lacquered (requiring tedious sanding in between the frets). Most bolt-on replacement necks—even if they come with a sealer already on them—need a few coats of clear. In the repair business we also need to refinish maple fretboards during some refretting jobs.

We add an optional touch here—amber staining on the bare wood with a weak wash of amber waterbase stain to give a vintage look. Bare-wood staining can be blotchy however, so practice on scrap (see Chapter 9, Step 2: Transparent Stains on Bare Wood).

RECIPE 35	FINISHING A BOLT-ON MAPLE NECK
Optional: 2 ounces of weak amber stain 1 pint clear lacquer Lacquer thinner Optional: 4 ounces vinyl sealer 320-, 500-, and 800-grit wet-sanding paper	1. Optional: On the bare wood wipe or spray a coat of amber stain. Let dry one day if water-soluble, or two hours if alchohol/NGR soluble. 2. If the wood is not already primed, spray a thin wash coat of 4 parts thinner to 1 part clear lacquer or vinyl sealer. 3. Spray three coats clear lacquer one hour apart. Dry overnight. 4. Scuff-sand with 320-grit. Spray one smooth coat carefully. Let dry several hours. 5. Spray three or four coats of lacquer, one or two hours apart. Let dry overnight. 6. Level-sand slowly and carefully with 500-grit so you don't sand through the finish into color. Watch the edges in particular. 7. Spray one last flow coat (see Chapter 9, Step 9) of well-thinned lacquer (4 parts thinner to 1 part lacquer) to melt any scratches and gloss the finish up. Hang to dry for a week or so. 8. If the flow coat was smooth enough you may leave it as it is, or wet-sand the finish with 800-grit or finer wet-sanding paper before buffing. **Variations** Use shellac for your wash coat. Make a 1-pound cut and apply as above. This will add an aged look to even new maple. For a vintage look without staining the bare wood, after Step 4 spray a well-thinned coat of Antique Binding Toner (see Recipe 2), or use a weak colored, extremely thin wash coat of amber NGR-stain with a dash of lacquer added to give it enough body to help it cling and keep it from running. Let dry an hour or so before touching it. For a vintage, dull-looking finish, spray an extremely thin coat of either a lacquer flattening agent, satin lacquer, or dull-rub lacquer with thinner added to it, after buffing the finish. Any of these coats must be almost all thinner. The flat lacquer left behind by the evaporating solvent takes the gloss edge off the finish.

Gretsch's Flagship Finishes

In the early 1950s, when Gibson was making its fabulous golden sunbursts and brilliant gold-finished Les Pauls and Fender put the blonde Telecaster and two-tone sunburst Stratocaster on the map, Gretsch defied convention by flaunting custom color when custom color wasn't cool. Gretsch catalogs advertised the "un-equalled spotlight sparkle" of the 6129 Silver-Jet and Bo Diddley's 6131 Jet Firebird's "ebony-finished body with brilliant oriental red top." For some, even the putrid two-tone "smoke-green" of the 6125 Anniversary was a sight for sore eyes.

Though Gretsch reigned as the king of color in the 1950s, often it's not the gawdy finishes that first come to mind when we think of them. Instead, we envision Chet Atkins, Eddy Cochran, Duane Eddy, or George Harrison playing Chet's namesake guitar models finished simply in clear lacquer over figured maple stained orange, red-brown, or walnut brown.

Even if these guitars were stained simply, then were named with flair. Gretsch called the orange it used on the 6120 Chet Atkins and 6033 Rancher models "western-style amber red"; the red 6016 Corsair's red-brown was "Bordeaux burgundy." The 6119 Tennessean sported "country-style wood grain cherry" (Gretsch's stain colors, by the way, preceded Gibson's dark cherry red SG and ES-series guitars by several years, although it could be argued that Gibson used the colors on its red-mahogany finishes of the teens, '20s, and '30s). And don't forget the walnut-brown colored "mahogany-grained country style" finishes of the 6122 Chet Atkins Country Gentleman. All these great-looking stain-under-clear lacquer finishes are applied the same way, and are easy to reproduce. We compared our color-matching boards to actual vintage guitars to come up with the colors used here.

- **Brown Country Gentleman Lookalike:** 3 parts stain solvent to 1 part medium brown concentrated liquid stain. If desired, add a little red brown to this mixture to match a particular year since they were not all the same.
- **Tennessean Lookalike:** 5 parts stain solvent to 1 part red mahogany concentrated liquid stain.
- **6120 Orange Lookalike:** 15 parts stain solvent to 1 part orange concentrated liquid stain.

GRETSCH'S FLAGSHIP FINISHES RECIPE 36

1. Wipe on the peghead stain, let it dry, and scrape the binding. Seal the face with a washcoat of clear lacquer and let it dry.

2. Tape off peghead face, fretboard, and binding (or leave binding unmasked and scrape it later if you prefer). Tape off heel plug dowel if you want it to contrast.

3. Spray or wipe the entire instrument with stain. Study the instrument while it's still wet (that is how it will look under lacquer), to determine if you have gotten the right strength and tint of stain. If too weak, cover with another coat

Peghead stain: 2 ounce brown mahogany or ebony stain for peghead

8 ounces of overall body stain: concentrated stain and stain solvent (water or alcohol)

8 ounces vinyl sealer, clear lacquer, or shellac in a wash coat consistency

1-1/2 quarts clear lacquer

Optional: Antique Binding Toner (see Recipe 2), well thinned

500- to 800-grit European P-grade or Japanese (JIS) water-sanding papers (consider mixing the stain stronger before applying another coat, but test on scrap). If too strong, use a clean rag with the correct solvent for your stain to remove some of the color. Shift the color if needed by lightly adding a separate colored stain (see "Shifting a Finish" in Chapter 3). If you've made adequate test boards before hand, color shifting is usually not required on the instrument itself. Let dry completely.

4. Apply one thin coat of vinyl sealer or clear lacquer to lock in the stain. Shellac is a nice alternative if you have experience with it. Let it dry for two hours.

5. Remove masking and scrape bindings.

6. Spray 4 coats of lacquer, one hour apart, and let dry overnight.

7. Scuff-sand lightly with 320-grit, watching that you don't sand through to color.

8. Optional: Spray one coat of Antique Binding Toner and let dry an hour or more.

9. Spray 4 coats of lacquer, one hour apart, and let dry overnight.

10. Level-sand with 500- to 800-grit European P-grade or Japanese (JIS) water-sanding papers.

11. Spray flash coat of clear lacquer (1:4, lacquer to thinner).

12. Let dry a week or more; and wet-sand and buff as normal.

The PRS Secret

We met Paul Reed Smith when he displayed at his very first National Association of Musical Merchants (NAMM) show. In the midst of showy industry display setups, his "booth" consisted of a small folding banquet table, a chair, and a large album with photos of his repair work and instruments he'd built. As we recall, he brought nothing else besides one guitar, from which he took orders. And take orders he did—about 500 by show's end. He was happy, that's for sure, since he was able to go to the bank to finance what later became the very successful PRS Company. Paul's first NAMM-show guitar had the features he's famous for today—in particular, a superbly finished curly maple top that stopped passersby in their tracks.

We'll probably get in trouble for giving away the secret to Paul Reed Smith's beautiful finishes, but we must: PRS is a perfectionist who keeps an extremely close watch on quality control. His finishing "secret" has little to do with the finishing steps. Instead, it's all about painstaking wood preparation. The rest is cake.

PRS VINTAGE SUNBURST — RECIPE 37

If you want this to look like a Paul Reed Smith, start with the most beautifully charactered maple you can find for the top. The neck, back, and sides of a PRS are mahogany (Paul did get his inspiration from the flametop Les Paul you know). A signature of a PRS guitar is its "binding," which is really a thin strip of the unstained maple top itself.

1. Prep the instrument, then inspect it very carefully. Sand, inspect, sand again, inspect again—until it is flawless. We understand that PRS finishers prep-sand to 220-grit (and to 320 and finer for a metallic finish).

2. On tops that are to receive just one transparent color, instead of a sunburst, mask the entire side, right to the edge of the maple top. Then mask the maple edge using pinstriping guide tape for smooth tight curves. This guarantees that the "binding" is protected from stain (the top edge of the binding will receive stain, but can be scraped and sanded off).

3. Wipe top with stain, yellow in this case. Wait 30 minutes.

4. Scrape the color from the thin top edge of the maple, which will appear like a binding. Let guitar dry several hours or overnight.

5. Sand binding line with 320-grit and round off the corner at the top. These scraping and sanding steps will remove all of the color from the wood, making the maple strip resemble binding.

6. Spray a very thin layer of wash coat or sealer. Let dry overnight in a warm room.

7. Even though it's sealed, mask off the maple top and the exposed binding edge with a good vinyl tape that will keep filler from running under.

8. Fill the mahogany grain with a dark walnut grain filler, clean off residue, and

---

Masking tape and pinstriping guide tape

220- and 320-grit no-load sandpaper

4 ounces yellow-amber waterbase stain (enough to wet your rag or sponge)

6 to 8 ounces thin wash coat

2 ounces dark walnut grain filler

2/3 quart sealer of choice: polyester base coat, vinyl sealer, lacquer sanding sealer, or clear lacquer

220-grit Fre-Cut sandpaper

8 ounces cherry red lacquer toner (add a little brown)

1 to 1-1/2 quarts clear lacquer

unmask the top. Dry for a minimum of several days if it's an oil-base grain filler, several hours or overnight for a waterbase filler.

9. Spray sealer of choice: One thick polyester base coat would work because of the fast build created by its low solvent content and heavy build. Several coats of vinyl sealer, lacquer sanding sealer, or clear lacquer would give an equivalent build. You will need enough build to level-sand. Let it dry for two nights in a hot room.

10. Sand very smoothly and carefully with 220- or 320-grit no-load paper. (This is how PRS gets his superb finish.) Don't rush this stage. If there is not enough finish to prevent sanding through, go back and spray some more. If you still end up sanding through into top color, you can touch it up because it's water stain.

11. Mask the top and exposed binding edge carefully, and spray all the mahogany surfaces with the cherry lacquer toner.

12. Unmask the top but leave the binding edge taped. Sunburst the top with the same cherry lacquer toner (for tips on spraying a sunburst, see Chapter 9, Step 8). Let dry for several hours.

13. Spray a thin layer of clear lacquer over the entire instrument to lock in the sunburst and let dry overnight.

14. Remove the binding mask and scrape the thin top edge of the binding one more time if necessary.

15. Spray six to eight coats of clear lacquer, waiting two hours between coats. Wet-sand and buff as normal.

A

Abrasive Grading System 44
Acetone 14
Acrylic lacquer 4
Acrylic spot putty 19
Acrylic wood putty (wood dough) 19
Aerosol 32, 98, 110
Air compressors 33
Air control knob 62
Air lines 33
Air pressure 11, 35, 59, 62, 65
Alcohol 13
Alcohol stain 83, 95
Antique binding toner (antiquer) 105
Artist's oil colors 28, 31
Atomization 35, 59, 62
Auto-body filler 19
Automotive paints 30

B

Barrier coat 3, 86, 90
Bar compound 54, 74
Base concentrate 27. *See also* Liquid pigment
Basic gold bronzing lacquer 113
Basic Martin-style finishes 118, 118–120
Binder 26, 27
Binding 97–98
   antique binding toner 104
   masking 82
   melting scraps 80
   PRS 168, 169
   trimming, scrapers 50, 72
Blackening the peghead face 105–107
Bleached alder 159–161
Bleachtone 145
Blockers 25
Blond 146–153
Blushing 14, 32, 59
Bolt-on maple neck 165
Bridging solvent 14, 29
Bronzing powder 112
Brushing varnish 12
Buffing 53–56
   buffs 54, 74
   compound 53
   tools used for 55
Build coats 90
Burnisher 51
Butyl Cellosolve 14

C

Candy apple red 117
Catalyzed acrylic resin 19
Cherry red 75, 134–142
   '58 vintage cherry sunburst 136
   cherry red filler 20, 135
   close-to-the-wood cherry red 139
   easier cherry red 140
   ES-335 137
   faded cherry red on mahogany 141
   modern factory cherry red 140
   mostly waterbase cherry red 141
Clear fillers 79
Coalescing finish 9
Cold checking 2
Color-sanding (wipe-sanding) 71
Colorants 20, 21, 28, 95
ColorTone 10–12
   ColorTone Retarder 12
   ColorTone Waterbase Brushing Varnish 12
   ColorTone Waterbase Grain Filler 17
Color matching 85
Color theory 24
Complementary colors 24–25
Compressed-air 32–36
   spraying 32
   spray guns 34
Contaminants 66, 77
Corrective colors 25
Craters (fisheyes) 66
Craze, crazing 2, 101
Cremona Brown 21, 124–126
Cross-grain scratches 68
Crystal clear (water white) 101, 149
Cut, shellac 4, 104

D

Danish oil 8
Dark salem maple shader 161
DA sanders 49
Denatured alcohol 13, 60
Drop-fills 71, 72, 80
Dry-sanding 43–47, 70
Drying oils 7
Dull-rub lacquer (satin lacquer) 4
Dye 25–26
   colors 24
   stain 26

E

E-Z-make blond 151
Earth colors (fresco powders) 31
Easier cherry red 140
Electrician's tape 41
ES, Gibson 128–138
   cherry red 335 137
   ES-125 tobacco sunburst 128
ES-350 93
Ethanol (grain alcohol) 13, 29
Evaporative finishes 1, 9

F

Faded cherry red on mahogany 141
Fan pattern 61–65
Fender sunbursts 154–164
Fiesta Red 108–109
Final sanding 81, 99
Finish contamination 66
Fisheyes (craters) 66
   eliminator 67
Flannel buffing pads 74
Flattening agent 4
Flow coat, flash coat 58, 71, 99
French polishing 5
Fresco powders (earth colors) 31
Fullerplast 155

G

Garnet sandpaper 46
Gel finish 8
Gibson Guitar Company 21, 121
   master model 122, 125
Gibson SG 139
Gibson sunburst 22, 126, 128–133
Glycol ether 14, 95
Golden Orange 123
Gold bronzing lacquer 113
Gold top finish 115–116
Good looking old blond 152
Grain alcohol (ethanol) 13, 29
Grain enhancement 81, 132
Grain filler 16–20, 87, 119, 137
   cherry red grain filler 135
Grain raising 69, 81
Gravity HVLP gun 34
Gretsch 22
   flagship finishes 166
Gun cleanup and maintenance 62

H

Handle for necks 40
Hand rubbing 53, 73
Hand staining 84
Hi-tech finish 8
High-solids lacquer 2
Highlighting 84, 93
Holding devices 38–40
Hook and loop sandpaper 45
HVLP guns 34

I

Isopropyl (rubbing alcohol) 13

J

J-200 130
J-45 128
Jamb guns 34, 96
Japan colors 31

Index

L

L-4C 128
L-5 130
L-7C 128
Lacquer
    nitrocellulose 1
    sanding sealer 2
    shaders 27
    thinner 12–13
    toner 95, 104
    water-white 1
Lake Placid Blue 112–114
Lap marks 84
Les Paul
    cherry sunburst 136
    gold top 112–113, 115–116
    junior 139
    special 143
    TV 143
Level sanding 70
Lighting 38
Limed mahogany 143–145
Linseed oil 7, 8, 16, 20
Liquid compound 53
Liquid pigments 30
Liquid stains 28
Liquid universal concentrated dye 95
Lloyd Loar 21, 122

M

Martin-style finish 118–120
    sunbursts 22
Mary Kay Stratocaster 151
Masking 81–83, 107
    supplies 40
Matte finish 4
Metallic blue 113–114
Methanol (wood alcohol) 13, 29, 95
Mineral oil 6
Mineral spirits 13, 16, 20
    cleaning 67, 78
    wet-sanding 72, 100
Modern factory cherry red 140
Modern factory color job 129
Mostly waterbase cherry red 141

N

Nail-stand 39, 157
Naphtha 13, 16, 20
    cleaning 67, 78
    wet-sanding 72, 100
NGR (non-grain-raising)
    reducer 29
    stain 95
Nick Lucas 130
Nitrocellulose lacquer 1–2, 30
No-load sandpaper 45
Nondrying oils 6
Nonstearated no-load papers 45

O

Oil-base grain filler 16
Oil varnish 6–8, 12, 16, 121
Opaque lacquer 30, 108
Orange peel 14, 59
Orbital (oscillating) sanders 49, 68
Overlay veneer
    blackening the peghead face 105
Oxidation 6, 102

P

Padding lacquer 6
Paint 27
Paraffin oil 6
Paste compound 54
Paste filler. *See* Grain filler
Paul Reed Smith (PRS) 168
Pedestal buffers 54–55, 73–75
Peghead face, blackening the 105–107
Piano varnish 5
Pickled finishes 143
Pigment 26–31
    colors 24
    liquid 30
    stain 26, 27
Pin striping guide tape 41
Plastic Wood 18
Polyester 6, 8
Polymerize 6
Polymerized tung oil (linseed oil) 8
Polyurethane 6
Pore filler. *See* Acrylic spot putty; *See* Grain filler
Post-'56 two-tone or pre-'64 three-tone sunburst on alder 163
Post-'64: yellow toner 161
Post-'64 three-tone sunburst on alder 164
Powdered stains 29
Power buffing 54
Power sanders 49
Pre-'56 two-tone sunburst on ash 162
Pre-'64: yellow stain 160
Pre-'64 three-tone sunburst on alder 163
Pre-mask 116
Pressure-feed guns 34
Primary color 24
Primer 91, 146, 149. *See also* Sealer
Production gun 35
PRS (Paul Reed Smith) 168
Putty 19

Q

Quick-mask 82

R

Random-orbit sander 49, 55, 68, 73
Ratios for thinning lacquer 58
Razor blade scraper 50
Reactive finishes 6
Ready-to-spray 86–87, 98
Red Diamond 131–132
Red mahogany sunburst 125
Resin 5–11
Retarder 12, 14, 59
Rich dark mahogany 123–125
Right-angle polisher 56
Rubbing out 99

S

Salem maple 156
    dark salem maple shader 161
Sand-through 29, 47, 89
Sanding 68, 75, 80
    blocks 51
    dry-sanding 47
    level 70
    power 49
    scuff 70
    strip 71
    table 51
    techniques 68
    wet-sanding 48
    wipe 71
Sandpaper 43–47
    abrasive grading system 44
    aluminum-oxide sandpaper 46
    garnet sandpaper 46
    silicon-carbide sandpapers 47
Sap staining 84
Satin lacquer (dull-rub lacquer) 4
Scrapers, scraping 50, 72, 98
Seafoam green 108
Sealer coat 89
Semi-drying oils 6
SG 139
Shader, shading 26–29, 83, 93–96, 161
    dark salem maple shader 161
    top o' the line shaded finish 130
Shellac 1, 4, 12, 13, 62, 86, 89, 104, 121–123
    enhanced shellac 5
Sheraton brown 123–126
Sherwood green 112
Shifting a finish 25
Silex 16
Single-stage guns 34
Siphon-feed guns 34
Slush filling 88
Soldering iron 51
Solids content 2, 58, 87
Solid color spraying with aerosols 110
Solvents 1, 12
Sonic blue pastel 109

Spirit varnish 5, 122
Spraying stain 85
Spraying technique 64
Spray booths 36
Spray carousel 39, 158
Spray guns
    adjusting 61
    cleaning and setup 60–61
    cleanup and maintenance 62–63
    gun capacities 103
    techniques 64–67
Spray table 157–158
Staining 26, 28
    color matching 85
    hand staining 84
Stationary buffer. *See* Pedistal buffer
Steam technique 79
Stearated no-load sandpapers 45
Sunburst 84, 92–97, 128–133, 154–158, 159–161
    '58 vintage cherry sunburst 136
    ES-125 tobacco sunburst 128
    modern factory color job 129
    post-'56 two-tone or pre-'64 three-tone sunburst on alder 163
    post-'64 three-tone sunburst on alder 164
    pre-'56 two-tone sunburst on ash 162
    PRS vintage sunburst 168
    top o' the line shaded finish 130
    vintage-style sunburst on figured maple and spruce 132
Super-400 130
Swarf 45
Swirl marks 68

T

Telecaster Blond 146. *See also* Blond
Thinner 12–15, 60
Thinning lacquer 57–58
Tobacco sunburst 128
Toners, toning 27, 92
    Post-'64: yellow toner 161
Top o' the line shaded finish 130
Transparent dye stain 26, 83
Troubleshooting, spraying 65
Tung oil 7, 8
Turbine HVLP spraying 35–36
Turntable 39, 157
Turpentine 5, 13
Turpine 7
TV-finish 143
TV Yellow 143–145
Two-stage guns 34

U

UTCs (universal tinting colors) 30

V

Value, color 24
Vintage-style sunburst 132–133
Vintage cherry sunburst 136
Vinyl sealer 3, 89–90
Viscosity 12, 57
Viscosity cup 87
VOCs (volatile organic compounds) 2, 13, 23

W

Wash coat 3, 85–87
Water 15
Waterbase
    basic martin-style finish using waterbase lacquer 119
    brushing varnish 12
    coalescing finishes 9
    grain filler 17
    lacquer 9, 11
    pigments 30
    pre-'64: yellow stain 160
    stains 28
Water putty 19
Water white (crystal clear) 1, 101, 148
Weights and measures 103
Wet-sanding 48
White undercoat 91
Wipe-sanding (color-sanding) 71
Wood alcohol (methanol) 13
Wood doughs 18
Wood patch 79
Wood preparation 43, 77, 80

Y

Yasuhiko "Yas" Iwanade 154
Yellow base coat 84, 94, 96
Yellow stain
    pre-'64: yellow stain 160
Yellow toner
    post-'64: yellow toner 161